An Imagined Geography

Contemporary Ethnography

Kirin Narayan and Paul Stoller, Series Editors

A complete list of books in the series is available from the publisher.

An Imagined Geography

Sierra Leonean Muslims in America

JoAnn D'Alisera

PENN

University of Pennsylvania Press

Philadelphia

Copyright © 2004 University of Pennsylvania Press
Printed in the United States of America on acid-free paper

10   9   8   7   6   5   4   3   2   1

Published by
University of Pennsylvania Press
Philadelphia, Pennsylvania 19104-4011

Library of Congress Cataloging-in-Publication Data

D'Alisera, JoAnn.
    An imagined geography: Sierra Leonean Muslims in America / JoAnn D'Alisera
        p.   cm. (Contemporary ethnography)
    ISBN 0-8122-3781-1 (alk. paper) ISBN 0-8122-1874-4 (pbk. : alk. paper)
    Includes bibliographical references and index.
    1. Sierra Leonean Americans—Washington (D.C.)—Social conditions.   2. Sierra
Leonean Americans—Washington (D.C.)—Ethnic identity.   3. Muslims—Washington
(D.C.)—Social conditions.   4. Immigrants—Washington (D.C.)—Social conditions.
5. Transnationalism.   6. African diaspora.   7. Washington (D.C.)—Ethnic relations.
8. Washington (D.C.)—Social conditions.   I. Title.   II. Series
F205.S54 D35   2004
305.896′640753—dc22   2003061628

For my son, Alexander

Contents

Note on Transliteration

Arabic words have been transliterated according to the system adopted by the *International Journal of Middle East Studies*. Diacritical marks, the initial ayn, and long vowel markers are not included.

Chapter 1
Multiple Sites/Virtual Sitings:
Ethnography in Transnational Contexts

The "homeless" mind is hard to bear, and there is widespread
nostalgia for the condition of being "at home" in society, with
oneself, and with the universe: for homes of the past that were
socially homogeneous, communal, peaceful, safe and secure.
—Rapport and Dawson (1998:31)

It is not so much a rending to be separated from your own, to be
rendered ineffective as it were; no, the pain is in being disconnected
from normalcy and eventually to become the living experience of
the fact that exiled memory is the slow art of forgetting the color
of fire.
—Breytenbach (1991:70)

In a world of constant movement, recently torn asunder by a vicious
civil war, Sierra Leonean Muslims living in the Washington, D.C. metropolitan area express the longing of exiled memory and the pain of dis-
connection in powerfully affecting narratives of homeland and
displacement. Constructing community boundaries around the complexities of urban American life and their ongoing connection to Sierra
Leone, self, and community identity is ever shaped by a pressing need
to affiliate on adopted soil with both multi-ethnic and multi-religious co-
nationals, and with fellow Muslims from diverse geocultural backgrounds, a process that is played out against the complex social field of
the American urban landscape, particularly in the cosmopolitan
national capital. In this book I endeavor to rethink long-held anthropological paradigms of separate, bounded, and unique communities, geographically located and neatly localized. In particular, I examine how
ethnically diverse transnationals from one African nation utilize religion

to fashion a sense of community; how their interactions with a broader Muslim population shape a sense of both belonging and alienation within the American context; and how they and their children, many of whom are American-born, struggle with and accommodate to different senses of what it means to be Muslims, Africans, and Americans of African descent. On a broader level, I also investigate the way a universal religion is being transformed on American soil by a multiplicity of transnational communities, such that a unique American Islam is emerging. The Sierra Leoneans with whom I work are at once shaping this transformation and being shaped by it.

When I first set out to do fieldwork with Sierra Leoneans in Washington, D.C., I had imagined that the community would conform to the standard models of immigration and immigrants that are rooted in both the historical past of the United States and my own personal past as the granddaughter and great-granddaughter of immigrants. I soon discovered that these models are inadequate for describing what the popular media have called the "new immigration," and what others more appropriately call transnationalism. Like others who study transnational processes, I discovered that the lifestyles of my informants speak to something more than the "images of permanent rupture, of the abandonment of old patterns of life and the painful learning of a new culture and often a new language" (Basch, Glick-Schiller, and Szanton-Blanc 1994: 3–4). Nor did my informants' experiences conform to the images of migrant populations that leave their native homeland to work temporarily elsewhere and who will eventually return.

Unlike immigrants of the past, or some present-day migrants, the Sierra Leoneans I have encountered are developing a lifestyle that spans a multiplicity of sites across the globe. At a wedding I attended in suburban Maryland, I discovered that the bride and groom had been conducting a long-distance relationship between London and Maryland, and that their marriage had been arranged in Sierra Leone by elders from each of their families. How can one make sense of such long-distance networks that allow traditional patterns of arranging marriages to prevail across three continents? The more deeply I have immersed myself in the community, the more impressed—and confounded—I have become by the new lifestyles and ideologies that Sierra Leoneans have developed that span homeland and host countries.

"Home"—and ultimately the loss of home—becomes an important base upon which Sierra Leonean identities are constructed in the new American diaspora. As such, any definition of "community" that overlooks the ways my informants (re)imagine themselves as Sierra Leonean Muslims living outside Sierra Leone, and instead focuses on the "persistence" or "loss" of "traditions" (especially away from "home"), negates the reality that individuals constantly select strategies to define themselves within their current contexts. As they align and realign community boundaries to reflect their understanding of the social space that they occupy, the significance of social relationships in multiple settings transcends locality to become a "dizzying array of crosscutting transnational spaces within zones of multiple contestation" (Stoller 1996:776). Community, then, is not a fixed construct with definable attributes, but is instead a fluid "field of practices and meanings" (Stokes 1994:7), constructed, contested, negotiated, and ultimately maintained across fixed national boundaries in self-defining terms. Recognizing, and attempting to fathom, what Arjun Appadurai has called the ambiguous "ethnoscapes" (Appadurai 1991:192) of transnational flows, the challenge facing me has been how to incorporate theory into active fieldwork, to gather field data and to write a descriptive ethnography that situates and analyzes the life experience of transnationals. As such, my primary goal in bringing this project to print is to produce an ethnography of transnational identity that locates my informants in the physical, cultural and emotional movement back and forth between an African homeland and an American metropolitan center, where they live, work, and raise families in a place that is never quite "home" in the classic immigrant sense.

Long a staple of anthropological inquiry, the ethnographic case study provides a much needed focus that has been lacking in research on African and Muslim immigrants in the United States. In response to this gap, my study focuses on individuals as they narrate their stories, capturing the dynamics of immigrant experience, the triumphs and disappointments of diaspora life in a world characterized by the unprecedented movement of people, goods, and ideas across national boundaries. When Sierra Leoneans speak of "Africa" they do not speak in purely cartographic terms. Rather, they remind us that we may find "Africa" in Harlem, where West African vendors hawk their wares on street corners (Stoller 1996, 1997, 2002; Coombe and Stoller 1994); in Georgetown, where a hailed cabbie may well be Ghanaian or Malian; in the District, where Sierra Leonean and Ethiopian women "man" corner hot dog stands (D'Alisera 1999, 2001); or in Fayetteville, Arkansas, where our African students remind us that the "Black Atlantic" (Gilroy 1993) links West Africa to the rich and diverse cultural traditions of the Caribbean, Latin, North American, and European diasporas.

American history is in many respects the history of "the transplanted" (Bodnar 1985). Like earlier scholars of American immigration, I am concerned with stories of "desperate individuals fleeing poverty and disorder," "bearers of proud, long-established traditions," and "aspiring individuals whose ties to tradition were loosened in their homelands and who moved to America eager for opportunity, advancement, and all the

rewards of capitalism" (1985: xvi). Yet, I situate my work more specifically within a growing corpus of studies that seek to explore—and with
ever greater nuance—the life experiences of those who embody what
has come to be called the "new" immigration following the Second
World War and especially the "winds of change" that swept aside the
old colonial world, those whose experiences both validate and challenge
traditional imaginings of American immigrant history and sociology
(see, for example, Foner 1987, 2000, 2001; Basch et al. 1994; Mahler
1995; Schiller and Fouron 2001).

Still associated in the minds of most Americans with the massive influx
of eastern and southern Europeans at the turn of the last century, immigration is again profoundly transforming the American social landscape.
Sierra Leoneans, while relatively few in number, are nonetheless representative of the growing number of sub-Saharan Africans who have
established themselves in the United States since the late 1960s, and they
exemplify the complex ways in which recent immigrants reinvent social
geography, creatively adapting to and transforming American life (Stoller 1997, 1996, 2002; Coombe and Stoller 1994; Holtzman 2000; Abusharaf 2002). As in other immigrant narratives, this transformation of self
and society entails a complex process by which indigenous—in this case
Sierra Leonean—cultural practices and norms are transplanted and
become sycreticized in a foreign context. Yet, ever aware that immigrants bring much of their "old world" with them, we should be wary
of searching too hard for "traditional African" or West African Muslim
linkages in the way they situate themselves on American soil.

Many of my male informants drive taxis. This may have something to
do with a proclivity for Muslim men to dominate a similar public transport sector back home. At the same time, taxi driving has long been a
staple profession for newly arrived immigrant males of many ethnic, religious, and national backgrounds, including Sierra Leonean and other
African non-Muslims. Likewise, women in Freetown and other Sierra
Leonean market centers clearly dominate the sale of rice and other staple foods. But while informants like Aminata and Maryama may on one
level look to be American "rice hajjas," they are also part of a much
wider network of recent arrivées who have gravitated toward food carts
and street-side vending. The same might be said for those who turn to
domestic work and health care provision. Recognizing that deep-rooted
cultural practices still come into play, we need to look deeper into the
process by which Sierra Leonean cultural identity is, through the dislocation from homeland, reorientation on American soil, and constant
trans-Atlantic gaze toward West Africa, both deterritorialized and reterri-
torialized, often simultaneously. This then challenges us further to
(re)examine what it means for such immigrants to speak of "home,"

"origins," "continuity," and "tradition," in the context of migration across multiple spaces and with the recognition that they stand betwixt and between homeland and (at least for the present) adopted home (Fortier 2000).

Theorizing Transnational Processes—Rethinking Community and Culture

Transnational processes, producing what Roger Rouse has called the "crisis of spatial representation" (1991:8–9), have become a growing arena for anthropological inquiry in recent decades, posing significant theoretical and methodological challenges to contemporary anthropology, and compelling us to rethink such core concepts as community and culture (Abu-Lughod 1991). In order to make sense of the complex ways in which immigrants sustain multi-stranded social relations across home and host societies, we have begun to devise research methodologies to account for the fluidity of space and place (see Gupta and Ferguson 1997a; Olwig and Hastrup 1997; Stoller 1997; Ortner 1997; Basch, Shiller, and Szanton Blanc 1994; Amit 2000). Arjun Appadurai, one of the most insightful theorists of transnationalism, has pointed to

some brute facts about the world of the twentieth century that any ethnography must confront. Central among these facts is the changing social, territorial, and cultural reproduction of group identity. As groups migrate, regroup in new locations, reconstruct their histories, and reconfigure their ethnic "projects," the *ethno* in ethnography takes on a slippery, nonlocalized quality, to which the descriptive practices of anthropology will have to respond. (1991:191)

As the link between cultural identity and specific places becomes more ambiguous and the "landscapes of group identity" that have come to embody the anthropological project are challenged, we as anthropologists can no longer assume separate domains of existence for our subjects and ourselves in which groups are seen as "tightly territorialized, spatially bounded, historically unself-conscious, or culturally homogeneous" (191). As such, we need to focus increasingly on ways delocalized communities maintain and enhance a sense of social identity in conditions in which the "totality of their relations" is not "played out within a single geographic location and a single universe known to others," but rather "is played out at a given point in time and across time" (Ortner 1997:62). So how do we capture the experiences of people living in the criss-crossed spaces of the postmodern world or the shifting positions and meanings that enter into transnational conversations (Stoller 1996, 1997)? The global flow of commodities, information, ideas, and people renders the concept of separable cultures, our imagined ethnographic landscapes, ever more problematic. Moreover, as the anthropological subject moves into our own backyard, and as our backyard in turn extends beyond the boundaries of the nation-state, we need to ask how we might engage and represent a world in which cultural reproduction is lived out globally and in which social relations appear "fragmentary, mixed-up but not interlinked" (Fox 1991:5).

As we recognize that culture is increasingly shaped by the interplay of the local and the global, we have begun to question traditional methods and key concepts, especially a place-focused understanding of culture that is rooted in the history of our scholarly discipline (Hastrup and Olwig 1997:4; see also Handler 1985; Malkki 1992; Gupta and Ferguson 1992). Arising from "an implicit internalization of the idea of culture, reflecting the romanticist idea of the nation, as a set of beliefs and customs shared by a people living in a well-defined area and speaking a particular language" (Hastrup and Olwig 1997:4), culture has generally been understood to be possessed by all people, but in distinctly separate, bounded, and unique configurations. Consequently, with the exception of nomadic peoples, cultures could be divided into bounded geographical locations, categorized, and documented (Gupta and Ferguson 1997b). This vision of the anthropological project was cemented and made solid by the paradigm of "the field" and "home," which rests on a distinct spacial separation that is manifested in the field as the "site where data are collected" and home as "the place where analysis is conducted" (Gupta and Ferguson 1997a:12). This place-centered concept of culture, reified by methodological paradigms of close cultural encounters of a particular kind, gave rise to the classic ethnography that has subsequently fallen out of favor with many leading theorists of the discipline.

The point is not to abandon ethnography. Rich, empirically based, "thickly" described ethnographic studies rooted in particular localities will and must continue to be written. The challenge now is to reapply our traditional tools to the shifting flows and amorphous boundaries of global culture. As Hastrup and Olwig assert, the "classic monograph documenting unique and self-contained cultures must . . . give way to a new genre, taking its point of departure in those nodal points in the networks of interrelations where there is a mutual construction of identities through cultural encounters" (1997:5). Following this, we need not only "write against" culture (Abu-Lughod 1991:137–39), but reinvent our very definition of culture by (re)exploring the "place" in both the experimental and discursive spaces in which people situate themselves physically and imaginatively (Hastrup and Olwig 1997:3). Recognizing that the neat, bounded introductory course and textbook designations of the "Peoples and Cultures" of Africa, the Middle East, and so on conceal the possibility that movement may be a significant factor in the self-definition of any people we study, we need to reposition the subject of our anthropological gaze and take into account the "siting of culture" (Olwig and Hastrup 1997) as a dynamic process of self-understanding. By doing so we are then able to resist broad categorizations of experience and turn to the diverse experiences of people's everyday lives, daily practice, and discourse (Bourdieu 1977), all of which in the global context clearly overlap and intersect, blurring boundaries of place. Thus posters of Madonna, Michael Jackson, and the Ayatollah Khomeini hanging side by side on a bedroom wall in Freetown, or the simultaneous voices of Qur'anic recitation and football play-by-play at a naming ceremony in a suburban Virginia home can be understood as creative improvisations structured on the basis of experiences generated by deterritorialization and the reterrorialization of constructed places of identification (Appadurai 1991). This allows us to view—and hear—the world as a global space of relations in which "people's actions alter the conditions of their existence, often in ways they never intend or foresee" (Rosaldo 1989: 102–3).

Sites of Community

For the Sierra Leoneans with whom I have worked, the construction of an "imagined community" (Anderson 1983) in the American diaspora is intimately linked to the powerful and unifying symbol of a remembered place: "back home." Precisely because this community ("here") is envisioned in relationship to nostalgic memories (Connerton 1989; Nora 1989; Swedenburg 1995) of their homeland ("there"), I maintain that the "site" of community should be understood to be moving and moveable—even a multiplicity of "sites"—in which realities are defined by discursive practices rather than by pre-established social structures or the fixed coordinates of a semantic space (Ortner 1997). As noted above, anthropologists have classically defined community in terms of a people sharing a common culture within a bounded, unmoveable territory. However, as recent studies have shown (see, for example, Rouse 1991; Stoller 1996, 2002; Coombe and Stoller 1994; Naficy 1991, 1993; Basch et al. 1994; Ortner 1997; Gupta and Ferguson 1997b; Fortier 2000; MacGaffey and Bazenguissa-Ganga 2000), the "continuous circulation of goods, money, people and information . . . have become so closely woven together that, in an important sense, they have come to constitute a single community spread across a variety of sites" (Rouse 1991:14), what Rouse calls the "transnational migrant circuit" (14), in which the distance between seemingly separable worlds is brought into close juxtaposition, creating complex heterogeneities.

This "circuit" challenges classical notions of "core" and "periphery." The presumed dominant core of cultural activity has held a privileged position because it has been understood to shape the way in which the periphery, the perceived margins, of a particular cultural sphere, are influenced and ultimately shaped by the dominant discourses of the center. From its historical origins to contemporary practice, Islam in sub-Saharan Africa, for example, is still often discussed as an import from the Arab center that has been transformed, even corrupted, on the periphery by indigenous African cultures. Equally problematic have been assertions that individuals or groups who move from the periphery into the center, for whatever reasons, are fundamentally reshaped by the dominant discourses and practices that they encounter.

These perspectives leave little room for understanding the ways such individuals and groups negotiate their understanding of those dominant central narratives and practices. As I will discuss later in this text, many of my informants both accommodate to and resist the particular practice and articulation of faith that they encounter at the Islamic Center where they congregate to pray, celebrate holidays, and otherwise express personal and communal religious identity. Their interaction with a cosmopolitan but in many respects Arab-centered Muslim community is not unproblematic. However, it is ultimately based in the way Sierra Leonean Muslims have come to internalize a peripheral sense of self that is very much a part of the discourse of Islamic institutions in the United States, where official narratives of what Islam is and should be are extremely powerful. When a peripheral community is defined in relation to a central core culture, the connections and links that bind crash into those that divide, and the mix that results can provoke as many if not more questions than it answers.

Because it challenges established notions of space, the very nature of transmigration renders the binary view of center/periphery problematic. As transnationals establish links between multiple sites, situating themselves exclusively in neither one nor the other, community can no longer be understood in terms of a single central orientation. Rather, community must be understood as increasingly deterritorialized (Appadurai 1996; Gupta and Ferguson 1997b, 1992; Bhabba 1994; Hannerz 1996; Clifford 1988, 1992, 1997; Lavie and Swedenburg 1996; MacGaffey and Bazenguissa-Ganga 2000). They now include the physically dispersed populations who live and work within the boundaries of other communities, other nations. As these transnational communities grow in number (and size), the ways they organize meaning and action become embedded in both the displacement and juxtaposition of cultural forms. This reality has been an important strand in changing how we as anthropologists look at the world. But we must remember to ask what the juxtaposition of cultural forms produces. And we ultimately need to pose the question of how we set about understanding and portraying cultures that are becoming ever more shaped by the continuous and comprehensive interplay between the indigenous and the foreign (Hannerz 1996). This is especially pertinent for the study of transnational adherents of a universal religion such as Islam.

Islam in the Diaspora—Metanarrative Traditions

This book also engages an emerging discussion among scholars of Islam that challenges us to reconsider ways Muslims practice, conceptualize, and redefine Islam in non-Muslim environments. For my Sierra Leonean informants, religion has become a focal point of transnational identity. Their interaction with a culturally diverse Muslim community has strengthened a sense of religious identity and reinforced nostalgic recollections of "back home." Confronting them with a metanarrative of faith and "proper practice"—what I will hereafter refer to as "global Islam"—this broad-based religious community challenges them to (re)explore their own religious understandings and customs. Muslim identity in the diaspora is increasingly expressed via personal attire and the decoration of private and public spaces—mosques and Islamic centers, domestic doorsteps and interiors, personal space in or at the work site, and vehicles—with religious markers (Metcalf 1996; D'Alisera 1998, 2001). In so inscribing their world, my informants simultaneously reach out to opt into the culturally diverse American and American Muslim societies in which they reside and endeavor to express their unique cultural and religious identity.

On a broader level I also investigate how a universal religion is being transformed on American soil by a multiplicity of Muslim communities, such that a distinctly "American" Islam is emerging (Haddad and Lummis 1987; Haddad and Smith 1994; Haddad 1991; Nyang 1999; Smith 2000; Haddad and Esposito 2000). African immigrants such as my informants are at once shaping this transformation and being shaped by it. By examining how they define and express "self," we may learn much about both the changing American cultural and religious landscape, as well as about identity formation and transformation within the wider Muslim world where ethnicity and nationality, often contradictory impulses, increasingly intersect with a broader community of believers.

In his path-breaking analysis of Islam in "local" context, Dale Eickelman underscored the need to study world religions in terms of how "ideology and practice are elaborated, understood and subsequently reproduced in particular places at particular moments" (1982:1). However, he cautions that simply to study the local and avoid the universal,

while perhaps a natural response to the Orientalist search for an ahistor-
ical, essentialized Islam, "provides a conceptual end product which likewise reduces Islamic tradition to a single, essentialist set of principles"
(1), and ignores the fact that Muslims do believe there are universal
principles that are essential to an understanding of Islamic belief and
practice. The challenge, Eickelman asserts, is to examine the ways local
interpretations play themselves out against the universalistic principles,
to study how Islam has "been realized in various social and historical
contexts without representing Islam as a seamless essence on the one
hand or as a plastic congeries of beliefs and practices on the other"
(1–2).

The issue becomes far more complex in the transnational context, in
which locality is not so clear cut. So how do we analyze the interrelation-
ships not just between a local and a universal, but between a group of
local Islams and the global? How do we assess the complexity of multiple
systems of meaning and the ways they are produced and transmitted
across national spaces to form a multiply inflected, shared system of
meaning that judges itself against changing forms and contexts in which
Islamic ideals are expressed? How do we reach beyond the notion of
national and regional contexts in order to explore the transnational and
transregional?

In the case of many Sierra Leonean Muslims with whom I work, an
idealized Islam rooted in part in the metanarrative of global Islam, one
that often conflicts with indigenous customs and practices "back
home," transcends location. This vision is enacted on many different
terrains, but the most powerful are the collective rituals of faith that are
shared equally by all Muslims: prayer, especially the communal Friday
prayer; fasting during Ramadan, going on and celebrating the return of
those who go on Hajj (pilgrimage to Mecca); and observing the two
major feast days (Id al-Fitr and Id al-Adha). These rituals and holiday
celebrations enable the Muslim community to disregard "local" differences and to transcend their given locality. At the same time, a gathering
of Muslims in a transnational setting speaks to the universal. Diverse in
dress and style of celebration, in indigenous language and worldview,
Muslims from virtually every Muslim land gather at the mosque to perform the prayers, which are the unifying element in what is otherwise a
swirl of differences. Locality is multiply complex in that it is not associated with one place, but is instead defined in the collective rituals of
many places. The congregation gather into straight lines to follow the
ritually prescribed prayer, each individual performing similar movements, reciting identical phrases in one holy language (Arabic). The
question is, to what extent do these rituals ultimately inform and shape
social experience or, conversely, to what extent do the congregants

return to their own disparate identities once the communal ritual has ended and the believers file out into the courtyard to converse, eat (on Fridays and holidays), or head back to work?

This is the problematic of defining Muslim community—or communities—in the transnational diaspora. To understand how people internalize and understand their religion in such contexts we must look beyond the interrelation of local/universal toward the ways in which locality is produced, (de)constructed, and then (re)produced across a series of imagined localities in which a globalized Islam has become a dominant and, for many, a persuasive discourse. Addressing rigid distinctions of great/little (universal/local) traditions, Eickelman warns that to "understand such transformations, concern with the internal differentiation of belief and practice within 'local' societies is essential" (1982:11). In the transnational context we need to take this a step further, to concern ourselves with the multiple differentiations within the local, defined within global Islamic discourses of American Islam, and the ways the multiple "locales" contest and accept dominant discourses.

The notion that there is a singular center in which a valid Islam exists suddenly faces challenges. The ways Muslims begin to perceive spaces defined by religion are informed by a more complex sacred geography, one that creates a sense of heightened identification that is encoded with the multiple ambivalences that emerge out of contact with an *umma* (community of believers) who speak multiple languages, who belong to various sects, and who come to the community with a variety of different customs and systems of knowledge (Tapper 1990). Muslims who travel outside their own perceived religious centers on pilgrimage or study missions and who encounter the "Muslim other" (Eickelman and Piscatori 1990:xv) often return to advocate a greater, universal orthodoxy. As such, established local order based on local customs is supplanted (see Launay 1990; Ferme 1994). However, in the transnational case, where a sense of local order is transplanted into a new setting, how does that order become reinvented, if at all? Or does a new order emerge? What are the processes at work in this case? What is the impact of migration on religious thought? Is there a direct link between migration and a heightened sense of being Muslim?

As my Sierra Leonean informants reveal, migration enables Muslims to reflect on the ways Islam has been understood and practiced in their country of origin. Many find themselves questioning for the first time what it means to be Muslim. The answers they often receive center on tensions between locally defined understandings that emerge out of a multi-ethnic and similarly displaced group of believers. Out of these tensions emerge boundaries, not simply those boundaries between local/universal, but rather, those constructed out of conflicts of practice and understanding within the confines of the broader transnational community. Muslim communities are imagined, constructed through the vision, faith, and practice of its members. However, when the vision, faith, and practice of community members transcend space, place, and time, similarities and differences of belief and practice are brought face to face. How this face-to-face encounter constructs a set of beliefs and practices that takes on the aura of a universal set of fixed practices is the fundamental question this book seeks to address.

Studying American Islam

To date, the experiences of Muslims living in the United States remain extremely under-studied by social scientists and other scholars. Until the late 1980s much of what had been written about Muslims had been subsumed in the small but growing literature on ethnic, primarily Arab immigration that dates back to the latter decades of the nineteenth century (Naff 1985; Abraham and Abraham 1981, 1983).[1] Recent studies of Islam in North America have continued to focus on the more deeply rooted Arab American populations, with growing recognition of the role played by South Asian and Iranian immigrants and African American converts in defining American Islam since the 1960s (Haddad and Lummis 1987; Haddad and Smith 1994; Haddad 1991; Smith 2000; Haddad and Esposito 2000). The diverse Arab American community in the Detroit metropolitan area and the large Iranian community in and around Los Angeles have by now become major fields of study in a variety of disciplines (Abraham and Abraham 1981, 1983; Blair 1991; Naficy 1991, 1993; Mandell 1995; Aswad and Bilgé 1996; Abraham and Shryock 2000). Within the small growth industry of American Islamic studies, African immigrants, migrants, and transnationals have gone woefully unnoticed until very recently (see Stoller 1996, 2002; Coombe and Stoller 1994; McGown 1999; D'Alisera 1997, 1998, 1999, 2001, 2002).[2]

The general thrust of the literature on Muslims in America places them within the context of traditional immigration studies, focusing primarily on the tensions between immigrant and American-born generations, the struggle to retain culture in the face of assimilationist tendencies, the ways Islamic institutions come to reflect the American social and cultural landscape, problems of popular stereotypes and political under-representation, and the adaptation of social norms that in many ways challenge Islamic values (Haddad and Lummis 1987; Haddad and Smith 1994; Haddad 1991; Nyang 1999; Smith 2000; Haddad and Esposito 2000). Much of the European literature also reflects this political-sociological orientation, with a strong emphasis on religious institutions, political organizations, and issues of immigration and assimilation (see, for example, Nielsen 1992; Werbner 1990a,b, 1996a,b, 2001).

The above comments are intended less as criticism than as a call to anthropologists of religion to join in the construction of a new and still understudied field of American Islam. I hope that the emphases of this book will also help to refocus part of the discussion away from more traditional, immigrant-based approaches (which should not deny their validity for certain communities) to the construction of religious identity among transnational Muslims, including but certainly not limited to Africans, and the ways in which identity is constructed not so much within bounded ethnic communities as within multiple locations of the transnational experience (see Metcalf 1996).

Siting Fieldwork

My data were collected over a two-year period (1991–93) when I lived and worked within the Sierra Leonean community spread throughout the Washington, D.C. area. Fieldwork in an urban American setting was greatly enhanced by an earlier field project in Sierra Leone (1989), during which time I came to know the "homeland" that is so important to my current informants. In Washington, I attended life cycle rituals, communal prayers, Muslim, Sierra Leonean, and American holiday celebrations, religious instruction for adults and children, and Sierra Leonean cultural events and community meetings. At such events, as well as in private and group settings—face-to-face or by telephone—I interviewed a growing circle of informants. I also spoke to members of the larger Muslim community in order to explore the complex interrelationship between Muslims of different nationalities. A central focus of my work was the Islamic Center of Washington, the primary mosque that most of my informants attend on a regular basis. But I also visited other mosques, and many of the events noted above took place in private homes and rented halls throughout the Washington metropolitan area.

Taped or scribbled interviews, observations, notes, and still photographs helped document my informants' lives. Formal interviews, lasting anywhere from twenty minutes to several hours, took place in coffee shops and taxis, at food-vending stands, in the mosque, in people's homes, and on the telephone. I attended Saturday classes at the Islamic Center as well as Sunday classes at the Fullah Progressive Union's Islamic school in Maryland. I regularly participated in life cycle rituals—weddings, divorces, naming and graduation ceremonies, and forty-day memorials. Less formally, I would spend my days "hanging out" with my informants, riding with them in their taxis while they cruised the streets for fares (I always sat in front), visiting and helping out at their food-vending stands, attending prayers and special holiday events at the mosque, sharing food and company in their homes, and, not least, chatting by phone. These less formal, everyday encounters, were the most significant ones I had in the field. As I became less visible, less "the white woman asking questions," as they often described me in the beginning, and more a part of their daily lives, my experiences took on deeper and thicker meanings.

By the end of my fieldwork period I had interviewed and come to know several hundred people. In all but the rarest instances, Sierra Leonean men and women were willing to share with me in great detail the intricacies of their lives. Working in an urban setting is indeed a challenge, nevertheless the landscape of the city and its outlying suburbs eventually became as familiar and intimate to me as a small African village. The anonymity that is often part of urban life did not exist for me—it was a rare day that went by without some contact with an informant. I would occasionally run into an informant at the grocery store, at a bus stop, in a Metro station, or on the subway.

The Sierra Leonean community is spread out geographically. It is not a bounded community in the sense of other ethnic or immigrant communities or neighborhoods in American cities. Nor is it a "vertical" community occupying entire apartment buildings, as in the case of West Africans living in New York City's Harlem (Stoller 2002:7). It is, rather, in a sense a "horizontal" community extending across the District of Columbia and outlying suburban areas in two states, Maryland and Virginia. Instead of being linked physically, the Sierra Leonean community in this area is linked by a range of affiliations that are connected to ethnic, religious, and national constructions of identity. This "horizontal" spread reflects the way in which the Sierra Leoneans in America situate themselves in a transnational circuit that has become home.

For the community in which I work, this transnational circuit is defined differently at different times. But the primary parameters are ethnic and national identity and, increasingly, religious affiliation to a broader Muslim community. All of these parameters entail constant negotiation and renegotiation. To the casual outside gaze, Washington, D.C., like other American urban centers, has become increasingly African—particularly in some of the transport, food vending, and service sectors that I will treat throughout this book. To Sierra Leoneans who are most immediately concerned with issues of ethnic, national, and religious identity, "Africa" and even "West Africa" are problematic homogenizing constructs. They follow continental and especially regional politics—civil conflict in Liberia, Guinea, and the Ivory Coast—along with other domestic and international issues, but few who I know are currently involved in any manifestation of pan-African identity politics.

The same might be said with regard to the relationship of my informants to the African American community, alongside whom many Sierra Leoneans live and work, and for whom they—and especially their children—may be mistaken. The relationship is not without its historical complexities (see Stoller 2002). Sierra Leoneans who came to this country to further their education know the relationship of their homeland to the Middle Passage as a major disembarkation point and later a British-sponsored haven for returnees, counterpart to the American Liberia. Yet, as with the broader African population around them (many of whom are from half a continent away), Sierra Leoneans remain focused on their own particular identities as members of a global faith and natives of a particular postcolonial state. Their trans-Atlantic gaze is focused on the here and now—toward family and friends trapped by war, in need of medicines, financial support, and basic resources to which they, however much they may struggle in the United States, have far easier access than those "back home."

As best as I could establish at the time of my fieldwork, there were from 3,000 to 5,000 Sierra Leoneans living in the Washington metropolitan area. These numbers have undoubtedly risen in the wake of the civil war that had threatened to engulf the country by late 1990, when I last visited Sierra Leone, had ravaged it by the mid-1990s, and still smolders, occasionally flaring up, despite a succession of cease-fires and compromise governments. My rough estimate is based not on any official statistics or scientific calculation, but rather on numbers that were cited to me by community leaders who attempt to keep track of how many Sierra Leoneans reside in the area at a given time. Accurately counting members of immigrant groups in this country is particularly challenging.[3] When I asked informants who had been here for fifteen years or more if they had ever filled out a census, they generally responded with a negative and often wondered what I was talking about. Because so many transnationals are never "counted," I resist using official Immigration and Naturalization Service (INS) statistics, as well as those compiled by immigrant-watch groups. In most cases such statistics group all West African immigrants together, rarely categorizing them by nation, let alone indigenous ethnic group.[4] Consequently, I rely on my informants' own assessments of the numbers. When all is said and done, I feel that it is their own calculation, however accurate, that really matters.

My informants hold different types of jobs, but the majority of the men are taxi drivers, while the women primarily operate outdoor food carts or are health- or child-care providers. By American standards, these men and women live working-class lives. However, I find such categorizations of socioeconomic class simplistic, essentializing, not fluid enough to describe the lifestyles or worldviews of the people I have come to know, too rigid to take into account the way Sierra Leoneans view their own class status and the way those visions intermingle with predominant American visions. My informants certainly do not see themselves as members of the American working class and often find themselves at odds with Americans who view them as such. For one thing, most of the men and women I worked with are college-educated. Many came to this country to pursue higher education, and quite a few have completed their degrees.

The age range of my informants is a difficult matter, one about which I can only speculate. Early in my fieldwork my informants instructed me not to ask anyone his or her age or name. Having read deeply in West African culture and visited Sierra Leone on two occasions, I was not surprised at this reticence. It was only the American-born children, ranging in age from ten to their early twenties, who would offer me their age, often before I even asked. Nevertheless, I can assert with some degree of certainty that the age range of my average informant is between thirty-five and forty-five. I did not actively seek out this group. They were the ones who proved most willing to share their experiences with me, and in many ways they proved to be the most intriguing informants. I attribute this to several things. Most of the young people whom I met and to whom I spoke were born or brought up in the United States. They therefore had little if any memory of or exposure to the Sierra Leone or the Islam of their parents. Consequently, my questions that dealt with the nature of living between two worlds seemed meaningless to them. By contrast, many of the older people I encountered were not immigrants or transnationals, but temporary visitors to this country. In Washington simply to see their families, they tended to spend little time interacting with the world beyond the homes of children, other relatives, or community members. Out of place, many were anxious to return home and would usually be gone within a year of their arrival. My interest in them lay more with the way their children, my primary informants, responded to their many demands. These demands, as key incidents described in the pages that follow will demonstrate, often serve to highlight the ambiguities that characterize the lives of so many of my informants.

Many of my informants have been in the United States for twenty years, although some had arrived much more recently. Before the civil war made return trips virtually impossible, many traveled back and forth between the United States and Sierra Leone on a fairly regular basis, dependent of course on their ability to afford the air fare. Born and raised in Sierra Leone, some in the capital, others in villages or towns, many of them came to the United States after 1965, in the wake of the dramatic changes written into United States immigration policy.[5] Their reasons for coming varied. Some came as students and stayed, often not finishing the education for which they set out. Others came to "make money" in order to support their families back in Sierra Leone. Many of these informants often expressed their disappointment at the difficulty in fulfilling this goal. As one man told me, "In this country you make money to pay bills; there is nothing left to send home. Sometimes I think I should just go home and starve there. At least I will be with my family." This informant, who has a master's degree in business administration from an American university but drives a taxicab for a living, laughed when I asked him why he did not look for work more suited to his credentials. "My family must eat, and working papers are hard to come by," he answered. "So I drive a cab. No one asks if you're legal."

Holding seemingly degrading occupations associated in the popular American mindset with poor immigrants and illegal aliens, these cabbies and hot dog vendors view their jobs not as symbols of a failure to succeed in America (as indeed some "successful" Sierra Leoneans with whom I spoke would have one believe), but rather as a means to allow them to live as they like, with particular emphasis on religious devotion. Several male informants described driving taxis as a liberating experience: "You come and go as you please. No one can tell you what to do." And for my male informants who are devoutly Muslim, driving taxis allows them to stop work for their five daily prayers without having to answer to a "nonbeliever." One informant commented that he could get a better paying job—he had a green card [6] and was a gifted electrician—but that would mean not being able to go to the mosque at least once a day.

Likewise, women informants who are food vendors, while situated in one spot, view themselves as free to explore the world of their choosing. One woman who owns her own food stand told me that working outside "in the middle of the coldest part of winter was better then being cut off from friends for the whole day, stuck in somebody's home watching their baby, or being a nurse's aide." She, like many other women operating hot food carts is visited frequently by Sierra Leonean cabbies who stop to eat, pass on news, and not least discuss matters of faith and religious practice.

The group I found most interesting and who thus comprise the focus of my work are those Sierra Leonean Muslims who, in one way or another, and to one degree or another, actively practice their religion. My informants offer daily prayers, attend the mosque regularly, and claim that Islam is the most significant guiding force in their lives. By no means do they constitute the only group within the very multifaceted Sierra Leonean transnational community, but it is their encounter with Islam in America that I find so instructive and compelling. They come from virtually all the predominant ethnic groups in Sierra Leone. Ethnic and national identity are also important components of their self-view, as are gender, parentage, education, and a sense of—or lack of—accomplishment.

Underscoring a shifting sense of community—with fellow Sierra Leoneans, as with a broader Muslim and American community—is an ever present longing, a nostalgia for what other immigrant groups called the "old country," and what they simply refer to as "back home." Their transnational identity has been circumscribed during the last decade by an inability to return, even for a short visit (although some have gone at times of relative quiet on fact-finding missions or to bring out family members). As an idea, a sense of permanent displacement—even for those few who have become citizens—continues to define their lives. One way of finding a place on foreign, but ever more familiar soil is to express an attachment to a broader religious community in which many are, like them, albeit for different reasons, displaced—and nostalgic. Embraced, and yet at times corrected in their practices and understandings, by a community of believers that struggles to define normative activity in an imagined universality, the road has been rocky. The mosque both welcomes and admonishes. The broader society, still adhering to an official dogma that welcomes those seeking the American dream, is ever and increasingly torn by counter discourses. And the immediate domestic space that is home, however inscribed with religious-national-ethnic markers, is also a site of contestation, between transnational parents, displaced from "back home," and their children, for whom home is not "back there," but rather "right here."

Chapter 2
Field of Dreams: The Anthropologist Far Away at Home

Imagining the Field—Double Arrivals/Double Visions

Since my first introduction to anthropology as an undergraduate, I have dreamed of a fieldwork experience in which I would find myself in an exotic place, notebook and tape recorder in hand. I would explore, document, and ultimately describe and analyze a different, remote, and unknown way of life. My imaginings often centered on mysterious, extraordinary, at times frightening phenomena. As such, they reflected the constructed images of "stories from the field" that my instructors had woven through their lectures. Their hardship stories, tales of snakes, bugs, and unstable governments held an undeniable aura of romance. Imagining similar field encounters for myself, I ate, slept, and dreamed anthropology. And so in 1991, when I found myself in my own car as my husband drove me to my field site in Washington, D.C., I must admit that I felt despondent, doubting the validity of my proposed project, and skeptical of my claim to be an anthropologist.

We set out that day from our home in Pennsylvania for the three-hour drive to northern Virginia, where I was to live with a Sierra Leonean woman, Ami, and her ten-year-old daughter, Mhawa.[1] The car was filled with typical fieldwork equipment: a tape recorder, portable typewriter, notepads, pens and pencils, vital source books (my Qur'an, Krio-English dictionary, a history of Sierra Leone), a few diversionary novels, clothes to suit the climate and my informants' perceptions of propriety. But missing were my Katydin water filter, my canteen, my medical kit with snakebite anti-venom syrup, syringes, anti-malaria pills, and my copy of *Where There Is No Doctor*. The ride south to Washington was uneventful and I found myself chatting about everything but fieldwork.

The closer we got to the metropolitan area, the more intense the traffic became. Joel turned his attention to the road; I sat silent. As we traversed the Woodrow Wilson bridge, crossing the Potomac into Virginia, I looked up and out the window to my right. There, gleaming white and majestic in the clear, bright winter sun, picture-postcard perfect, was the Washington, D.C. skyline. Unique for an American city, it is dominated not by skyscrapers but by neo-classical and Egyptian-revival monumental architecture. The Capitol building, at the time under scaffolding for renovation, marks the beginning of the vast Mall promenade of nine-teenth-century exhibitionism and cultural warehouses. At the opposite end of the Mall stands the Lincoln Memorial; in between, the Washing-ton Monument towers over both. As I contemplated this familiar skyline, my eyes moved to the seemingly empty spaces between the three domi-nant "monuments."

In a flash I remembered bouncing down the steps of the Lincoln Memorial as a child, my sister and I dressed in identical sunsuits, my father, 8 mm film rolling, telling us to wave to the camera. I remem-bered myself years later a college student driving down from upstate New York to demonstrate on the Mall against United States involvement in Central America ("U.S. out of El Salvador!") and the proliferation of nuclear power plants ("No Nukes!"). These memories fused into the present, underscoring for me a harsh reality: I was going into the field in my own backyard.

This was not my dreamed-of entry into "the field." The landscape evoked too many personal memories—of family, holiday fun, under-graduate idealism. Inscribed with these multiple remembrances, it seemed void of adventure. "This isn't Africa," I mused. "This isn't even rural. This isn't really fieldwork." Horns beeping, angry traffic faces, icy river below, English spoken all around me—familiarity.

The bridge finally crossed, we entered Alexandria. I had never been to this part of Virginia before, and my spirits lightened somewhat. We wound our way through Old Town—a colonial neighborhood of upscale shops and historic row houses, well-kept homes of elite Washingto-nians—in search of the garden apartment complex where I was to reside. As we drove on, the neighborhood began to deteriorate. We soon found ourselves driving past more modest Depression-era and postwar homes, a borderland between exclusive Old Town and the north-side ghetto. Suddenly, we pulled into the parking lot of an apartment com-plex for low-income residents in the midst of a middle-class neighbor-hood. We climbed the stairs to a second-floor apartment, where we were greeted warmly by Ami and her daughter.

I moved into my bedroom, which until that day had been Mhawa's. She would now move in with her mother. The room was large enough for a twin bed, small desk, and chair. The bare walls desperately needed a paint job. The window looked out onto the back side of the property, which was dark and garbage-strewn, and evoked the dangers of urban America—dangers that, unlike the "bush," carried no romantic aura. I closed the curtains and rarely opened them again.

As I unpacked, my mind raced. I had never been trained to do field-work in an urban environment. I felt disoriented, out of place. I regret-ted that in my rush to salvage an aborted project in Sierra Leone, I had not had time to really explore the nuts and bolts of doing fieldwork in an American city. Even though I had grown up in a city, I could not imagine trying to make sense of the urban landscape. I had surely read urban ethnographies, but certainly not as project-models, and in any case my mind now drew only a blank.

In June 1989, having trained as an Africanist and finished my required coursework and preliminary examinations, I set off for West Africa to study the Susu, an ethnic group in northern Sierra Leone. With the help of a small summer grant from my university, I embarked on a feasibility study to focus my project, make contacts, and select a village field site. I spent the summer traveling through Susu land. By the end of my stay I had chosen a small village in Kambia district. Situated between the dis-trict seat and the seat of the Chiefdom, the village seemed an ideal site. I was greeted warmly by village elders and had my plans approved by the paramount chief. I left Sierra Leone in August convinced I would return the following year, with no inkling of the problems, both personal and political, that would soon arise to frustrate my plans. When I returned to Sierra Leone in November 1990, I found that the country to which I had returned had changed dramatically.

In the year between my first and second visits, the Liberian civil war had erupted and spilled over into neighboring Sierra Leone. The few reports in the American press in the months before I planned to depart had begun to make me apprehensive. Was the Liberian situation too close for comfort? I had heard tales of Liberian refugees streaming into Sierra Leone, further straining an already overburdened country. The price of rice, the index by which Sierra Leoneans judge the state of their nation, had skyrocketed and everyone was reportedly on edge. My Sierra Leonean friends in the States were thrilled that I was to live in their country for an extended period of time, although they felt uneasy about my going alone. My husband and I tried our best to ascertain the situa-tion in the country—from the press, the State Department, even retired officials engaged in business ventures—to gauge the feasibility of my traveling to, living in and, if necessary, getting out of an up-country vil-lage. All that we heard led us to believe that the situation was stable, and I determined to go ahead with the project. I did, however, formulate a clear list of what conditions needed to be met in order to leave Freetown and head up-country (regular truck service, petrol, certain medicines, and so forth).

I arrived at Lungi airport at about midnight, exhausted and ready for bed. I knew the ferry across the bay to Freetown did not run until morning, so I had made arrangements to stay at the airport hotel just across the road from the terminal. I collected my bags and went in search of someone to help me lug them to the hotel. A young man offered his services; we settled on a price and set off. As we approached the road, a soldier—I thought at the time he was Liberian—emerged out of the tall grass, bobbing and weaving, clearly drunk. He asked in Krio what the young man was carrying, then turned his attention to me. As he began to approach, a sense of panic overcame me. I dropped my bags and in the most authoritative voice I could muster asked what he wanted. The young man helping me said to me in English, "Quick give him money!" Without thinking I threw him all the *leones* I had on me, picked up my bags and started to walk away. The young man followed me down the road to the hotel with the rest of my luggage. I turned back briefly to check if we were being followed, only to see the soldier sink to the ground and fall face down in the dust, unconscious.

When we finally reached the hotel I realized I had no *leones* to give to the young man who had helped me. Flustered, I handed him a five-dollar bill. He seemed more than satisfied, wished me good luck, and turned to leave. Suddenly he looked back and said, "I am sorry for what happened out there. There are a lot of bad people roaming around this country these days. Please don't judge us all by that evil man." I smiled, promised him I would not, and thanked him once again for his help. Much to my delight, my room was ready. I undressed and got into bed, only to discover that I was too anxious to sleep. So I got dressed, went down to the hotel lounge, ordered something cold to drink, and began to chat with several taxi drivers who were hanging around. I arranged for one of them to drive me to the ferry the next morning. Then I returned to my room and slept until dawn.

The year before, the ferry had run regularly every few hours. But this morning, as I loaded my bags into the taxi in a leisurely way, the driver informed me that for the last several months the ferry had been running only once or twice a day due to fuel shortages. "If we don't hurry, you will miss it," he warned me. We tossed my backpack, sleeping bag, and several large suitcases into the taxi and quickly set off. Trying to be helpful, the driver put his foot to the floor. "Slow down, please!" I screamed. Exasperated, the driver reminded me that if I missed the launch I would have to stay on this side of the bay another night, or suffer what he described as a long, arduous trek around the bay by land to Freetown.

The road from Lungi to the ferry launch runs through several villages, and as we flew through one I noticed a chicken on the road. "Watch out for that chick . . . !" An explosion of feathers cut me off. "Shit! We ran over a chicken!" I screamed. I turned to spy the flattened bird on the road. Children ran from all sides to see what had happened. Horrified, I sensed that this was anything but an auspicious beginning to my field-work. "Stop!" I insisted. "I have to pay for that chicken! Go back!" The cab driver laughed. "You will miss the ferry. Don't worry," he said, and drove on.

We arrived at the launch to find several women with bundles waiting for the ferry. They assured me that I had not missed the boat, but they were uncertain if it was running that day. Apparently the ferry ran even less frequently than the cab driver had suggested. I sat down by the launch and waited, watching the local fishermen casting their nets out on the bay. The sun shone brightly and I began to relax, but that chicken still bothered me. In due course—about an hour—the ferry did indeed arrive, and as the women and I boarded, I wondered if the dead bird's owner had cursed me.

The summer before, when I had taken the ferry from Freetown to catch my flight home, I had stood on deck watching the mountains that surround Freetown fade and become distant. I had regretted not having enough money to stay on and do my fieldwork at the time, but I knew that I would return the following year one way or the other. Now as we approached Freetown, I looked again to the mountains. Forgetting about the chicken, I imagined them welcoming me back to their country. This was the beginning of the rite of passage that would make me an anthropologist.

When we arrived in Freetown I asked the taxi driver—he had accompanied me on the ferry—to take me to the Paramount, an old colonial hotel in the heart of the city, not far from the American Embassy. "Forget that place," he told me. "It's filled with rich Liberians. And besides, Charles Taylor [then a Liberian warlord and currently president] stayed there and kicked a Sierra Leonean woman down the stairs! Don't go there. Stay at the beach hotels." But the beach hotels were too expensive and too far from town. The previous year, the Sisters at St. Joseph's Convent had allowed me to stay in their guest house for several days, so I asked the taxi driver to drop me there.

The welcome refuge the sisters offered could not change the reality of a city teeming with refugees from neighboring Liberia and the adjacent border zone—even worse, a country clearly facing its own imminent civil war. Freetown faced shortages of food, petrol, and medicine. The anti-malaria drug I had counted on purchasing locally was nowhere to be found. The truck traffic north on which I counted for supplies and— God forbid—evacuation was irregular at best. No one could tell me definitively what I might find in Susu land. I spent the next few weeks coming to terms with the impracticality of heading up-country. Crushed, I had to acknowledge that not only might I not get up-country, but that even if I could, I should not go. I left Sierra Leone mourning my own unfulfilled project, and a country that was destined for calamity.

Back home, caught between my ambition to be an anthropologist who worked in a small village in Africa and my disappointment at the obstacles that made this impossible, I turned to friends and teachers for advice on how to salvage my project. My advisor suggested I look into research that was being carried out with Francophone West Africans in New York City. But that would mean major retooling. I would have to learn spoken French (and French-based creoles) and familiarize myself with new groups of people from Senegal, Mali, and other countries. Feeling down, drained of energy, I contacted a Sierra Leonean friend who had moved to Washington, D.C.

I had met Samuel some years before, in the Africana room in the University of Illinois library. At the time I was in the midst of deciding where to do fieldwork. I knew I wanted to work in an Anglophone African country, and I had narrowed my choice down to Sierra Leone or Liberia. As I sat looking at a map of Sierra Leone, Samuel peeked over my shoulder and asked, "Why are you looking at that map?" We quickly became friends. Samuel introduced me to his country in long chats over tea and on the telephone (a presaging of fieldwork to come). Having decided upon Sierra Leone, I next needed to choose a group that I could work with. As my enduring scholarly interest has always been Islam, my criterion was simple: I wanted to focus on practicing Muslims. I researched the country and found a scant literature on a small Muslim group, the Susu, in northern Sierra Leone. Samuel introduced me to Ahmadu, the son of a Susu paramount chief who was also studying at my university, and when I went to Sierra Leone in 1989 to do my preliminary study both he and Ahmadu sent me with letters of introduction. It all seemed so easy.

Now, as I dialed Samuel's Washington phone number after my disastrous second trip to Sierra Leone, I wondered if he could he help me this time. The phone rang several times. Just as I was about to hang up, I heard his cheery "Hello." Samuel listened quietly as I told him news of his country and of my failure. Very calmly, he said, "Come to Washington. There are a lot of Sierra Leoneans here and I'll introduce you to them. I will even find you a place to live." The idea of working with a group of Sierra Leoneans in the United States had never crossed my mind. "I'll call you back; I have to think about it," I said. Would it work? And how would it be received, especially from a junior scholar with little "real" experience in the "real" field? How many times had I heard people insist that American anthropologists who work in the United States are "not really" anthropologists? Those whose work went unquestioned had usually established their reputations in a foreign setting before turning their gaze homeward (e.g., Myerhoff 1978).

Nevertheless, I deemed this my only alternative and determined to proceed with the new project. The reaction of many teachers and most fellow students—all envisioning their own "entry" to the field in romantic terms I knew all too well—ranged from lukewarm to hostile. Many thought my project unexciting, insignificant, somehow less valid than an African adventure. With Sierra Leone not yet in the headlines, the tales of horror yet to become common knowledge even to many Africanists, few lent credence to my earlier decision to pack up and come home. Fortunately, my advisor and the key professors to whom I turned to reconstitute a thesis committee stuck by me. None of us were quite sure where my project would take me either theoretically or thematically. But in January 1991, within two months of my return from Sierra Leone, I began my new adventures.

Eager to leave behind the frustration of my aborted village study, I decided to forgo the background research one usually does before entering the field. I would just plunge in, a fieldwork technique that in retrospect I have come to value immensely. At least I knew something of the background of my future informants. And I had spent some time in their home country. Still I found my lack of focus daunting. During my first weeks in the field I constantly wondered where and how to begin. I was not even sure where "the field" was. My interest had always centered on Muslim peoples, so clearly that was where I should start. But where would I find them, and how?

Fieldwork in a Familiar Place

Fieldwork, our basic research tool, the adventure that drew many of us to anthropology in the first place, has been a primary target of recent theoretical debates on the focused notion of culture (Rosaldo 1988; Clifford 1992; Appadurai 1988). Our tendency since Malinowski has been to study indigenous peoples living in bounded locales. In an ideal anthropological world, one in which people and their things stay put, this might work. However, when I embarked upon fieldwork in what Paul Stoller has called the American "bush" (1997:82), I quickly discovered that people and their things rarely stay put. I did not yet recognize just how the complex interplay across disjunct spaces allowed for the persistence of community, no matter how decontextualized people appeared to be. I grappled constantly with the problematic of defining my field site. In Sierra Leone it was to be a small village in which I would be "on location" twenty-four hours a day—distinct and bounded, a research field in which I could define and delimit my time and movements, or at least attempt to.

Our mentors teach us that the first months of fieldwork are trying. Alma Gottlieb had described to me in graphic detail her own frustrations as she waited in Abidjan until she met the Beng student who would introduce her to her eventual field site (see Gottlieb and Graham 1994, Chapter 1). As students we imagine those difficulties through a romantic lens: this is part of the rite of passage that makes us anthropologists. And so, as I sat watching soap operas with Ami in our living room in Alexandria, I wondered whether or not what I was doing was anthropology. I had turned to anthropology in search of "otherness," and here I sat watching American television with a roommate—albeit an African roommate—in America. Clearly, I could not spend a year like this. I began to press Ami for information. Where was the community? Was there a building, a neighborhood, an area where I could find a concentration of Sierra Leoneans, of Muslims? "No, we don't have neighborhoods, we are scattered all over this area," she would respond to my endless inquiries. Unable to abandon the notion that a community needs to be centered in one bounded place, I spent my first month frustrated at my inability to pinpoint a specific field site—a neighborhood or cluster of people that seemed like a village in which I could immerse myself physically, to observe and participate in daily life and ritual.

In my search for a "fieldsite," two concurrent discussions, the reconceptualization of community and the changing nature of "anthropological locations" (Gupta and Ferguson 1997c), quickly emerged as problematics I needed to address if I was to move forward with my project. Confronted with the immensity of the Washington, D.C. metropolitan area and the physical distances that separated my prospective informants, I was at a loss as to how to begin. After all, scattered people do not traditionally constitute a community, or do they? In her recent work on the "Class of 58" (1997) Sherry Ortner challenges us to rethink the very concept of community. The concept, she believes, is "worth keeping" only so long as we do not identify it "with harmony and cohesion, nor imagine that the sole form of community is a group of people in one place" (1997:63–64). We need to treat people as "contextualized social beings," describing the "thickness" of their lives in terms of the "fact that people live in a world of relationships as well as a world of abstract social forces and disembodied images" (64). Those relationships, as Joanne Passaro discovered in her work with the homeless in New York City, may play themselves out in a field that is "chaotic, uncontrolled and unmanageable" (151).

For an anthropologist trained to sit in a village, to observe and participate twenty-four hours a day, this created what George Marcus has termed "methodological anxieties" (1995). My predicament speaks to the issue of the place of locality in anthropological discourse, particularly in the study of transnational communities, especially when the ethnographic focus is the Western metropole, even more so when the metropole is your home. Clearly a new kind of fieldwork was called for— one that utilized the subway, the automobile, the interstate highway, and the telephone—but most important, one in which the boundaries between distance/nearness and foreign/native are abandoned.

According to Deborah D'Amico-Samuels, the notion of the field site "functions as an ideological concept which erects false boundaries of time and space and obscures real differences . . . [and begs the question] where does the field begin and end, if ever?" (1991:69). "The field," conceived as a bounded set of distinct activities, informed by the notion of participant-observation, and framed in the context of a distant, far-away place separate from the rest of a fieldworker's life, came into question when I was confronted with the field in my own backyard. Clearly, to be a participant-observer one must separate, be "other." Is this possible within an indigenous context? As Passaro reminds us (1997:147), the notion that the distant/romantic/dangerous location legitimates the ethnographer is "a holdover from the colonial mentality that once delighted in harrowing ethnographic accounts of the conquest of physical landscapes and of native reticence, when wresting 'secrets' from remote 'natives' was the raison d'être of the endeavor." While references to "the native" have "generally disappeared from anthropological discourse, conceptions of 'the field' that constituted and defined those natives persist. The world as viewed by anthropology is still broken up into 'areas' and 'sites' sanctioned for study, peopled with those who might no longer be exotic but are still coherent Peoples and necessary Others" (1997:148). Consequently, "the localizing strategy of anthropology, and the accompanying regionalization of ethnographic accounts, . . . crumples under the weight of manifest global relations" (Olwig and Hastrup 1997:2; see also Gupta and Ferguson 1997c).

Challenging the long-held anthropological paradigms of far/near, here/there is even more problematic as our encounters with cultures thought to be separate and unique converge on the same stage, especially in our own front yard. With a sense of irony and wonder, Lavie and Swedenburg (1996:2) have asked, "What would Margaret Mead have made of Samoan gangs in Los Angeles, or of the L.A.-Samoan gangsta rap group the Boo-yah Tribe, named after the Samoan term 'boo-yah,' for a shotgun blast in a drive-by shooting?" What is our point of departure? Recent arguments for changes in fieldwork practices by theorists such as Appadurai (1991), Clifford (1992), Gupta and Ferguson (1997a), Marcus (1986, 1995) and, Ortner (1997) challenge us to reconfigure the "site" as delocalized, moving and moveable, even as a multiplicity of sites (Ortner 1997:62). Increasingly we find that "realities are defined in practice rather than by pre-established social structures or the fixed coordinates of a semantic space" (Olwig and Hastrup 1997:5). This seems to speak to Michel de Certeau's assertion that "space is a practiced place" (1984:117).

In Washington, I found myself constantly on the move. "The maps in my dissertation will be of the Metro line and the Beltway," I often joked. My husband bought me a T-shirt depicting the Metro stops, and I would tell people I was wearing my field site. On one such occasion a colleague of mine who works in rural Mexico admitted that he was baffled by my ability to do fieldwork in an urban American setting. "I tried doing fieldwork in [a city] once and it didn't feel real," Stan told me. In a small, bounded Mexican village he felt in control of his work. "I went to the village and people talked to me and I took notes. I didn't move much beyond the village. I am not sure how you managed." As I had earlier done, Stan drew a classic anthropological distinction between home and field. I too at times found myself caught in both the immensity and the narrowness of my chosen site. Was I still "in the field" when I was riding the Metro back to Ami's apartment from the mosque, a memorial service, or a naming ceremony? This all came home to me one Sunday when I was going into Washington with Ami and Mhawa.

"We'll hop on the train at the King Street Station today," Ami shouted from the bedroom as she dressed for a visit to a mutual friend. We walked to the station to catch the Yellow Line into the District. All lines originating in Northern Virginia eventually have to cross the Potomac, but the Yellow Line goes above ground. I always enjoyed this part of the ride. Crossing the river into the city raised the hope of a new adventure. Crossing it coming home meant I was closer to a hot shower, my bed, and sleep. I had come to love the river for its beauty and often spent leisure time wandering along its banks in a preserve near our apartment.

But Ami often warned me about the river and became anxious when I went there for walks. I did not know why and, frankly, did not want to, because the moment I knew her reason I feared I would have to give up my recreation. This Sunday she was not going to let me get away with my studied indifference to her concern. As we crossed the river I automatically turned my gaze to the glistening surface of the water. "Don't do that," she whispered. "Stop immediately, now!" Shaken out of my daze, I asked her why. "You might see a Mami Wata," she whispered.

"What's a Mami Wata?" I asked.

She is half fish and half human and has long straight hair. You call them mermaids, I think. If you see one and look at her, you will go crazy. I knew people in the village who went crazy. Men fall in love with her and can never get married.

"So you think Mami Wata lives in the Potomac?" I asked.

I don't know. I never saw one. But yes, all water has them. You must be very careful, and don't walk near the river.

Right then and there I knew I had taken my last riverside stroll. Now that I knew about Mami Wata, ignorance was no excuse. Ami would never let me walk there again, and I could not defy her. In that instant the boundary between home and the field had completely dissolved.

First Encounters

One month into my fieldwork I still had not met the Muslim Sierra Leoneans with whom I wanted so desperately to work. A friend in Sierra Leone wrote informing me that a member of the Susu family with whom I had stayed in Freetown was now living in the Washington area. I contacted Mariama, hoping that this would be my entree into the Sierra Leonean Muslim community. I even wondered if there were enough Susu people in Washington to allow me to continue my research with this specific group. But Mariama, I discovered, was married to a Krio man, a Christian, and she was deeply uncomfortable talking about Islam. Although she claimed not to have converted, clearly she was in conflict with her family, whose members, like most Susu I met, were deeply devoted to Islam. After our first meeting, Mariama ignored my calls; when I did finally reach her, she was curt with me. I could not force her to talk to me, but she was the only Muslim I knew.

Once again I turned to Samuel, who always seemed able to solve my problems. "Of course I know Muslims," he assured me. "Meet me tomorrow and I will take you to meet a good friend of mine." It is this meeting that opened the door to my field site.

Joel and I met Samuel at his apartment on a Sunday morning. "My friend is Ahmed," Samuel informed us. "He is a Muslim and a Temne. He has a master's degree in sociology, but is presently driving a taxi. I am sure he will talk to you because I've spoken with him already and he is willing."

Ahmed lived in a public housing apartment in northwest Washington. The neighborhood was run down, the streets almost deserted. We parked and walked to the front door of the building, where a security guard let us in. We entered with several other residents. In the elevator I noticed we were being eyed suspiciously, and I grew increasingly uncomfortable. "What are they staring at?" I wondered. I tried a smile and a friendly hello. This was greeted with averted eyes and grim demeanors.

I asked Samuel later what he thought the problem was. "They think you are social workers," he replied.

A bit unnerved, we entered Ahmed's apartment. The walls of the apartment, which were covered with tourist art from Sierra Leone, pictures of the Ka'ba (the holy Muslim shrine at Mecca), and various Qur'anic verses, caught my eye. Finally, a Sierra Leonean who was clearly a practicing Muslim—why else would he have the Ka'ba on his wall?

After preliminary greetings filled with blessings and thanks, Ahmed asked us to sit down and offered us a glass of cola. "What beautiful pictures you have hanging on your wall," I commented. "Are they all from Sierra Leone or did you buy them here in the States?"

"Mostly back home," he replied. "I don't think there is anywhere to buy this stuff here." Wary of inquiring too abruptly about matters of faith, I avoided any mention of the Islamic art. "Have you been to Sierra Leone?" he asked me. For the next half hour we joked about my adventures in Sierra Leone, especially about my first trip through the countryside on a bus packed, inside and topside, with people and livestock. As we laughed I found my own fond memories of Sierra Leone becoming intertwined in Ahmed's nostalgia for his homeland.[2]

Feeling I had established a good level of rapport with him, I began to formulate a general question to broach the subject of religion. Before the question was out of my mouth, Ahmed said, "I understand you are interested in Islam."

Inwardly ecstatic, I responded as calmly as I could: "Yes, I am. Would you be willing to talk with me about your religion?"

"Yes, of course. It is great blessings for me to spread the word of Islam. I am what some of us are calling a 'born-again Muslim.' What do you want to know?"

The question silenced me for a minute. What did I want to know? The phrase "born-again Muslim" swirled in my head. In all the years that I had known Muslims, both in the States and abroad, I had never heard people describe themselves in quite that way. This was the language of American Evangelical Christians, a language I never imagined Muslims would use. "Are there other Sierra Leonean Muslims who call themselves 'born-again'?" I asked.

"Yes. Would you like to meet them?"

Ahmed gave me several telephone numbers and encouraged me to visit the Islamic Center on Massachusetts Avenue. "You will find a lot of us there," he told me. I felt I was onto something but was still unsure what that something was. After our meeting with Ahmed I asked my husband, who has worked in the Muslim world for many years, if he had ever heard a Muslim use the phrase "born-again." He had not. Fascinated by the discourse, he reminded me that Ramadan had just begun and that many Muslims spend this month reflecting on their religious lives. Was Ahmed's intense introspection influenced by a similar heightened sense of holiday devotion? Would it last beyond Ramadan? In fact, I soon came to understand that Ahmed's self-reflection went deeper than Ramadan piety. My meeting with him would lay the foundation for my study as it developed.

Soon after, I began to call the Sierra Leoneans whose telephone numbers Ahmed had given me. Much to my pleasure—and surprise—everyone I contacted agreed to talk with me and to introduce me to others. Mustafa was the first of Ahmed's friends whom I met, and he ultimately became my most significant informant. After several telephone conversations he agreed to take me to the Islamic Center and introduce me to other Sierra Leoneans, as well as to the director. Like many of Ahmed's friends who regularly visit the Center, Mustafa is a cab driver.

Mustafa and I entered the mosque for midday prayers; intending to participate, I walked toward the women's section. Surprised that I had not stopped to sit on the chair placed just inside the door for non-Muslim observers, he asked me if I knew how to offer prayers. When I told him I did, Mustafa smiled and walked over to the men's section, where he proceeded to tell all the Sierra Leonean men in attendance that I was present and that I wanted to talk with them. After prayers I walked to the entrance and waited. Several men came up to me, handed me their phone numbers, and said they would be more then happy to talk with me. I had found the access I had been struggling to find for over a month; it seemed I was being accepted.

My fieldwork had truly begun. But I still wonder whether Mustafa had initially been apprehensive. While my ability to offer prayers may have opened doors that would not have been open before, did my knowledge of Islam, my ability and willingness to participate in such devotional acts, to wear *hijab* and modest dress, close other doors? By participating to such an extent, was I closing the door of naive inquiry? Would I be able to make mistakes and then be able to claim ignorance? In offering prayers that day, had I effectively said that I did not need to learn the basics? Many times during the months that followed, when I asked a question that my informants deemed elementary, they would reply incredulously, "Why do you ask that? You should know the answer!" Frustrated by this response, I soon learned to recite what I knew and have them fill in the blanks. The day I set foot in the Islamic Center was my true entry into the world that I was to study. Increasingly, the community unfolded before me, and within weeks I found myself caught up in the swirl of their transnational, beltway-oriented lives.

My reevaluation of what the field is supposed to be began one afternoon soon after I had arrived in Washington. Ami, Mhawa, and I were sitting in the living room talking when the phone rang. Ami answered calmly, then immediately flew into a rage. In Krio she told the person to hold, then turning to me said, "Listen to what this bitch and her friends have to say!" She pressed the button that made the call come through the speaker in the phone. I heard a female voice raging, then another, and finally a male voice. They were also using a speaker phone. Everyone was screaming at once in Krio. Lost in the cacophony of curses and accusations of witchcraft, I dutifully grabbed my notebook. Would Ami draw me into the fray? We had lived together for a month now and had become very close. She called me sister and Mhawa called me mother. Ami accepted that I wanted to be a part of the lives of Sierra Leoneans and actively included me in all her adventures, arguments, pleasures, and sorrows, but I had never heard her this angry. Would I be forgotten or excluded?

In a flash Ami jumped up, beckoned to Mhawa and me to follow, and ran out the front door screaming at the top of her lungs. As I grabbed my notebook I heard the other voices, unaware that Ami had left, still ringing out from the speaker phone. Ami ran out into the parking lot, heading for another section of our apartment complex with Mhawa and me on her heels. She entered a building, ran to the second floor, and began banging on the front door of an apartment; familiar voices answered, the same voices on the other end of the phone. A shouting match ensued, separated by the still-closed door. "Open the door, you illiterate cowards!" Ami screamed. "I want my money!" After hurling a few more choice words and giving the door a swift kick, she turned on her heels, triumphant. "They are afraid to come out and confront me," she boasted. "This proves that I am right and they are wrong. Hmmm! They are illiterates!" She mumbled under her breath all the way home. Mhawa followed quietly, skipping, smiling, seemingly unconcerned with the events that had just transpired. I also followed quietly, my mind racing with the implications of this event.

Clearly the telephone was playing a significant role in the lives of what I had felt to be a community-less people. I would have to pay it more attention. I began to take notice of how the phone was being utilized. Nevertheless, for many months to come, the phone's role in my project remained ambiguous. It may play a significant role in the lives of Sierra Leoneans, but was it a valid fieldwork technique? In fact, I resisted the idea that real field encounters could take place on the telephone.

My dilemma centered on the notion of participant-observation.

Always connected by a hyphen, this term implies that one or the other of its two components is not sufficient to do "real" anthropology. Just to participate and not observe is to "go native." Going native, according to the dominant anthropological view, is to lose the scientific edge, the distance, the ability to observe that one needs to truly understand the society one studies. On the other hand, simply to observe is to remain too distant, to be an "armchair anthropologist," to succumb to the tendency to treat people as distant curios, objects to be collected, categorized, and shelved. The anthropologist's job is to find just the right balance between participating and observing. The telephone did not seem to lend itself to this standard. Could one participate in a foreign culture, let alone observe it, over the wires?

A significant American cultural icon, the telephone loomed large in the popular images of teenage lifestyles when I was growing up.[3] It was too close to home, part of my own socialization, an object to be taken for granted, a means to make appointments or gossip with a friend. It was intrinsically part of the American landscape that, as a backdrop to my fieldwork, I was trying my best to ignore. Moreover, I assumed that the phone symbolized the very lack of community I struggled to overcome, and therefore it could not provide the closeness to my informants that I needed to achieve. Yet, as I soon came to appreciate, the telephone was in fact constructing a connected space by which a community was being created, one that transcended the limitations of disjointed living arrangements. Sierra Leoneans in Virginia could "meet" with Sierra Leoneans in Maryland via the phone, negating distance. As the telephone began to seep into my field encounters I grew increasingly comfortable utilizing it to participate and observe, to query and be queried, to check in with informants scattered over a vast urban landscape. Phone calls never precluded face-to-face contact or attendance at group functions or ceremonies. But when I was on the phone with an informant, or group of informants, I was on-site—often multiple sites—just as were my informants.[4]

When I opened my eyes I quickly discovered that speaker phones were just the beginning. "Call waiting," conference calls, multiple telephone lines in one home, answering machines, and "caller ID" are the norm in most Sierra Leonean transnationals' homes. These services are utilized in original ways precisely to transcend distance. For example, Sierra Leoneans use "call waiting" to carry on simultaneous conversations with two or more people on two different lines for extended periods of time. I would often find myself a participant in these round-robin calls.[5]

One evening I was talking simultaneously via a speaker phone to Mustafa and several other Sierra Leoneans who happened to be visiting him.

The beep of "call waiting" came through. When I first started talking on the telephone with informants and this happened, I would offer to call them back later. "No, no, just hold on," they would always insist. I would find myself waiting for ten minutes or more, during which time I would write notes or think of further questions. I became used to these inevitable time-outs and looked forward to the opportunity to jot down notes in silence.

However, when the beep came this evening, Mustafa, having asked me to hold, immediately came back. We had been having a serious discussion about "bluffing Islam"—pretending that you are a pious Muslim through extreme acts of public worship. "Ahmed wants to join our talk, so I will hang up and call you back with a conference call," Mustafa explained, This was a first for me; I was not sure how it worked, but I was certainly curious. Within five minutes the phone rang, and Mustafa greeted me. Before I could respond, I heard another greeting. It was Ahmed! In the background I heard the voices of the other men at Mustafa's, as well as those of several people at Ahmed's—he too was on a speaker phone in his living room. There I sat at midnight in my room in northern Virginia talking with one group of Sierra Leoneans in Mustafa's living room in the District and another group in Ahmed's living room across town. We talked for hours in animated spirit about prayer, propriety, the evils of ostentatious behavior, and inner versus outward conviction.

It was after this experience that I realized that the telephone was prominent not only in the lives of Sierra Leoneans, but in mine as well. I no longer shunned the phone and came instead to regard it not only as an essential field work tool but as a field site in and of itself. I put an Islamic greeting on my answering machine and ordered "call waiting," which I learned to manipulate masterfully. When I was not out and about doing fieldwork, I was home doing it on the phone. As I became more comfortable with the telephone I would often wonder how something so familiar had become so foreign and then familiar again in a different way.

My telephone experience raises some interesting questions. As anthropologists turn to study their own societies, the notions of familiarity and distance shift, and the notion of doing fieldwork at home "can recede infinitely," as Marilyn Strathern points out, raising the question of "how one *knows* when one is at home" (1987:16). Like Judith Okely, who worked with Gypsies in her native England, I too "had to learn another language in the words of my mother tongue" (1984:5). Inverting the anthropological paradigm of making the foreign familiar, the familiar needed to be made foreign. It became clear to me that familiar cultural categories of home had to be reinvented in my mind. How did

Sierra Leoneans understand that which I took for granted? What did the telephone, the television, hot dog stands, taxis, the Washington Monument, movies, and all else that had seemed so commonplace to me mean to the transnationals whose lives I was trying to understand? In trying to make the familiar different, I had to ask questions that initially seemed to have too-obvious answers. As my fieldwork progressed, I soon discovered that the notions of familiarity and distance collapsed in on each other in confusing and sometimes emotionally charged ways.

Distance and Familiarity

We study and prepare to enter the field hoping against hope that we will be funded. We are given advice about what to bring and how to keep healthy. The plane ticket purchased, we leave home. Scared, unsure, appearing to leave everything behind, we enter the secret world of fieldwork. We don indigenous garb, study and ultimately hope to communicate in a new language, suffer the indignities of the occasional cultural faux pas, and ideally learn what makes "our" people tick. Finally, when we are confident that we have enough data to prove that we are worthy to be called "anthropologist," the process of reintegration occurs. Tearful goodbyes, feelings of having changed, we are again unsure and fearful of what lies ahead. We return and spend several months complaining of reverse culture shock, claiming confusion and feeling as if we are, or wishing that we were, back in the field.

The central theme of this narrative is a distancing of the familiar, the acquisition of a new sense of the familiar, and then the (re)discovery of the old familiar. Yet, working in my own country, even as I made my contacts and found my site, I often felt frustrated by the cultural landscape in which I was doing my fieldwork. At times the familiarity seemed intrusive, and I often became angry when it invaded my research space. The taxi drivers with whom I rode would often stop in mid-sentence to point out to me the usual tourist attractions—the White House, the Washington Monument, the Supreme Court—sites that they either assumed I wanted to see or had just grown used to announcing to their passengers as a matter of habit. I would smile, then try to ease them back into whatever we happened to be talking about. It never occurred to me to ask what these so very American places meant to them. I was not, after all, in Washington to sightsee. I did soon become aware of my mistake, but I am not convinced that I fully realized its import.

One spring Friday afternoon I was driving around the District with Mustafa. He was unusually quiet and we spent a good portion of the ride in silence. Suddenly he said, "Hey, look to your right. Do you know what that is?" I looked, expecting to see some war memorial or embassy.

Instead I saw a building that seemed familiar, but not immediately important. "What is it?" I asked. Mustafa laughed loudly. "It's the Watergate Hotel!" It was! I knew it from photographs.

Suddenly it hit me: what could this possibly mean to a Sierra Leonean? "Do you often take tourists here?" I asked.

Sometimes, but not often. Do you remember Watergate? Where were you when it all happened?

"In New York, in junior high school," I answered. "Where were you?"

Here, in D.C., driving a cab. Oh, oh, these people are crazy! We laughed because some of us never believed this kind of thing happened in the U.S. Only in Sierra Leone! I pass here often and think how foolish I was back then. This place is as corrupt as home!

I listened, taken aback. In an attempt to imagine myself away from home, I had totally negated the landscape before me, and in so doing I had negated the very context of my research. No, this was not a spirit village, or the three ancestor trees in Kukuna that had been pointed out to me the summer I spent in Sierra Leone; it was the Watergate, thick with meaning and part of *my* American identity. But clearly its meanings ran further than I had imagined, and I realized that the Washington landscape was as much my informants' as mine, and that our ownerships intertwined and separated to form new and significant meanings. At that moment the city became alive for me in newly significant ways.

Having belatedly realized the importance of the local urban land-scape, I began to consider how I could navigate around and through the myriad meanings embedded in it. I had learned to negotiate a community living across two states and the Capital district. The Metro had become my home away from home as I moved from place to place. "I can drive the inner and outer beltways with my eyes closed," I once told a friend as we sped through my field site in my green Toyota wagon, weaving in and out of traffic, racing to a baby's naming ceremony in Maryland. I did not close my eyes, but as we crossed the Potomac I kept them focused on the cars ahead of us, careful not to let my gaze turn toward the river even for an instant. After all, Mami Wata might be watching.

Chapter 3
Icons of Longing: Homeland and Memory

For the vast majority of Sierra Leoneans I came to know, the phrase "I am Sierra Leonean" is the foundation upon which recent and distant memories are evoked and in which definitions of self are woven. Informed by a complex array of individual and group perspectives, these definitions extend beyond the physical realities of a place to construct and mobilize a sense of community that "exists in relationship with a whole ensemble of notions which many others possess: with persons, places, dates, words, forms of language" (Connerton 1989:36). Sierra Leoneans position themselves in relation to an intricate system of social relations both within and outside the community, presenting themselves to each other and to the world beyond through interconnections that extend across multiple social and cognitive spaces (Hannerz 1996; Giddens 1990). When asked the seemingly simple question, "Where are you from?" my informants generally respond with an insistent series of refrains about place that reveal how displacement informs their positionality and also the degree to which they feel displaced in an American society that, in general, knows little of the rest of the world. When I first met a new acquaintance, I would invariably have to establish my credentials, not only as an Africanist, an ethnographer who had spent time in and traveled through Sierra Leone, but more generally as an American with fundamental knowledge of world geography. In what became a predictable "test," some variation of the following exchange would often ensue:

Me: Where are you from?
Informant: I am African.
Me: Where in Africa?
Informant: I am West African.
Me: Yes, but where in West Africa?
Informant: I am Sierra Leonean. Do you know where this is?

My intention in asking Sierra Leoneans I had just met where they had come from—followed up by queries about ethnic affiliation and religion—was generally a simple attempt to situate them back home (spatially and culturally) to establish my own credentials as a person who knew their culture and history and, not least, to break the ice of a first encounter. I was often introduced to these potential informants by other Sierra Leoneans who had known me for a time and knew that I had visited Sierra Leone, had traveled to several regions within the country, and was well aware of the ethnic diversity that existed there. Moreover, they had often introduced me as such to new informants. What then compelled these new acquaintances to respond to me with a series of restatements about who they where in relation to place?

As Eric Hobsbawm (1991:67) reminds us, the first question adults often ask in order to situate themselves among strangers is one of place. The response, in the case of Sierra Leoneans, is to name in succession a continent, an area of the continent, and a country. In so doing, they craft boundaries that point to the way in which "everyday subjectivity is constructed out of a sediment of understandings" (Ganguly 1992:30) that refer not only to the past, but to the complex interplay between past and present circumstances. As such, the boundaries of a shifting personal-place-narrative point to an ever increasing need to carve out a niche within a society that has little understanding of the complexity of social life in the diaspora and equally little about the diversity of a home continent. In their attempt to negotiate the gap between competing notions of "my-self-here" and "my-self-there," actual geography becomes the site of an ongoing process in which the crafting of boundaries, in this case, Africa/West Africa/Sierra Leone, points to the way in which self-representation is connected to a series of complex negotiations that serve to bridge past and present experience, illustrating how Sierra Leoneans negotiate the fragmenting experience of difference and marginality in the present. At the same time, geography becomes an "object of memory" (Slyomovics 1998) that is "open to the dialectic of remembering and forgetting, unconscious of successive deformations, vulnerable to manipulation and appropriation, susceptible of being long dormant and periodically revived" (Nora 1989:8). It serves to remind Sierra Leoneans of events, people, moods, and practices by condensing and compressing the present and past into memory. As such, "forms of solidarity and identity that do not rest on an appropriation of space where contiguity and face-to-face contact are paramount" are created (Gupta and Ferguson 1992:9).

For Sierra Leonean Muslims living in the Washington, D.C. metropolitan area, narratives of homeland, and increasingly narratives of homelessness, have become the most salient features of expressing places of belonging and exclusion. As Rapport and Dawson (1998:27) describe, "For a world of travellers and journeymen, home comes to be found far more usually in a routine set of practices, in a repetition of habitual social interactions, in the ritual of a regularly used personal name." As such, home and ultimately the loss of home become an important base upon which identities are developed and maintained. In this chapter I will explore the ways homeland is conceptualized and made manifest in the everyday lives of my informants. I examine the practices and narrations of homeland that serve to challenge the notion that communities exist in definable, single, bounded spaces. Traditional theoretical understandings of community that stress homogeneity, its members sharing a singular understanding of the world based on a commonality of rules, values, and beliefs, overlook the possibility that the actions of people often confound "the fiction of cultures as discrete, object-like phenomena occupying discrete spaces" (Gupta and Ferguson 1992:7). For the Sierra Leoneans with whom I work, a definition of community that overlooks the ways in which they (re)imagine themselves as Sierra Leonean outside Sierra Leone, and instead focuses on the persistence or "loss" of "traditions" (especially away from "home"), negates the reality that individuals constantly select strategies to define themselves within their current contexts. Hence, as they align and realign community boundaries to reflect their understanding of the social space they occupy, the significance of social relationships in a multiplicity of settings transcends locality (Stoller 1996:776; also see Stern 1991). Hence, conceptualizations of homeland serve as a means through which Sierra Leoneans embody the experience of living in the diaspora, bringing "memory and longing, the ideational, the affective and the physical, the spacial and the temporal, the local and the global" into relief (Rapport and Dawson 1998:8).

As Eric Hobsbawm has pointed out, "humanity has learned to live far from its roots, even under some of the least attractive conditions. But nostalgia . . . still moves us" (1991:65). The nostalgia Hobsbawm refers to is not the nostalgia of the face-to-face childhood experience of home life, but that of a reconfigured homeland in which the present only acquires meaning as a consequence of Sierra Leonean response to displacement. How Sierra Leoneans respond when asked where they come from, how they situate themselves in relation to non-Sierra Leonean others, is a vital clue to the way in which they negotiate identity. As Keya Ganguly (1992) discovered in her study of middle-class professional Indians who emigrated to the United States in the 1960s and early 1970s, it is displacement that makes apparent the "*relational* character of memory" (1992:30), in which recollections take "on a special import because they represent the only set of discursive understandings which can be

appropriated and *fixed*," permitting people to "make sense of the uncer-
tainties of the present" (1992: 31). Like Ganguly, it is clear to me that
identities constructed in the immigrant context are fraught with ambivalence. Displacement creates a social space in which the constant struggle
to negotiate difference and marginality is actively played out in the public and private arenas of Sierra Leonean lives. Through the (re)presenta-
tion of a nostalgic homeland in ritual, ceremonies, images, gestures,
utterances, and decoration, Sierra Leoneans recall and localize memories of a prewar Sierra Leone in which the disjunctures between the distant past and the present are fused. As such, images of homeland are a
way of localizing memory within the space of displacement. Those
spaces ultimately become imaginative (re)constructions in which the
illusion of rediscovering the past in the present becomes the central paradigm for defining group and individual identity (Connerton 1989).

How is imagined geography produced and (re)produced? What are
the sites upon which the social construction of homeland becomes an
"active *practice*" in which experience is transformed into "tangible
power—an exercise in empowerment—by restructuring both the social
self and the relation between the self and the dominant Other(s)" (Stoller 1995:25)? What is the process by which collective cultural memory is
produced and made manifest in everyday experience? In *How Societies
Remember* (1989), Paul Connerton demonstrates the way in which commemorative ceremonies, like other rituals, share two characteristics,
"formalism and performativity," which as Connerton rightly asserts
allows them to "function effectively as mnemonic devices." However,
commemorative ceremonies, unlike other rituals, achieve their effect by
reference to "prototypical persons and events, whether these are understood to have a historical or mythological existence." These ceremonies
serve as "ritual *re-enactment*." That is social experience is enacted, negotiated, and ultimately encoded and (re)presented as (re)enactments of
"prior, prototypical actions" (1989:61). For Connerton, what is remembered in commemorative ceremonies is an image of the past in which a
"community is reminded of its identity as represented by and told in a
master narrative . . . a making sense of the past as a kind of collective
autobiography" (1989:70).

However, that is only part of the picture. For as Connerton asserts, a
master narrative is "more than a story told and reflected on; it is a cult
enacted" (1989:70). Master narratives are imparted and maintained
through their (re)enactment. What is remembered in a commemorative
ceremony is something more than a (re)constructed history of the past.
It is in fact a (re)collected set of images in which that which has disappeared (re)appears in new and intriguing forms. For Sierra Leoneans,
an imagined homeland provides the terrain upon which the displaced

and marginalized collective-self is performed. Community is embodied in the multiple discourses and enactments of their everyday lives. Sierra Leoneans map the boundaries of their community by defining and employing symbols that represent their social realities. Social perform-ance, understood as a practice in which social realities are generated, manipulated, and authenticated (Bourdieu 1977), renders meaningful socially defined situational contexts.

Performance is an especially powerful means of looking back on one-self. For Sierra Leonean men and women, identity is constructed in and authenticated more by the images and the performative action sur-rounding those images than by ordered sets of explicit values and beliefs. In this sense the performance of community is a primary mode of discourse that generates and authenticates cultural realities (see Geertz 1980, Turner 1982, Bruner 1986). Through image, words, objects, and bodies, versions of the past are (re)presented, legitimating present experiences. The presentation of the past has little to do with historical "truths," but much to do with the way in which displaced iden-tities are negotiated and made "real." Private memories of home are (re)worked to accommodate dominant representations of collective-self in the multiple public and private domains in which Sierra Leoneans move and, as such, create and maintain a communal history of a dis-placed community. As Connerton (1989:37) notes:

Groups provide individuals with frameworks within which their memories are localised and memories are localised by a kind of mapping. We situate what we recollect within the mental spaces provided by the group. But these mental spaces . . . always receive support and refer back to the material spaces that par-ticular groups occupy . . . no collective memory can exist without reference to a socially specific spatial framework. That is to say, our images of social spaces, because of their relative stability, give us the illusion of not changing and of rediscovering the past in the present. We conserve our recollections by referring them to the material milieu that surrounds us.

Of the multiple ways in which Sierra Leoneans perform community, the construction of the imagined geography of homeland provides a ter-rain on which boundaries of differentiation from the host society and continuity of community identity are simultaneously realized. Home-land, narrated, represented, and made concrete in souvenir-objects, realized in religious and ritual contexts, and continually reinvented, is both a potent metaphor and a central focus through which Sierra Leoneans weave the complex fabric of their identities. Marked through religious and American-inspired ethnic labeling, homeland is a mirror image, a place from which one can look back upon oneself and contem-plate the meaning of life as lived. So then we need ask, how does the construction of homeland produce a history through which identities are created and ultimately maintained?

Sierra Leoneans relocate themselves through expressive representations of homeland. These expressions form the boundaries that are the site for the construction of a homeland narrative, a densely packed space imagined to provide a means by which people recognize the identities, places, and realities that separate them from the perceived American Other (Bruner 1996b), but which also provide a social space in which an image of continuity with the past is maintained. The social and cognitive spaces that Sierra Leoneans construct and occupy provide a terrain upon which to retrace past and present experience, and allowing for memories to reappear forming a "whole ensemble of thoughts" that are common to the group and serve as the thread that binds (Connerton 1989:37).

The Cotton Tree

On the cover of the maiden issue of *Sierra Leone Today* (June 1990), a magazine published quarterly in the early 1990s in the Washington, D.C. metropolitan area by a group of Sierra Leonean academics and journalists, is a picture of the massive Cotton Tree that dominates the central square in downtown Freetown, the capital of Sierra Leone.[1] Inscribed over the image of the tree is a stirring call to national unity:

This great tree of ours, standing in our midst, should give all citizens an underlying sense of purpose, striving and effort, of social co-operation, an endurance, and of unity finally triumphing over all our several and ephemeral diversities, tribal, religious, and political.

In his introduction to the accompanying article, Ritchard M'Bayo, the editor, photographer of this particular picture, and a professor of communications at an American university, writes: "The mere symbolism this tree represents, and the wish that if only such a symbolism could guide the way we relate to each other, motivates our sharing of the piece with our readers" (20). In the same issue E. F. Sayers, the author of the lead article of the issue, "Our Cotton Tree,"[2] articulates similar sentiments:

Since a big Cotton Tree of great age, presiding over any town or village, must have witnessed and been familiar to the succeeding lives of the present and many past generations, they [the trees] tend to be held in veneration, almost as though they might be the after-life abode of ancestors whose souls may clingly [sic] inhabit the mysterious deep recesses and crevices between the immense buttresses of the trunk, and together with the bats and vultures—reincarnated

Figure 1. Cotton Tree, Freetown, Sierra Leone, cover of *Sierra Leone Today,* June 1990. Photograph by Ritchard M'Bayo.

in them—may flutter round and among the spreading branches and the kindly concealing foliage.

The author continues:

How many human joys and human sorrows has our Freetown Cotton Tree not seen, and how many tragedies and comedies must have been enacted within the sight of it and within its sight? Freetown's Cotton Tree stands to-day for a sense of continuity in our corporate life, symbolic link between our past and our future.

In asking the community to envision the Cotton Tree as a communal icon, M'Bayo points to the way objects of memory serve as a bridge between the past and present. The community response to this plea further illustrates the active and constructive nature of memory. While the editor's plea presents the tree as a storehouse of images, feelings, and history that Sierra Leoneans can evoke at will, it is nevertheless an attempt at (re)capturing an authentic past that is ultimately changed through remembering. As Colleen McDannell (1995:39) has noted in another context, Sierra Leoneans "look to spaces, gestures, images, and objects to embody memory" connecting them to their present circumstances. For Sierra Leoneans living in the United States, the Freetown Cotton Tree has become a powerful "key symbol" (Ortner 1973) of homeland and community identity in which a romantic and idealized past is articulated and through which a community is imagined and constructed. A place remembered becomes the "symbolic anchor" (Gupta and Ferguson 1992:11) of a displaced people, a site in which the complex narrative of home remembered is woven. Assuming sacred qualities, the tree embodies distance from home; at the same time it denies one's separation from it.

How do we account for this seeming contradiction? Gottlieb (1992:43–43) points out that, for the Beng of Côte d'Ivoire, the kapok tree, symbolically significant in much of West Africa, is both a "symbol of difference and, simultaneously, the obviation of that symbolic difference . . . [in which the] oscillation between the connections, on the one hand, and disjunctions, on the other, [embody] the richness that is the mark of the most powerful of symbols: ambivalence" (see also Turner 1967). Likewise, for Sierra Leoneans living in the United States the Cotton Tree has come to represent the ambivalence of living between two equally powerful social spaces. The tree represents both "home" and the longing for "home" that comes from living abroad. Symbolizing the distinct identity of the nation as a separate space, and thus constructing difference and separation, at the same time it creates a symbolic bridge between homeland/nation and host country that merges both spaces into a transnational flow. As a symbolic representation of transnational flow, the tree not only blurs the boundaries between here and there, it is also the vehicle through which the resulting continuity is produced. Not unlike the kapok tree Gottlieb has analyzed, the Cotton Tree's meaning revolves around a fundamental contradiction, and, "like many other powerful symbols . . . stands both for a certain concept and for the negation of that concept" (1992:43). In the final analysis, "it becomes itself by going beyond itself, turning into its conceptual opposite" (44). The Cotton Tree becomes a symbol of the complexly configured identities that emerge out of transnational experience while at the same time facilitating the production of those identities. Its meaning, oscillating between disjuncture and continuity, encapsulates and ultimately defines for my informants the relationship between the ambivalence of a world characterized by and experienced as conflict, dislocation, relocation, and, conversely, the fear of exile.

Domestic Decor

By their utilization of images of the Cotton Tree in both personal and communal spaces, Sierra Leoneans create a complex juxtaposition of home/abroad. For many of my informants, the Cotton Tree has become increasingly significant. The tree acts as a perpetual source of recollection that triggers memory. Khadi told me that when she saw the tree's picture on the magazine cover she realized that "everything in Freetown is centered there." The tree, she explained, is

very old, and because of its age it is a symbol of a country that has always been there and always will be. That whole picture is a memory. That tree is Sierra Leone; it is a reflection of Sierra Leone. I do not want to lose it. If you are not careful you forget. You have to have something so you don't lose your Sierra Leonean-ness. I don't want to melt in.[3]

The memory of the past embodies the present that Khadi desires, and in this sense the reality of the present is discredited. Memory becomes the medium through which experience is measured and understood. As Susan Stewart (1984:23) points out, "By the narrative process of nostalgic reconstruction the present is denied and the past takes on an authenticity of being, an authenticity which ironically, it can achieve only through narrative." Creating a longing for a past that has never really existed and "continually threatens to reproduce itself as a felt lack" (1984:23), Sierra Leoneans deny their present circumstances. For Khadi, images of the Cotton Tree capture traces of an "unrepeatable original experience" (McDannell 1995:41), and like Stewart's notions of the souvenir, function to "create a continuous and personal narrative of

Figure 2. Cotton Tree. Photograph by Ritchard M'Bayo.

the past," present, and future (1984:140). However, this narrative ultimately produces a tension between remembering and forgetting in
which only certain experiences are remembered. In essence, Khadi, like
many of my informants, uses objects, images and narrative to (re)make
homeland in order to forget what is in fact absent. As such they attempt
to fill a void, one that evokes loss, with what increasingly is out of their
reach (Forty 1999).

In her living room Khadi has what she calls a "sofa sized reproduction" of another picture of the Cotton Tree from the same issue of *Sierra
Leone Today* (21). This photo, shot from above, shows the tree and its
surroundings in the square. For Khadi, the impact of the picture lies in
its ability evoke memories, as well as the shifting boundary between present and past circumstances. The fluctuation between continuity and displacement is also deeply embodied in her three children, Ali, Fatmata,
and Ibrahim (at that time seventeen, twelve, and ten years old). All Khadi's children were born in the United States, a fact she often lamented.
Like many fellow community members, Khadi wants her children to
view themselves as Sierra Leoneans. "American children equal failed
parenthood," my informants often say, and Khadi is no exception. Our
discussions about community and the importance of homeland would

often turn toward the problems of raising children in the diaspora. She would often tell me:

If they [her children] view themselves this way [as not American] then I know I have been a successful parent. I have that picture of the Cotton Tree on my wall in the living room not only to remind me of who I am, but to remind them. It shows them who their parents are. Who they should be.

For Khadi, the importance of her children not identifying themselves as American is intertwined with the wish not only that they perceive themselves as Sierra Leonean, but that they never make the mistake of perceiving their parents as American.

Khadi and other Sierra Leonean parents constantly confront the reality that their children, born and raised in America, often embody what they fear most. For Khadi this was illustrated clearly by an incident at a local supermarket.

Fatmata and I went to Three Brothers to get a salad for dinner. There was a young man behind the counter and Fatmata noticed that he had an accent. She asked me: "Where do you think he is from?" "Why don't you ask him?" I told her. She wouldn't, so I said I would. Can you believe this child told me not to? She said I would embarrass her! So I asked anyway.

Much to Khadi's dismay, the conversation (all too familiar to me) went like this:

Khadi: Where are you from?
Young Man: Africa.
Khadi [exasperated]: And?!
Young Man: West Africa.
Khadi [more than exasperated]: And?!
Young Man: Sierra Leone

Fatmata, she related, stood there giggling the whole time. Upon discovering that he had mistaken a Sierra Leonean woman for an American, the young man was mortified. Khadi for her part was livid, and as she told me this story several days later, neither her anger nor her consternation had abated.

I get so mad when people think I am American! It has happened one too many times lately! My kids think it is funny! How could that boy think I was American? How could he not know?

For Khadi, as for many of the Sierra Leoneans I know, being recognized as a Sierra Leonean by other Sierra Leoneans is of paramount importance. This element of daily life becomes the site for the construction of identity in relation to home. Despite significant situational differences, the phenomenon is not unlike that which Stef Jansen describes when viewing post-Yugoslav identities. Sierra Leone, not disbanded but far away, becomes the "discursive background against which different cultural frameworks [are] invoked in the creation of a sense of belonging" (1998:91). From a diaspora vantage point, homeland is imagined as a place with a distinctive national character that is to be sustained and conveyed to those who have not ever had the privilege of being born or residing there. Sierra Leone, similar to Yugoslavia, becomes a "polysemic and dynamic reservoir of discursive material for the construction of one's identity" (Jansen 1998:93). Fluctuating between continuity and discontinuity it ultimately rests, if only for brief moments, "at the intersection of dwelling and travelling" (Trinh 1994:14). Homeland exists in traces and memories of the past and in the fear that forgetting will slowly corrode and ultimately destroy the foundation upon which collective and self identity is based. Daily acts of representation through objects, images, and narration act as a strategy to construct the illusion of continuity in the face of discontinuity. And as illustrated above, the illusion of continuity can instantly be fractured in a moment of nonrecognition by a fellow countryman and the response of an American daughter who views the incident as humorous.

Like many Sierra Leonean parents, Khadi often wonders how best to convey the importance of an emerging national-ethnic identity to her children. On several occasions during my stay in Washington, parents met specifically to discuss this "problem." Solutions were many, but the solution of choice at the time of my fieldwork was to send children home to be educated in the hopes that they would become "more Sierra Leonean" (though the civil war, March 1991–2002, foreclosed this option for many and led some to ultimately bring their children back to the States). Khadi and her husband Ahmed chose this strategy for their eldest son, Ali. In general, parents could rarely afford to send more than one child home. So they selected the eldest child. When I first met Khadi, Ali was still in Sierra Leone. She explained:

Ahmed insisted that Ali go home. At first I was unhappy; he was only thirteen. I knew I would miss him terribly. But Ahmed insisted that he wanted at least one child who was truly Sierra Leonean. I am glad Ali is in Sierra Leone now. Raising children here is hard. I have to work hard to make them understand that they are Sierra Leonean. It's not easy but it's possible.

For Khadi and Ahmed, Ali's return home became yet another qualifying symbol through which they could express their Sierra Leonean identity to themselves and to the community, and imbue it in their other children. They would often invoke Ali, particularly when their two younger children challenged the very foundation upon which their parenting skills were built. At such times they would remind Fatmata and Ibrahim that Ali was "suffering, living without the conveniences of an American life so that he could call himself Sierra Leonean. You should be proud of your brother" they insisted, "and try to make him proud of you."

The living room in Khadi and Ahmed's house is a canvas on which Khadi enacts her struggle to communicate her own sense of identity to herself, to her children, and to anyone who enters her home. Khadi would often (re)arrange furniture, pictures, and objects in the living room, and I would find myself in a "new" room when I would next visit her. Family pictures, photographs of her parents and parents-in-law taken in Sierra Leone many years earlier alongside photos of her children at various ages, were constantly (re)positioned. The room seemed to be perpetually in motion, and when I asked her one day, as she moved about (re)locating family pictures, why she felt compelled to redecorate so often, Khadi replied, "I just can't seem to get it right. It all seems a bit off center."

Amid all her rearranging, Khadi never moved the photo of the Cotton Tree. It hangs fixed in the center of the living room wall, facing the front door, and is the first thing seen upon entering the room. As such, it provides a lens into the way in which the boundaries of individual, family, and community identity are articulated. I asked Khadi why she never moved the Cotton Tree. After pausing a moment to reflect, she answered:

When I was last in Freetown I stopped and looked at the tree. I said, "Okay, the tree." I don't think it means anything [politically] to the average Sierra Leonean back home unless he or she is a Krio, but here [in the United States] it is more meaningful. Hanging on my wall, people will look at it and say: "Aha, this person is Sierra Leonean." Or they can ask, and I can tell them I am Sierra Leonean.

For Khadi, the tree has come to embody her sense of displacement and her related need to be recognized as a Sierra Leonean. When she says that the tree has no meaning to the "average Sierra Leonean back home," she means that while "back home" it may be a recognizable marker of Freetown, and hold particular meaning for the Freetown-based Krio population, it becomes a national symbol only in reference to transnational realities.[4] As a transnational symbol, it connects Sierra Leoneans in the United States to a place that they no longer occupy physically, but that they want to (re)create socially and intellectually in their current context. Thus, Ritchard M'Bayo deliberately uses the tree as a public national icon. Likewise, it is a central visual object that makes Khadi's and her family's Sierra Leonean identity visible, while at the same time pushing the knowing viewer to imagine the invisible, the rest of Sierra Leone.

The image of the Cotton Tree evokes the existence of homeland, one connected to a personal and historical past that appears to be stilled by the boundaries of the frame. But in its capacity to represent the multifaceted discourses of homeland, the image of the Cotton Tree (re)calls a past that is intrinsically tied to the present. It is a reminder of another world for which Sierra Leoneans long. The stillness of the image regenerates movement through the stories that are woven about it, infusing it with immediacy. The power of the image for Sierra Leoneans lies, as Bruner (1996b:302) has pointed out in another context, in its power to construct "dominant localities that define boundaries" in which Sierra Leoneans can center their narratives about home and abroad. In so doing they construct a transnational space that is infused with the experiences of displacement.

Iconic depiction of the tree confounds the assumption that the foundations of a national-ethnic identity need be situated either "here" or "there." Khadi describes the surrounding landscape of the Cotton Tree visible in the picture as a "resource center":

To the right of the tree stands the American Embassy. It's the fire that keeps Sierra Leone going; it stands for the support we can give our families if we can just get there [to America]. Also to the right of the tree is the Mobil gas station. It's the only place you can get gas in Sierra Leone most of the time, something you need to get you anywhere. For me that gas station means I can move, go anywhere. To the left of the tree stands the Archive/Courthouse. It is one of the oldest colonial buildings in Freetown. It represents justice, which we do not have in Sierra Leone, and stands for justice that if put in place would make Sierra Leone a better society. In Sierra Leone when you look at that tree it's just there, and you say it's always going to be there. It never occurs to you to say, "I'm never going to see it again."

Her description invokes the present in reference to the past. The past, however, can only have meaning through juxtaposition to the present, to a new way of life imagined in a reinterpretation of the past. The photograph systematically creates a filter through which Sierra Leoneans can construct a series of narratives that express their current circumstances. Sierra Leone becomes the "elsewhere" (Ossman 1994:19) of their dreams. In this expression it provides a way of knowing essential to the maintenance of identity. For Sierra Leoneans living in the United States, the "elsewhere" of the past is now home, the homeland now "elsewhere." In this sense, home is (re)imagined in terms of present experience, and it is the relationship between "elsewhere" and home that is shaping new and emergent identities. The image of the tree, its size mind-boggling, spreads across the photo to incorporate that imagined place beyond the border of the picture. It stands for the past, the present and the future of this community, validating an emerging sense of self that fights to situate itself in images of homeland. The Cotton Tree validates the claim that community is connected to a real place whose power and authority supersede any that my informants may encounter in their present situations. It establishes the legitimacy of calling oneself Sierra Leonean. It gives people a sense of self within emerging groups and frames the public world of Sierra Leone, merging it with the private world of a household. Through this picture Sierra Leone can be remembered, can become known to the children who have never been there, or those who left too early to have concrete memories. Negotiating the two worlds that Sierra Leoneans inhabit, the Cotton Tree embodies the transnational realities of their lives. It challenges the notion that movement into a new social space means an abandonment of one for the other. In its stillness it (re)creates movement.

Ritual Mapping

Throughout this chapter I have focused on the way my informants synthesize their identity into framed representations of homeland, while at the same time demanding that the gaze of the viewer go beyond the frame. But this is only part of the picture. Images keep the past and its locality in mind, but it is through social action that the past is materialized onto space, creating places of nostalgic remembering necessary for the reproduction of community. This is best exemplified in the heightened realities of ritual events.

Ritual provides a means through which participants (re)construct an imagined past and inscribe that past on to present locale. Space and place must be maintained carefully against all odds, and ritual provides the means by which the defining boundaries of community are maintained and managed. Hence, ritual brings a sharpened awareness to the dangers of instability centering and bringing to life that which can only be imagined by gazing at pictures of a Cotton Tree. As Appadurai has pointed out, "Ceremonies of naming and tonsure, scarification and segregation, circumcision and deprivation are complex techniques for the inscription of locality onto bodies" (1996: 79). As such, ritual, and in particular the naming ceremony, become the vehicle to produce memories of a nostalgic past, inscribing and incorporating those memories onto and into communal memory, producing a "structure of feeling" (Appadurai 1996:181; see also Connerton 1989).[5] The naming ceremony is the first truly public event in which an infant is presented to the community. Shaped in the context of a series of discourses and counterdiscourses in which issues of homeland, Islamic practice, and identity intertwined to configure and inscribe the terrain on which the event was taking place, this particular naming ceremony entailed a challenge to common practices among Sierra Leoneans in this community.

In its special capacity to evoke homeland, the naming ceremony maps and relocates, for both parents and their children, a sense of community that confirms and strengthens social identity (Cohen 1985:50).[6] Ordered to reflect the familiar (Sierra Leone), this ritual enacts the unfamiliar (America). In turn, how the American landscape, shaped and understood in terms of its juxtaposition to the Sierra Leonean homeland, deepens the boundaries, making them appear impenetrable. As such, the notion of locality is maintained in a dramatically delocalized world through the production of "local subjects" (Appadurai 1996:176). Homeland is produced and (re)produced in the naming ceremony, providing the social action for participants to recast boundaries in response to a series of references embedded in the opposition of self/other. That opposition, informed by the problematic of displacement, constructs multiple frames of reference and meaning in which the deeply territorialized imagined constructs of homeland/America encounter actual lived experience, simultaneously locating seemingly separate spheres of meaning within one social space (Bammer 1994). In their capacity to imbue geographic space with the imagined boundaries of a homeland, naming ceremonies continually recast boundaries in response to the ongoing negotiation of meaning, creating multiple domains within which participants respond to social, religious, political, and economic pressures, and providing the ground on which social experience is mediated through nostalgic rememberings in complex and differentiated ways. Hence, the naming ceremony does not simply imply a continuity with the past, but actively claims that continuity exists by ritually combining and (re)enacting a series of discourses in which memories become entangled with present circumstances creating the illusion of continuity across time and space. In this way, displacement is challenged and community made manifest in the evocation and embodiment of a central narrative centered on notions of homeland.

The Naming Ceremony—Thanksgiving Day, 1991

I turn now to a naming ceremony that I attended on Thanksgiving Day, 1991. My husband and I enter the living room of Abdul and Isha's suburban northern Virginia home, a modest second-floor two-bedroom garden apartment in a quiet working-class neighborhood. In the small room we encounter about twenty-five men and women who are engaged in a variety of activities. Most of the men sit on couches lining two walls of the room. Some are wearing pale blue or white embroidered African shirts, a few even wear patterned shirt-pants outfits, but most are dressed casually in American clothing. The women, virtually all wearing brightly colored dresses tailored from African cloth, move back and forth between the bedroom (where a three-week-old girl is being prepared for her ritual naming), the living room (where food is laid out), and the kitchen, where, as I would soon learn, a second table is covered with food). Abdul, his brother, and the imam who will perform the ceremony sit in folding chairs facing the row of couches. Abdul wears an African shirt, polyester pants, and a white cotton crocheted prayer cap. His brother and the imam are dressed similarly. Above the chatter of hosts and guests, Qur'anic recitation sounds from a battery-powered cassette player that sits on an end table by the sofa; concurrently a professional American football game blares from the 27-inch color television that dominates one corner of the living room.[7]

As in many Sierra Leonean homes, the walls are sparsely decorated with framed posters of Qur'anic verses, a black-framed color picture of the Grand Mosque in Mecca, and several pieces of tourist art from back home: roughly carved generic mini-masks and banana leaves with ink drawings of "natives" in "traditional" costume. Over the front door hangs a framed, glossy magazine photograph (*Time* or *Newsweek*, most likely) of Ronald and Nancy Reagan, by now ex-president and first lady. The Reagans, smiling, wave to an audience that is unseen but undoubtedly enthralled. My husband and I both note instantly the seeming incongruity of this particular image. However, to Abdul and his wife, the Reagans seem perfectly in place, simultaneously sharing the wall with both religious and homeland representations.

The juxtapositions of image and sound, particularly the Qur'anic recitation and football "sportspeak," intrigue me even more. Early in my fieldwork I might have presumed that the television would be shut off when the naming ceremony began. By now I am used to the swirl of sacred and profane sounds playing side by side at such occasions. This ceremony is one that purports to challenge such juxtapositions, to reassert an "authentic" over the "syncretic." Nevertheless, as the imam recites Qur'anic verses to open the naming ceremony, the televised play-by-play continues in the background, becoming part of the event. Eyes, at one moment fixed on the imam, drift to the television at any possibility of a dramatic play. Even the imam, my husband later claimed, "had one eye on the game," while never missing a Qur'anic beat.

The layout of the food and the corresponding swirl of smells also reflect the duality of the event. For today we are celebrating both a Sierra Leonean Muslim naming and the American holiday of Thanksgiving. The long table set up in the living room is covered with the usual West African-style fare for such events: *plasauce* (a leaf- and palm oil-based stew) and rice, roasted *halal* meat on skewers, somosas, salad, fruit, and ginger beer. The aroma of onions, pepper, ginger, and hot palm oil fill the apartment. Most ceremonies, whatever the occasion, are "potluck," with all participants expected to bring a dish—a "sacrifice."[8] I add my own offering, home-baked banana bread, my usual—and very popular—contribution, and compliment the women around me for laying out such a lovely table.

"Wait," one woman told me with a gleam in her eyes. "You haven't seen it all!" Taking me firmly by the arm, she led me into the kitchen, where a complete and very traditional American turkey dinner is laid out on a second table. Ordered from a local supermarket, cooked and ready to serve, was a fully stuffed and roasted fifteen-pound turkey. The aroma of the bread stuffing—rosemary, thyme, celery, and onion—wafted through the room. Alongside the turkey sat the usual American trimmings: mashed potatoes, corn, green beans, and cranberry sauce. If the aromas of the living room evoked memories to us all of Africa, the kitchen greeted me with all the sensory reminders of childhood holidays with family and friends.

The naming ceremony, a combination of Qur'anic recitation and a sermon during which the mother and child sit at the center of the room with the imam, cannot commence until Isha is satisfied that she and her three-week-old daughter are properly attired. Dressed in Western clothing—a colorful skirt and top reserved for special events, and unveiled—Isha will not let the ceremony start until she has draped a large piece of patterned cloth from Sierra Leone over her head. In arranging this cloth she makes sure that her baby, also dressed in Western clothing (a two-piece white knitted outfit that I had given as a birth gift) has a bit of the cloth draped over her as well. When Isha is satisfied that she and her daughter are properly covered, the naming ceremony begins.

It was only after I had given birth to my son two years later and was given a bolt of African cloth by a Zimbabwean friend—"So you can wrap your child in Africa"—that I understood the importance that Isha gave to covering her daughter and herself with a bit of cloth from Sierra Leone. Dressed in the "Sunday best" of the American world in which her child was born, Isha's insistence upon "wrapping herself in Africa" dramatized the importance of homeland to the participants. Using the cloth to mask the realities of their American context and connecting herself and her American-born child through that cloth to homeland, Isha blurred the boundaries of the seemingly separate worlds that were symbolized in a Sierra Leonean-born mother and father and an American-born child, and by the multiple representations of the two worlds in which they lived. The cloth linked the incongruous juxtapositions of the event, symbolizing the importance of connecting two worlds so that the newborn was not abandoned to the world of her birth.

"This Child Is Being Named Properly"

The ceremony begins with Qur'anic recitation. The imam, the father, and the mother, holding the infant in her arms, all sit in the center of the room on metal folding chairs. The guests grow quiet; the tape player has been shut off, but the football game plays on. The imam, who has arrived recently from Sierra Leone, is a follower of the Saudi-trained Imam Bashar, a religious teacher who has been gaining prominence in Freetown and whose influence was beginning to reach into the Washington, D.C. community at the beginning of my fieldwork.[9] The imam begins his sermon, which he delivers in Krio, by praising ":the Arabs" for their "proper" practice. He implores all present to follow their example:

If you practice as the Arabs do, then you will reap the same benefits. Your children will be trained properly and have the tools not to give in to the evils of America. This child is being named properly. There is no drink here. I have seen too much of that in America.

Focusing on the correct behavior of Muslims in general, and the proper way in which to name a child in particular, he continues:

When naming a child in the U.S., many parents give big parties. They serve alcohol. This is not proper. When a child is born, after seven days you are to call the *adhan* (the call for prayer) in her ears and name the child. This is our obligation to the child. How will the child know who she is until we name her? How will she know she is a Muslim? This child will be brought up properly. Her parents have set her feet on the right path.

In challenging what he perceives as the syncretic, corrupted practices of some Muslim Sierra Leoneans, this imam implores his followers to search for authenticity in purity of practice, a purity defined by what Stewart and Shaw (1994:8) have called "anti-syncretic" discourses. In his sermon he attempts to dismantle elements of practice in the United States that he deems alien. His assertion that he has seen too much evil in America is ultimately directed at practices within his own community, rather than an abstract evil Other called America.

To many of the participants at this event, the imam's words hit home. Turning back to perceived "traditional" practices—in this case, naming children within a traditional time frame (the first seven days of a child's life), rather than within the prolonged time frame that has emerged in the United States (whenever enough money is saved to have a big party)—is for many a strategy whereby new parents can regain a sense of self that they feel has been lost living in a foreign context.

The sermon ended, the imam names the baby. Taking her from her mother, holding her close to him, he whispers the *adhan*, then her names into both her ears, so that only she can hear. The infant lies quietly in his arms while all look on. The imam then turns to the parents and asks if they have reached agreement together on the child's name. They affirm this quietly and the imam announces the baby's name aloud several times. Her name, we are told, is Adana. It means "the beginning of humanity." It is this name, first whispered to the child and then announced publicly, that introduces the newborn to her community.

The naming ceremony complete, the food is served. Having done their best to ignore the football game during the proceedings, the men now turn full attention to the television. The older children present, all either American-born or having lived most of their lives in the United States, also sit down to watch the game. I hear them complaining quietly to each other that they have missed important plays. The women begin to serve the men, piling Sierra Leonean food onto heavy-duty paper plates. Sitting to the side writing notes, I am ordered by the women to "Get up and serve your husband," who has become drawn into the men's discussion of the game. The women instruct me to fill his plate with Sierra Leonean food first; the turkey will be served afterward.[10]

All the Trimmings

This particular event was shaped in the context of a series of discourses and counter-discourses in which issues of homeland, Islamic practice, and identity intertwined to shape and inscribe the terrain on which the ceremony was taking place. It also entailed a vigorous challenge to practices common among Sierra Leoneans in this community. Most naming ceremonies that I attended were elaborate affairs, "big parties" held in rented halls with a hired disc jockey blasting "party music" through over-sized speakers, and often with alcohol present for those who wished to consume it. As one informant told me, an elaborate party "is more important now than naming your child was in the traditional time. You don't want your child to grow up thinking you didn't give them the best." Parents often scrimp and save for a year or more to afford the event. As a result, many children are well into toddlerhood before they are officially named. Yet some Sierra Leonean Muslim parents worry that unnamed children are in danger of spiritual anonymity. One informant feared for her one-year-old daughter: "What if the child dies before she is named? It would be a disaster! The child would have no identity before God!"

Increasingly, some parents have begun to contest the "big party" (see Chapter 7) naming ceremonies, Abdul and Isha among them. Their turn toward practices defined as more "authentic" cannot be seen as the simple erasure of elements deemed foreign. Rather, they continually recast imagined traditional forms to construct an essentialized Muslim Sierra Leonean homeland.

Community, defined by the elusive construct of homeland, constructed and authenticated by the categories "Us" and "Them," and illustrated in the naming ceremony described above, forms the foundation on which Sierra Leonean men and women build their immigrant lives in the United States. But, as Angelika Bammer (1994:xii) has pointed out, "as we ever more obsessively attempt to specify our precise locations (the familiar 'I am a [fill in the blanks]' recitation), our sense of identity is ineluctably, it seems, marked by a peculiarly postmodern geography of identity: both here and there and neither here nor there at one and the same time."

Nothing demonstrates this more clearly than the finale to Adana's naming ceremony. After sharing the Sierra Leonean food prepared specifically for this occasion, in due course we move on to the kitchen to partake of the "American" fare. The men, who had expressed great enthusiasm for the "African" food, eat with gusto, but are markedly less animated about the turkey dinner. After my husband and I voice our own preference for the plasauce, some confess to us that they find the turkey rather bland (they were not wrong). The children, however, are a different story. They move with greater ease from living room to kitchen tables. Piling plates high with Thanksgiving dinner, they settle back down in front of the football game. The naming ceremony over, it is time to celebrate Thanksgiving. To the kids, the turkey and trimmings are a treat, a holiday break from the African food that constitutes so important a part of their normal daily diet. Much to their parents' consternation, the Thanksgiving dinner is familiar, delicious, theirs.

The Sierra Leoneans with whom I work not only struggle with changing notions of homeland, defined in large part by their distance from "home," as an ethnic-national marker, but are in the process too of redefining their religious—Muslim—identity. The question of what it means to be a good Muslim, especially in America, is for many a concern no less important than what it means to remain Sierra Leonean in the United States. This question confronts them with a variety of dilemmas to which I now turn. How these Muslim Sierra Leoneans square their indigenous religious traditions and practices with the often conflicting interpretations of Islamic religious authority in the United States places them very much on a sacred "borderland" between homeland and American Islam.

Chapter 4
Spiritual Centers, Peripheral Identities:
On the Sacred Border of American Islam

Friday afternoon prayer at the Islamic Center swirls with the smells, sounds, sights, and tastes of a diverse group of Muslims who for nearly fifty years have "Islamized" and "stamped into the earth" (Werbner 1996b:167) their claims to a piece of Massachusetts Avenue. The perfumes worn by men and women from Africa, the Middle East, Asia, and North America mingle with the distinct aromas of incense and lamb stew, imbuing every corner of the Center with the "smell of Islam." Congregants adorned in silk, satin, cotton, and polyester flow through a euphony of Muslim sound—the adhan, Qur'anic recitation, and whispered prayers—to form straight lines facing Mecca, the center of their world, to pray in unison, as one body. "This place is sweet," Ali tells me, as we sit savoring the lamb stew that is served to congregants after the prayer has ended. Swirling his spoon through a steaming plate of rice and meat, he continues:

It is here that I found Islam again. I spent years here [in the United States] being frustrated. Back home, my father taught Qur'an in a school without walls, but he never pressured me to pray. I could recite portions of the Qur'an, but it is here in America that I discovered the meaning of prayer. Here [at the Center] I learned that you pray and fast for God, not for yourself or material things. It is here that I learned to live every moment of my life as a Muslim.

We sit silently watching a self-contained world move all around us.

The Islamic Center of Washington, D.C. is a place in which my informants negotiate the stark contrast between nostalgic feelings for the Islam of home and the growing awareness of a markedly different engagement with the Islam that is embodied in this location. As they traverse the complex terrain of the Center, negotiating the social relations and practical knowledges of a locality that is informed by a complex set of diverse practices and understandings of what it means to be a Muslim living in the United States, their embodied practices in relation to all other congregants at the Center, constructs a *habitus*, which produces and (re)produces a dynamic spacial ordering of knowledge (Bourdieu 1977).

In this chapter I explore how my informants engage with a multiethnic Muslim community in which belief and practice are negotiated, defined, and (re)defined in the larger non-Muslim community. For this broad-based community, social and religious meaning is negotiated and intrinsically connected to a central point of reference, a perceived geographical center, in which notions of what it means to be a Muslim living in the United States are examined. The Islamic Center plays a multidimensional role in the lives of these Muslims. Participation in a culturally diverse congregation provides a framework for social and cultural interaction both between and within ethnic groups in the Washington area, creating dominant interpretations of meaning and practice as well as a multiplicity of voices that resist those interpretations. It is here that many of my informants turn to explore the complexities of a religious worldview that embodies broader spatial orientations, but that nevertheless has been localized in relation to competing interpretations of "proper" Islamic practice and belief in the diaspora. For many of the Sierra Leonean Muslims with whom I work, their understanding of Islam, a significant part of their identity, is being shaped by these many voices.

The Islamic Center is a place in which the cultural and social dramas of everyday life are acted out. Symbols and traditions are manipulated and given expression, relationships are negotiated, and new social identities formed. Multiple voices of religious discourse are incorporated into the everyday practice of religion, lending substance to a search for, and validation of, an authoritative definition of what it means to be a Muslim. For Sierra Leoneans redefining identity in an American context, this diversity of voices lends power to ideas that are understood to have objectified religious reality. In this community, as in other Muslim communities (Eickelman and Piscatori 1990), believers assert that Islam is universal and clear, a coherent closed system, and that their representations of practice and tradition are stable and uniform.

But daily encounters often highlight differences in politics, practice, social customs, even dress. For Sierra Leoneans, the social and religious meaning of these assertions creates a mirror through which "social relations subject to interpretation . . . focuses crucial questions about what it means to be human in a meaningful world" (Chidester and Linenthal 1995:12). When Sierra Leoneans look into that mirror they often see themselves caught between universal aspirations and an endless multiplication of meanings in which Islam, filtered through a broad range of interpretations, can come to signify almost anything. As such, Islamic knowledge is ultimately not defined by its connections to any particular set of practices or understandings, but instead by the limitless "claims and counter-claims on its significance" (18). The Islamic Center becomes the stage upon which the production of meaning is filtered through a diverse set of discourses that claim authentic ownership of a proper Islamic understanding and practice and the many voices that challenge those claims. This ultimately produces a space in which strategies of appropriation and exclusion are employed to advance the special interests of some and silence those of others. And, constructing a milieu in which inversion and hybridization are set in motion, ultimately laying the ground work for a resistance to that domination. This is the type of space that Foucault (1986:24) called a heterotopia, "a kind of effectively enacted utopia in which real sites, all the other real sites that can be found within the culture, are simultaneously represented, contested and inverted," a time-out-of-time site that alters the way in which congregants understand the world in which they reside.

Setting

Located in the heart of Embassy Row, the Islamic Center was built in the 1950s in response to the influx of peoples from the Muslim world into the District of Columbia. It was also, as the subtext of the official history reveals, the outgrowth of a longing for the "pure" Islam of an imagined shared past in which significant commonalities among Muslims scattered across the globe come to define for each member of the congregation a "memory-text." As the Center's chronicler recounts, "On a cold night during the dark hours of World War II in the latter part of November 1944, members of the diplomatic corps and representatives of Washingtonian society gathered in a funeral parlor in the capital of the United States of America to bid farewell to a distinguished Turkish diplomat." The mourners agreed that the absence of a mosque in which to hold a prayer service for their colleague was a "shame," and the idea of the Islamic Center was born. The Washington Mosque Foundation was formed in 1945 to facilitate the building of an Islamic Center to serve as a place of worship, as a facility for lectures, teaching and publications, and as a way to promote understanding of Islam in the United States (Abdul-Rauf 1978:12). The Center was, from the outset, a site upon which the desire to remember and to forget, to hold onto a fleeting sense of meaning, laid the foundation for the "creative cultural production" (Rosaldo 1989:208) of forms of representation that attempt to freeze in time an imagined past and solidify the emotions and desires of a diverse congregation.

Figure 3. Islamic Center, Washington, D.C., 1991. Photograph by the author.

Completed in 1957, the Center is open to all Muslims. The congregation, encompassing the foreign diplomatic and business communities, expatriates, naturalized citizens, and American converts, represents the breadth of the Islamic world. Its members come from all walks of life. They are taxi drivers, teachers, lawyers, doctors, corporate executives, service workers, food vendors, scientists, engineers, students, homemakers, and diplomats. The congregation reflects sectarian as well as cultural and national diversity. Unlike many other Islamic centers in the United States that cater to particular ethnic groups, this institution is truly international. Shii and Sunni pray together. The diverse nature of the congregation is reflected in the ethnic makeup of its staff. The director-imam is a Saudi. He has classical Islamic training, as well as a Ph.D. in psychology from an American university, and is fluent in both English and Arabic. The head of security is an Iranian; his assistants are Moroccan, Kenyan, and American. The librarian at the time of my fieldwork was Sudanese, the muezzin who calls the faithful to prayer an Egyptian, and the cooks Moroccan. The Islamic teacher was Pakistani, the general office staff South Asian, Arab, and American.

The mosque itself, the centerpiece of the Islamic Center, also reflects the diversity of the congregation. Aside from the *mihrab*, the prayer niche denoting the *qibla*, or direction of Mecca, there are no specific plans or designs prescribed for building mosques. Rather, each is constructed stylistically to reflect the community that sponsors it. In the case of this mosque, the diversity of congregants is most clearly seen in the building materials, which were gathered from many countries. The tiles are from Turkey, the *minbar* (pulpit) from Egypt, the carpets from Iran, and the marble from the state of Vermont. The universality of Islam is represented in the Qur'anic verses and names, or attributes, of God inscribed in Arabic on the ceiling and walls, as well as on the minaret. The crescent that sits atop the minaret, 160 feet above ground level, serves to represent the essential unity of the very diverse congregation (Abdul-Rauf 1978:68).

Located in the basement of the mosque is a lecture hall. At the time of my fieldwork this room served a variety of purposes. On Fridays it was used by women to offer prayer (during the week women pray upstairs, in a corner of the mosque, separated by a movable partition). Most Fridays the basement was filled to capacity. Wedding receptions were often held in this room following mosque ceremonies. Every evening during Ramadan women would gather in the basement to break their fast, each contributing food from her country of origin. Also located in the basement are classrooms where Islamic and Arabic language instruction for children and adults is held, as well as men's and women's rest rooms with facilities for the ritual ablution (*wudu*), which is required before prayer. Toward the end of my fieldwork, plans to renovate the basement had been drawn up, a response to the growing number of congregants. Women were to be relocated into a newly built structure in one of the outer courtyards.

The mosque is flanked by two wings. As one enters the Center, the wing to the right contains the director's office, the book store, and a gift shop. The wing on the left houses the library. There are several court-yards. The courtyard on the right is rarely used, except during the two major holidays, Id al-Fitr (the festival marking the end of Ramadan) and the Id al-Adha (the Feast of the Sacrifice), when extra space is needed for people to pray. The courtyard on the left is used every day and con-tains two structures. One is a kitchen in which daily meals for the direc-tor, his staff, and their guests are prepared, as well as meals for the congregation on Friday, when free food is distributed after the prayer. The kitchen has separate windows from which food is distributed to men and women. The other structure was built to accommodate the overflow of worshipers as the congregation grew through the 1960s and 1970s. It is often used on Fridays to accommodate men who want to eat indoors (as noted above, plans were underway to move the women's prayer here). Otherwise, weather permitting, the men eat in the courtyard. Women eat their Friday meals in the basement of the mosque apart from the men, but they do enter the courtyard to be served at the women's window in the kitchen. The central courtyard directly in front of the mosque was dominated by a fountain that was rarely in working order and which was finally removed several years after my initial fieldwork. On Fridays men often pray in the courtyard, and afterward sit around the fountain area discussing important matters.

For the many Muslims in the Washington, D.C. metropolitan area, the Islamic Center has come to be the single, central force of their commu-nity. Its administrative connection to the perceived centers of the Islamic world, through the diplomatic community, lends authority to the belief that a unified and authentic understanding of Islam exists and is embodied in a central geographical space. Religious communities, constructed through the imaginings of their members, are shaped, accepted, and sustained through symbol and metaphor (Anderson 1983:14–16; Eickelman and Piscatori 1990:4; Geertz 1973). For these Muslims, the Islamic Center represents a connection to a stable, unified understanding of religion, which in this case is seen as being derived from the central Islamic states of the Arab world, especially the Arabian peninsula, home of the Holy Cities. The belief that authority and power emanate from a central source is particularly important to people like the Sierra Leonean Muslims with whom I work, who perceive themselves on the periphery of the Muslim world.

For those Sierra Leoneans the Islamic Center is imbued with profound spiritual power. They describe it as the spiritual heart of the Muslim community of which they are a part. This spiritual power, defined as a memory of a past way of life in which the "evils" of modernity are challenged, is understood to be sedimented in the space, objects, and images that signify, affirm, and give significance to official interpretations of Islam at the Center. Through imaginative (re)collection and (re)presentation, notions of a common collective Islamic past are reified, and in the case of my informants, understood to emanate from the authoritative voices at the Islamic Center, the imam, religious instructors, and Arab believers who are taken to be proper practioners of the faith. How then is this illusion of centralized power created, validated and utilized in the social world of Sierra Leoneans?

The Islamic Center is the center of their world. It defines daily interactions with the Muslim and non-Muslim communities in which they reside. It is in this world of social relationships that people create and utilize concepts of power and authority, constructing not only individual but collective identities founded on sanctioned symbolic acts such as prayer and fasting. Through Islamic practice that is deemed legitimate and timeless, the reification of memory through practice at the Center "constitutes an apparent permanence of the recollected, organized in time and space" (Crane 2000:3). It is the place in which my informants weave into their lives ideas about the nature of the world enabling them to negotiate their understanding of Islam, validate and empower how they identify themselves as Muslims, and ultimately take that knowledge beyond the walls of the Center to become a central point of reference around which identities evolve and are enacted in everyday experiences (Crane 2000; Mandel 1990:153–54).

Knowledge and Practice

Through the multiple discourses available to them, Sierra Leoneans are able to make choices about how they will be Muslims. Religious belief and practice are influenced, religious identity is (re)constructed, and the feeling of being part of a unified community, which originates in belief and practice, is interpreted contextually. In other words, the diversity of the Muslim community, the encounter with "other" believers, gives Sierra Leoneans a heightened sense of how they are Muslim and in what ways their understandings and practice of Islam may be wanting, even inauthentic. The imagined bounded, distinctions between "us" and "them," sharpens an awareness of differences in religious beliefs and practices. That motivates a desire to reshape identity. Sierra Leoneans thus strive to redefine their own Muslim identity in relation to an imagined, dominant "other." Increasingly, their feelings of marginality provide a context for their newfound religious understanding (Eickelman and Piscatori 1990; Mandel 1990).

Sierra Leonean Muslims in the United States describe their religious life in Sierra Leone as peripheral, displaced, and disconnected, distanced from the central Islamic states. This feeling of distance is embedded in a self-consciousness about the quality of religious knowledge that they received in Sierra Leone, knowledge they often feel to have been shrouded in mysteries and dominated by the few who have learned access to religious truths. As Mustafa put it:

In Sierra Leone they do not go into details. They just tell you not to drink, but not why. When this imam back home, who studied in Saudi Arabia, came home and started to tell us why, the elders in Freetown became very disturbed. They felt he was revealing secrets.

In the United States, believers like Mustafa focus on learning the meaning of practice. "Good intentions are not enough," stated Abdul. "You shouldn't be afraid of knowledge." For Abdul, Mustafa, and others, the sense of being outsiders to such a significant, defining element in their lives are or have at times been framed by feelings of embarrassment, frustration, anger, and in some instances hostility to religion. In relating how his relationship to Islam has changed since coming to America, Abdul told me that

Many of us were hostile to Islam because of the methods of introduction in Sierra Leone. We did not have choice and there was lack of meaning in it for us, mainly because of language [Arabic]. Islam is by choice in America.

The feeling of being peripheral, passive followers of religious prescriptions they cannot understand, or recipients of incorrect traditions, is central to why and how these Sierra Leoneans continually redefine themselves as Muslims. For the Sierra Leoneans with whom I work, self-consciousness about the extent and quality of their knowledge of religious practice and meaning motivates them to seek alternative interpretations of their religion that they accept as more authentic. They crave knowledge that is both accessible and authoritative. The Islamic Center is the authoritative "text" to which they turn for that knowledge.

For many, the feeling of being peripheral is translated into an emphasis on "correct" practice. At the Center they observe and gauge religious practice and reflect on daily life. The first time I went to the Center was with Mustafa. It was during the month of Ramadan, 1991. It was actually the first time I had met him in person; prior to this we had only conversed on the phone. He took me to the Islamic Center to introduce me to others like him who describe themselves as "born again." As Mustafa tells it:

I came back to Islam a year ago. I did not quit, I was always a believer. Up until this time, 1973 was the last time I had prayed. I came back to Islam in the month of Ramadan last year, but I did not fast. I came back because I was living a bad life. I never prayed. My conscience was bothering me. I never drank or did drugs, I am very proud of that, but it was not enough. So I began to go to the Center, read books, learn to pray. I found out what you needed to do to be a good Muslim. You must do more every day to please Allah. If you are going to jump in the water you must get entirely wet.

For these men and women, being "born again" is not embedded in redefining belief. The essential question is not, "What is wrong with how I believe?" Instead the important question is centered on how one practices Islam, and more specifically on how one can be a "successful" Muslim in this world and the next.

My informants tend to focus on correct practice as the vehicle for success. For Mustafa, being a "good Muslim" came to mean that every action in his life needs to be informed by correct practice. Every moment is now a cleansing of his previous life's sins, bringing him one step closer to salvation. Salvation is defined by the acquisition of blessings, that is, the acquisition of grace, a sense of a spiritual influence that God sends down (Glassé 1989:64). Every action, every circumstance can be a vehicle for blessings. Even Mustafa's relationship with me is informed by these ideas. He feels the blessings he will receive from his willingness to facilitate my understanding of his and others' religious journeys will be well worth it:

I'll help you get what you need. You get many blessings if you help someone during the month of Ramadan. Blessings are important for me. I do not want the Angel of Death to hand me over to the tar-faced Angel when I die. During Ramadan you get 27 percent more blessings if you pray in the mosque than if you pray somewhere else. Many people park their cars far from the mosque because every step you take toward it, sins are rubbed off, and every step elevates you closer to Allah. I want the Angel of Death to hand me over to the two shiny-faced Angels who take you to Allah. You must pray or you will go to Hell.

Collecting blessings is profoundly important to Mustafa, and the blessings received this Ramadan were especially important, for it was the first anniversary of his "rebirth" as a Muslim. He was celebrating the triumph of having been a good practicing Muslim for one year.

Worship

For many of my informants, practicing Islam correctly is embedded in acts of worship, the most significant of these being prayer. *Salat*, ritual prayer, is performed five times each day. The basic unit is the *rak'a*, a round of ritual actions, including prostration and sacred utterances. Each prayer consists of a prescribed number of rak'as. Extra rak'as are permitted and, indeed, encouraged. If for a valid reason it is not possible to pray at the appointed time, the prayer can be made up (Glassé 1989:317). Prayer is a central means of worship. It brings the believer before God and works to purify him/her of all that is bad.

My informants believe deeply in the purifying power of ritual prayer. For these men and women the act of prayer represents their renewed Muslim identity. Many of my informants described prayer as making them "feel light." In describing how she felt before she began to pray again, one woman told me that when she does not pray she feels guilty about her behavior: "I feel like there is a heavy load on my shoulders." When I asked Mustafa about the importance of prayer he told me that before he was "born-again" he felt that life had no meaning or purpose:

Something was missing spiritually. I was feeling badly. Allah made me realize that all that partying I was doing was a dead end. You must pray, ask for forgiveness. Doing good things is not enough, you must pray for forgiveness.

For many Sierra Leoneans who prayed infrequently or who had stopped entirely, performing prescribed prayer is the first step toward reestablishing their Muslim identity. In subsequent relations with fellow Muslims, including friends and family, prayer becomes a focal point in the assertion of their newfound identity.

Central to that assertion of identity is the concept of *da'wah*, the act of calling, or inviting one to Islam. Doing da'wah is generally associated with those "who preach in the spirit of the contemporary Islamic resurgence" (Gaffney 1994:33), and in the American context is directed both at Muslims who do not appear to be practicing Islam correctly as well as at potential American converts. Mustafa's first attempt at da'wah was aimed at his wife, Sadatu, and was related primarily to her unwillingness to pray regularly. When Mustafa first started praying, Sadatu would not. They would have intense arguments over what he expected of her. She told me that she resented his intrusion into how she did or did not practice, but for the sake of peace she complied.

To avoid the arguments I began to pray, but my heart and soul was not into it. I would pretend to pray because, as you know, women stand behind men when they pray, so he couldn't see me. He never knew I was pretending. But then I started reading the books Mustafa brought home and I started to feel guilty about my behavior. So I pray properly now. Sometimes I still wish God was not always looking.

After confiding her feelings to me she went off to pray.

Toward the end of my fieldwork Sadatu, who had not been "reborn" entirely when we had this conversation, had completely "submitted." For Mustafa this was a profoundly triumphant moment, for he felt that how his wife practiced reflected directly on him. In a later conversation during which we discussed her past impressions of Islam, Sadatu told me:

> It feels good, my life is better. I was in limbo. Muslims in America get into limbo because it is a Christian country. I try to do what I am supposed to do, but it is hard for me. I work and can not pray when I am supposed to. I make up the prayers when I come home. Deep down I have always been a Muslim, but I need to pray more.

For Mustafa, Sadatu, and many other Sierra Leoneans in America, rigorous practice is the vehicle by which they choose to represent themselves as Muslims. Being Muslim is intrinsically connected to cleansing one's self of sin in the eyes of God, and representing that cleansed self to the world.

Friday noon prayer is the quintessential event in which one's cleansed self can be displayed to the community. The communal prayer is insisted upon not only as meritorious but as a duty. It is on Friday that the imam delivers the *khutba*, or sermon, which during my attendance at the Islamic Center lasted from half an hour to an hour. After the khutba, the worshipers perform prayer, in this case a two-rak'a prayer in place of the normal daily four-rak'a noon prayer (Glassé 1989:133–34).

For my informants, Friday prayer is the most significant moment in which the Muslim experience is interpreted and communicated. It is a event in which the community displays its Muslim identity to itself (Drewal 1992). It is a complex event in which people act out the experiences of their lives, utilizing ritual practice to express those experiences. The participants are actively engaged in the transformation of meaning. Religious identity is enacted, symbols and traditions manipulated, cultural forms given expression, and relationships negotiated. For the Sierra Leoneans with whom I work, Friday prayer is a particularly special event, one that creates and reinforces feelings of community (Cadaval 1991; Drewal 1992:164; Lambek 1990). It is a time in which they can come together with a diverse congregation of believers (umma) to fulfill a religious commitment. For these Sierra Leoneans, feeling as one with the broader Muslim community is embedded in that larger community's perceived mastery of correct practice. Friday prayer is a time and event in which they "mirror-off" the perceived authorities within the community, asking how they can correct their practice.

Friday prayer is also a primary time during which Muslim community leaders define and authenticate religious practice. Both official (the imam) and unofficial figure. These individuals consciously construct an atmosphere of authenticity and centrality by "direct[ing] the flow of symbols" (Laitin 1986:176; also see Drewal 1992:164). The imam through his sermon, members of the congregation in conversation and acts of piety—doing more than the required number of rak'as before prayer begins, putting money in the charity box, dress, and overall demeanor—continually redefine correct practice. Perceiving themselves as a peripheral community, Sierra Leoneans watch closely and weigh which forms of practice to adopt.

One Friday before prayer, Sadatu and I were sitting in the women's section of the mosque. A woman entered with her face completely covered. Sadatu suddenly turned to me and asked: "Why do some women cover their faces like that?" I told her I was not sure, and asked her what she thought about the women's particular style of Muslim dress.

It's their faces, why do they cover their faces? Should I dress like this? In Sierra Leone no one covers their faces like that. It confuses me. Is this the right way for a Muslim woman to dress?

Sadatu suddenly wondered if her traditional Sierra Leonean dress was improper, even immodest. Had this woman, with whom we never had a chance to speak, somehow figured out or been better instructed in proper dress for women? During the entire time we were there Sadatu watched the woman intently. By the time we left she had, after debating long and hard with herself, decided that this woman did in fact possess authoritative knowledge that she had not yet acquired, a knowledge to which she certainly aspired.

For Sadatu and the many Sierra Leonean Muslims who participate in Center events, the most fundamental questions they can and do ask themselves are, "What is my religion?" "Why is it important in my life?" and, most important for my informants, "How do my beliefs guide my conduct?" (see Eickelman 1992:644; Needham 1981). The answers to these questions shape their discourse and practice. Increasingly this discourse is one of return to "traditional" practice, the (re)institution of what are taken to be older, more authentic forms of religious understanding, which is shaping profoundly how these men and women define themselves as Muslims (Eickelman 1992:643). For religion to be objectified in people's minds it must be discussed for them by experts, or, as in the case of Sadatu, enacted by people whose behavior is perceived as exemplary. Of the many ways that the discourse of correct practice is sustained, the most significant for these men and women is the printed word. Literacy is the key, access to religious truth in a language that one can master (644).

Textual Authorities

For these Sierra Leoneans, the Center book store is a significant micro-center. Here are available instructional books and tapes, as well as translations into English of the Qur'an and *hadith*. Access to these materials allows them to explore and discover their religiosity on their own. This is extremely significant for men and women who feel that their knowledge of proper Islam is weak.

These English translations are so important that some of my informants become profoundly disturbed, even passionate, when confronted with texts in Arabic. As Mustafa and I left the Center one Friday after prayer, we were approached by a young man passing out Arabic flyers. "How dare they!" Mustafa fumed. "This is America! Anything to do with the Center and Islam should be in English!" He ripped the flyer into shreds and proclaimed he would have nothing to do with anyone who did not understand that English should be the language of communication for American Muslims. I tucked my copy away. When I had it translated I discovered that it was an advertisement for low-rate air fares to the Middle East.

For many Sierra Leoneans, the difficulty of learning written Arabic, which in Sierra Leone is traditionally studied only in the context of Qur'anic schools, colored Islam with an aura of secrecy. As a result, Arabic came to embody symbolically powerful knowledge used to facilitate secrecy (see Bledsoe and Robey 1986). Through contact in America with Muslims whom they perceive to be practicing Islam more properly, these Sierra Leoneans come to believe that this secretive knowledge actually served to prohibit them from practicing correctly. For some, like Abdul, the inaccessibility of the sacred language became a barrier to fulfilling religious obligations:

Understanding is important. I discovered this when I arrived in America. You must understand in order to practice Islam properly. Those who are educated back home understand that meaning is important, but their only route is to study Arabic. It frustrated me, so I quit practicing.

For Abdul and others, however, access to religious materials in English becomes a path to (re)discovery, to correct practice, and a reassertion of faith:

For those of us who are "born-again" Muslims, books and tapes in English have made it possible for us to practice correctly. You do not have to be fluent in Arabic to be a good Muslim. Thanks to being in the U.S., I have learned to pray. I have learned from books so I did not have to be embarrassed to ask someone to teach me how to pray. Being in the United States has helped me to find my religion.

As Abdul sees it, English translations of the central texts of Islam, the Qur'an and hadith, made available to him knowledge that had previously been viewed as inaccessible and secretive. For many of my informants, access to the central texts, as well as supporting materials lifted the veil of ambiguity that had surrounded Islam in Africa.

The Muslim Book of Prayer, one particular text published by the Center, instructs the reader step by step how, when, where, and why to pray. It emphasizes that:

Genuine prayer, based on humility and submission, illuminates the heart, purifies the soul and teaches the worshiper both the refinements of worship and his obligations to the great and almighty God, for it is through prayer that the glory and majesty of God is implanted in his heart. (Al-Sawwaf 1977:1)

It then provides the appropriate Qur'anic citation (29:45) to prove the authenticity of this assertion.

Thus he proves the word of Almighty God to be true, "Prayer retrains from indecency and evil. And remembrance of God is the greatest thing in life. And God knows the (deeds) that ye do." (Al-Sawwaf 1977:1)

In *Fasting,* another book published by the Center and distributed freely during the month of Ramadan, the author states in the introduction that

Fasting, as a major pillar of the Islamic religion has its meaning and detailed, yet precise rules. However, the full meaning of this pillar and its rules are not clear to everyone. For this reason many people have questions and need to find answers to these questions. (Khouj 1991:iii)

He goes on to explain that these answers are informed by the Qur'an and hadith, then goes on to describe and instruct in thirty-six pages the practice of fasting during the month of Ramadan.

Examining the role of these texts, how and by whom they are used, provides a framework for understanding the significance of textual knowledge in daily practice. The power of the texts lies in their ability to construct objectified knowledge and to make sacred knowledge accessible. The aura of easily accessible, universal knowledge contributes to an environment in which the religious authority given to these texts enables Sierra Leoneans to negotiate the quality of their understanding. Sierra Leoneans utilize available texts to establish order and direction in their lives, and help construct their Muslim identity (see Lambek 1990:24–25). However, the power of the text goes beyond the text itself. The process by which Sierra Leoneans come to understand texts to be authoritative statements of Islam lies mainly in the hands of the authoritative voices at the Center, for it is these people who imbue the available texts with power. It is they who stock the shelves and dispense religious instruction.

Religious instruction for adults is held every Saturday. At the time of my fieldwork one class met regularly in the morning. The teacher, Shaykh Muhammad, a Pakistani trained in Saudi Arabia, ran an informal discussion session that lasted one to two hours. The theme of the class may be described loosely as correct practice and proper behavior. Hadith were the focus of class discussion. Subjects ranged from specific ritual to discussions of morality and how to be a good Muslim. At the time I attended, the class consisted of a handful of regular participants. The instructor and the students were all adult males, but I was welcome to join the class and participate freely (as any Muslim sister would have been).

Shaykh Muhammad began each class with a recitation of the Fatiha, the opening *sura* (chapter) of the Qur'an. This passage, along with twelve Qur'anic verses, constitute the required minimum that every Muslim must memorize in Arabic in order to preform ritual prayer. Apart from this central place in ritual prayer, the Fatiha is often recited as part of individual or spontaneous prayer, or in any circumstance in which prayer is appropriate, such as marriages, funerals, and entering the mosque or other holy places (Glassé 1989:123). The teacher then initiated the discussion. During one session that I attended we discussed the issue of wudu, the ritual ablution before prayer. Shaykh Muhammad informed us that according to tradition wudu is an obligation, one of the conditions that make prayer acceptable, for it reduces sin and increases blessings. He then instructed us in method, paying particular attention to performing wudu in proper order. We were then instructed in the correct procedure for performing wudu and the proper utterances. Next we discussed possible circumstances that would render ablution invalid (contact with bodily fluids, sleeping, insanity, uttering negative things about Islam, touching a person lustfully, etc.). The teacher punctuated each instructive point with a reference to a hadith, and encouraged us to note these references so that we could look them up and read them ourselves.

Confronted with the many interpretations of Islam available to them in the literature, many of my informants turn to the imam at the Center to answer questions about what they read in books, particularly when it is corrective. For these men and women, validation that they are on the right path, interpreting what they read, see, and hear at the Center as correct, is of paramount importance. They judge and believe they are judged in terms of how they act, whether or not they are practicing correctly. Texts and their interpreters—in this case the Center's imam—

lend authority to that belief. In Sierra Leone the imam would be the unquestionable religious authority. In contexts in which the members of his congregation are not passive receivers of knowledge, but interpreters of his words, an imam is more likely to mold his interpretations to particular followers (Antoun 1989:3–12). This recognition lends power to his voice when he is discussing matters of practice with them. The imam of the Islamic Center carefully crafts both his sermons and his answers to congregants' questions in recognition of the multicultural setting in which he works. To underscore this, he delivers his sermons in both Arabic and English. The relationship between the imam and his congregation is a process of exchange that "has to contend with the often wide gap between popular and elite beliefs and styles of life" (17).

For the Center's imam, who is Saudi, accommodation of the diversity of belief and tradition of his congregation is of paramount importance. For example, when we discussed Sierra Leonean wedding ceremonies held at the Center, he admitted that he finds many Sierra Leonean traditions confounding. "Sierra Leoneans are very wild in their wedding ceremonies," he told me. "Much of what they do is not proper Islamic practice." Nevertheless, he indicated that simply to confront them and tell them that they were practicing incorrectly would drive them from the Center. "Our mission," he stated, "is not to drive them from the Center, but to guide them towards right practice."

Accommodation in this context is an interchange that moves both ways. In looking at this conflict, the critical role of the cultural broker to imbue the available texts with power is illustrated. For Sierra Leonean Muslims, the conflict emanating from a cultural broker who is of a different cultural background from the majority of his congregation is of paramount concern. These men and women are caught between the authority of the imam at the Center and their commitment to very strong Sierra Leonean community ties and traditions. Throughout the entire span of my fieldwork, Mustafa in particular was in a constant dilemma in his search for correct practice. He questioned virtually every aspect of his religious upbringing, beginning at the most elemental level, such as the proper way to pray and rules for fasting. He is most concerned, however, with the propriety of ritual and ceremony, weddings, naming ceremonies, memorial services, and holiday celebrations, all of which he perceives as practiced incorrectly by the Sierra Leonean community. For example, he was extremely upset to learn that the Sierra Leoneans planned to hold a celebration to commemorate the Prophet's birthday (Mawlid al-Nabi), for he had been told by non-Sierra Leonean congregants at the Center that this was improper.[1] Mustafa believes that "pure Islam" should not be "bounded by culture." Therefore the Prophet's birthday should not be celebrated:

It is a mixing of culture with religion. You shouldn't even celebrate your own birthday because it is like worship, and that means you are worshiping someone else besides Allah, and this is not good.

For Mustafa and others who have accepted the authority of the Center, all Sierra Leonean religious practices are suspect. This holds particularly true for practices such as sacrifices to ancestors and to the Prophet and prayers to gain blessings for any new undertaking. In their search for validation of their suspicions they turn to the imam for answers.

The imam's answers to questions of practice and propriety often highlight differences between my informants' traditional upbringing and that of the imam, who comes from an Arab country, and from Mecca, the holiest city to Muslims. Mustafa, for example, would constantly bemoan the fact that the imam did not understand him and did not understand the essence of his questions. At the same time, he praised the imam for his great knowledge of Islam, which he attributed primarily to his being a Saudi. Mustafa, who is attempting to embrace a constructed orthodoxy, deals constantly with the dilemma of negotiating multiple worlds (Sierra Leonean, American, Center-oriented Islam). At times he finds this situation confusing, painful, and even infuriating.

How can he resolve what is a very profound conflict in his life, a conflict that affects how he and many other Sierra Leoneans practice their religion? To some extent he does so by finding imams from his own community, of whom there are several. These men range from very traditional Sierra Leonean imams who have no connection to Saudi Arabia, to imams who have studied in Saudi Arabia and have internalized Saudi interpretations of Islam. For Mustafa and many others, those Sierra Leonean imams who have trained in Saudi Arabia are the most legitimate cultural brokers. Yet, while maintaining a connection to the Sierra Leonean imams, Mustafa ultimately accords highest legitimacy to the Saudi imam who directs the Center. The fact that the Saudi and Saudi-trained Sierra Leonean imams have studied in a context which Mustafa considers legitimate lends authority to his pursuit of knowledge through texts.

The role of these imams in answering questions and giving counsel, both publicly through sermons and in private conversations, validates the texts that Sierra Leoneans purchase at the Center. In turn, the role of the imam is validated by the materials available in the bookstore. In this case, religious authority is constructed and empowered in the context of conflict, a conflict embedded in a search for "correct religious interpretations," notions of authority, and Muslim identity.

In the American context, where Sierra Leonean traditional belief is challenged and where there is a trend toward "print-and-cassette-based

Figure 4. Sierra Leonean imam, Washington, D.C., 1991. Photograph by the author.

religiosity" (Eickelman 1992:648), a situation is being created in which meaning is embedded in objectified statements of belief that are inseparable from texts (655). Religious authority is constructed and empowered in the context of the Islamic Center in an atmosphere where traditional Sierra Leonean interpretations of religion are challenged. However, as Eickelman notes (1982:1), "any religion's ideology and practice are elaborated, understood and subsequently reproduced in particular places and at particular moments." For Sierra Leoneans in Washington, D.C. the main challenge to their understanding of Islam lies mainly in whether traditional Sierra Leonean interpretations of Islam can blend with the universalistic principles of Islam as defined and elaborated at the Islamic Center. Sierra Leoneans may assert that they cannot, and therefore work towards making a change in their understanding of practice and tradition, striving for a stable, uniform interpretation of Islam. But, does traditional understanding, of Islam erode in a context that supports the idea of a universal Islam, or is it integrated with universal Islamic practices and beliefs, forming new ways of understanding?

Chapter 5
I ♥ Islam: Popular Religious Commodities and Sites of Inscription

Leaving the weekly Friday prayer, I run into Mustafa outside the gates of the Islamic Center. My usual Friday routine after noon-prayer is to ride with one of my cab driver informants, and Mustafa readily agrees to some company. He tells me we have to hike to the cab. The side streets off Massachusetts Avenue are crowded with congregants' vehicles, a fair number of them taxis, but Mustafa purposely parks a few extra blocks away because "every step to and from the mosque earns us blessings." From the outside, his weathered black and white sedan appears to be a typical Washington, D.C. taxi. The inside is another story. Like many taxis driven by Muslim Sierra Leoneans, Mustafa's is inscribed with his personal vision of Islam. The dashboard is covered with stickers, Qur'anic verses in Arabic. On top sits an embroidered box that contains a copy of the Holy Qur'an. On the front seat are strewn multiple copies of various pamphlets that Mustafa gets free from the Islamic Center, and cassette tapes, all of which are Qur'anic recitation.

When we get into the car, Mustafa hands me a pamphlet. This one concerns fasting during Ramadan. Noting my interest, he hops out of the car, walks to the back, opens the trunk, and rummages around for a few minutes. He returns with a huge stack of pamphlets, hands me half of them, and places the rest on the seat between us. Mustafa keeps the free pamphlets in his trunk and on his front seat in order to give them to customers. I ask him how Americans react:

Sometimes they say, "No, thank you." Sometimes they just leave it on the seat when they get out, but sometimes they want to know what it is. So I tell them. You get a lot of blessings for bringing the word of God to non-Muslims.

Mustafa pops a Qur'anic cassette in the tape deck and we set off.

We cruise the streets of the District looking for fares, listening to the taped recitation and discussing the Friday sermon, in which the imam cautioned congregants against allowing religious observances to lapse in the aftermath of Ramadan. Mid-conversation, we are hailed by a man in his mid-twenties, wearing a conservative suit, the typical uniform of the mid-level federal worker. As Mustafa and I continue discussing the khutba, I gaze through the "vanity" mirror on the passenger-side visor. Our rider has suddenly become cognizant of his environment—the religious objects that surround him, the Qur'anic recitation sounding from the back speakers, Mustafa up front in his brightly colored African shirt and white skullcap. Eyes widening, his gaze moves to me. I am still wearing the bright pink hijab I always donned for Friday prayers. "I'll get off here!" he suddenly stammers. "But we are not at your stop!" Mustafa protests, "Besides, we are in the middle of traffic!" Not persuaded, our passenger reaches into his pocket, throws a handful of bills at Mustafa, and leaps from the taxi.

We sit stunned for a minute, then burst out laughing. "That fool!" Mustafa exclaims. "He thinks we are terrorists, maybe suicide bombers taking him with us!" I gather the money strewn on the seat and floor; it is far more than the fare for our passenger's short, disturbing ride. When I hand the money to Mustafa, he takes the correct fare from the bundle of bills and gives me the rest. Within blocks we see a blind, homeless man. Mustafa pulls over to the curb. "Give him the money," he tells me. "Maybe God will forgive that man's [our rider's] stupidity." I get out and hand the man the money, and we drive on.

This story highlights several key aspects of the experiences of many Sierra Leoneans living on the borders between homeland and a global Islam. The style in which my informants, most of whom are pious Muslims, choose to present themselves is characterized by the emergence of new cultural forms in which they image themselves in relation to others. The religious objects that decorate the interior of Mustafa's taxi are a means of "making Muslim space" (Metcalf 1996), of transforming a physical space into a site of cultural identity. While his display may have backfired in the instance described above, Mustafa remains undeterred. His humored reaction to the event—his joke about terrorism, in contrast to my own anger, even embarrassment—illustrates his self-confidence, as well as his familiarity with his broader environment. Having come to the United States nearly thirty years ago, Mustafa can contextualize the passenger's fears; he has heard it all before, too many times.

Mustafa's cab is a public site on which he encodes his world. His taxi is the conduit through which he converses with the world around him as he attempts to order and maintain a sense of self. However, as the above encounter indicates, his attempt to order his world may be disrupted, challenged by the society in which his taxi moves. As a site that is both private (his) and public (the passengers'), his taxi becomes a vehicle in which multiple social codes interact, at times in conflict. He "writes" his Islam onto his taxi in an attempt to display himself in relation to the people and places that he encounters while on the job (for the notion of "writing," see Austin 1996). Islam and Sierra Leone, his codes, and those of his passengers are all examined, tested, and reconstructed in the context of a space that becomes public the moment Mustafa picks up a rider.

This chapter explores problems and issues that arise when different cultures and perspectives come into contact over and through the display of religious objects in seemingly mundane places; in this case the taxis and food-vending stands in which many of my informants work. In particular, I explore the complexity of the multiple gazes and responses that give context to any site of inscription. As such, I will examine ways in which the display of religious objects are forums for the (re)presentation of a community situated in transnational spaces, a "visual narration of cultural negotiation" (Ybarra-Frauto 1991:83) in which meaning and understanding are mediated and articulated. Looking at how people use objects to make and maintain their worlds points to the act of display as physical manifestation of experience. Objects are regrouped and renamed in an act of (re)classification in order to produce meaning that accommodates and reveals cultural relations, becoming part of the defining frame, "the artistic creation of new sensitivities toward the world" (Yamaguchi 1991:61).

The juxtaposition of Islamic objects to work site illustrates the permeability of boundaries that enable the objects, their placement, and their significance to come into being in the first place. The contours of experience are a "dense network of evolving and often contradictory social practices" (Greenblatt 1991:42) and, I might add, understandings. As such, the display of Islamic objects on seemingly mundane work sites compels a "historicized gaze" (Karp 1991:17–18) in which popular notions of Islam and Muslims as exotic, other, and often dangerous in effect challenge the viewer to contrast and compare existing categories of knowledge, and to respond to the shock of nonrecognition. Non-Muslim American viewers—in this case consumers of goods (hot dogs) and services (transport)—either define what they see to fit existing understandings or reorganize that understanding to fit their own prior experience (Karp 1991:22). Thus, any discussion of religiously inscribed Sierra Leonean work sites raises the question of how isolated personal objects are combined with a public work site to create an atmosphere that implies the complexity of transnational relationships, an "affecting presence" (Armstrong 1981:3) in which some objects seem to possess the power and energy to resonate the complexities of social experience. For my informants the act of display is an act of constructing past, present, and future. This display is bound up with its "resonance," the "power of the displayed object to reach out beyond its formal boundaries to a larger world, to evoke in the viewer the complex, dynamic cultural forces from which it has emerged and from which it may be taken by the viewer to stand" (Greenblatt 1991:42).

Display is transformative in that it functions as a vehicle for turning experience into space, enabling my informants to use their work sites as a stage for the mediation of social experience (see Metcalf 1996). It is clear that Mustafa utilizes his taxi to articulate his religious identity in his own terms; he is equally aware that how he articulates that identity may serve to reinforce negative images of Muslims at home and abroad. Given that recognition, which all my informants share to one extent or another, how do they then choose to represent themselves, to articulate their identities?

The inscription of workplace conveys my informants' positioning in a community that is rooted in memories of a Sierra Leonean homeland that is ultimately (re)experienced through the (re)invention of an imagined Islam. As such, the objects by which they mark an invented collective memory are embedded within what Naficy (1993:xvi), in his discussion of Iranians living in Los Angeles, has labeled "ambivalences, resistances, slippages, dissimulations, doubling, and even subversions of *both* the home and host societies," all of which produce an "evolving syncretic and hybridized exile culture." Much like Iranian exiles, Sierra Leoneans inscribe and communicate "home, the past, memory, loss, nostalgia, longing for return, and the communal self" (xvi) onto their everyday lives, situating themselves between the "here" and "there" of present locale (America) and "home" (Sierra Leone). They map a complex set of meanings, creating a "shared discursive space" (2) in which their community can place itself on the larger cultural maps of America and a global Muslim community.

The objects and their placement condense and compress memory, becoming a perpetual source of recollection and longing for an imagined past. Islam, always an important source of "local" identity, entwined with other local identities (ethnicity, political affiliation), has in the American context become a powerful unifying symbol through which to create collective identity. As such, generic and by now highly commoditized Islamic objects serve to link Sierra Leoneans to a highly cosmopolitan community of fellow Muslims, while at the same time providing a means through which to recapture an imagined authentic past. Sierra Leonean Muslims use religious goods to tell themselves and the world around them who they are, easing the burden of physical and cultural displacement. These objects function as symbols of community affiliation, giving meaning to intersecting and at times conflicting understandings of what it means to be both Sierra Leonean Muslim and part of the broader religious community. Meaning thus materializes into—and onto—location, and this is illustrated best by how Sierra Leoneans "inscribe" their "presence" (Bammer 1994:xiii–iv), onto work sites that are by their very nature at once private and public.

The enactment of these representations in the public and private spaces of their lives provides significant clues into an emerging Sierra Leonean Muslim American identity. These representations are illustrated by the public world of religious celebration, as well as in the mediated private/public spaces of the home and workplace. The workplace is certainly not the only site of personal inscription. I have noted the presence of religious and cultural objects and wall hangings in Sierra Leonean-American homes (see also D'Alisera 1997, 1998). In such settings identity is inscribed for self, family, relatives, and guests—generally people who belong to one's Sierra Leonean-African-Muslim transnational community. What makes the workplace so interesting is that it is a place where one may inscribe identity for "others"—regular and one-time customers, competitors, (especially non-Muslim foreign rivals), above all strangers who are generally not of one's national, ethnic, or religious community (Coombe and Stoller 1994:254). This is especially pertinent to the taxicabs and the hot dog stands of people with whom I spent much of my time. Furthermore, because of their common features—they are out-of-doors, movable, relatively cramped, and settings for hasty social and economic encounters, these sites are natural venues for the display of highly commoditized and, in the case of religious items, increasingly available identity markers.

Inscriptions

As Mustafa and I ride from Northern Virginia into the District, we notice a car covered with green and white bumperstickers asserting: "Don't get caught dead WITHOUT ISLAM," "PRAYER: keeps together," and "ISLAM THE RELIGION of peace and security." The occupants of the car are bearded and dressed all in white. I ask Mustafa what he makes of the occupants and their adorned vehicle.

These are very pious people. Probably Pakistanis. You see, these bumperstickers are telling the world who they are. Everyone knows they are Muslims. Didn't you see the sticker on my trunk, back there, saying "I ♥ ALLAH"?

In fact, I had overlooked his bumpersticker. Prior to this conversation I had paid scant attention to popular cultural manifestations of Islam in the city, especially such seemingly simple marketed products. When I

Figure 5. Book store, Islamic Center, Washington, D.C., 1991. Photograph by the author.

ask Mustafa where I can buy a similar sticker, he directs me to the bookstore/giftshop at the Islamic Center. I had visited the bookstore at the urging of another Sierra Leonean informant when I had asked about particular religious texts that Sierra Leonean Muslims read. But heading straight for the bookshelves, I had walked right past the popular items for sale by the cash register counter.

Now, after my encounter with the bumper stickered car during my ride with Mustafa, I returned to the bookstore with a different aim, notebook in hand, to survey the non-print items. I suddenly found myself confronted with a plethora of items that I had always seen, even perused, but never looked at closely: prayer rugs, prayer beads, men and women's head coverings, bottles of perfumes and oils, incense sticks. But also bumperstickers and window decals, holiday cards, religiously inscribed bookmarks and key chains, coffee mugs adorned with either Qur'anic verses in English and Arabic, or assertions similar to those emblazoned on the bumperstickers (I ♥ Islam/Allah).

Over the next year I noticed that the stock changed often. Once a group of items were sold out they rarely reappeared on the shelves, for the stock was dependent on visits home by members of the congregation, Center employees, and the imam. In recent years a thriving business of Islamic goods has emerged in the United States and elsewhere

Figure 6. Bumper stickers for sale, book store, Islamic Center. Photograph by the author.

(see Starrett 1995). Along with more traditional religious commodities (prayer rugs, beads, perfumes, incense, standardized clothing), and the newer style commodities (mugs, stickers, key chains, holiday cards), one now finds a plethora of goods that touch upon—and Islamicize—virtually every aspect of life. In addition to bumperstickers, decals, and holiday cards, one can now purchase postcards of Qur'anic verse or one of God's ninety-nine attributes, in combined Arabic and English. Islamic alarm clocks and wristwatches announce the times of prayer. Timepieces of various sizes and models—usually the ka'ba or a domed mosque—"recite" the adhan. Religiously inscribed trophies and wall plaques for virtually any honor, halal soap, fund-raising cans, videos, and computer programs are all available. Videos range from religious sermons, including responses to leading American evangelical Christians, to children's programming. The latter include animated movies that depict the life of fictional and historical Muslim heroes and "Muppet"-like puppet programs, such as "Adam's World," that instruct children in Islamic ritual, practice, and morals. Many of these programs mirror both mainstream television and programming on Christian networks. Computer software runs the gamut from Arabic language writing programs to Qur'anic concordances. Moreover, whereas until recently such items were generally on sale only at Islamic centers and specialty stores (often in special aisles of ethnic food markets run by Muslims), there is now a thriving mail order business that can be accessed through a variety of catalogs and magazines of American Islamic affairs, as well as the World Wide Web.

Some of these products are not all that new, nor is the globalization of popular American symbols and their commoditization. In Egypt in the early 1990s I purchased bumperstickers that utilized the heart to express love for everything from country to sporting club, with the remainder of the phrase rendered in either English or Arabic. The political (I ♥ Egypt), the religious (I ♥ Islam), the social (I ♥ Ahli [Club]), often share symbology and venue. What is recent is the degree to which the Islamic items, previously imported, are now produced and marketed in the United States.

Looking at mass-produced religious goods in Egypt, Gregory Starrett (1995:65) argues that the way in which the meaning of "new types of commodities [are] constructed, contested and negotiated," makes religious goods "particularly sensitive markers of cultural transformation." Deeply embedded in a familiar context, in this case Egyptians (or other Muslims) buying Islamic goods in a predominantly Muslim country, such objects signify a cultural transformation in the way in which Muslims relate to texts at home, in a context where the dominant interpretive domains reflect familiarity with the symbols, terms of debate, and local discourses of authenticity. However, the case of an Islamically marked station wagon crossing the Potomac raises new questions about the significance of these objects outside the traditionally defined "Muslim world." What meaning do they impart when they become part of an evolving, transnational interpretation of what it means to be a Muslim here, there, and everywhere? How do these objects, as global religious "texts," construct a frame of reference through which experience is mediated?

For transnational Sierra Leonean Muslims, these commodities serve to reorder fragmented experience. Symbolically, they connect disjunct social space, constructing and announcing that "I am a Muslim." However, for Sierra Leoneans they also announce that Islam is deeply connected to an emerging national-ethnic identity that has become interwoven with Islam in the American context. The American context insures that these inscriptions serve not merely as amulets, means to attain blessings or insure protection, or, in the case of Qur'anic tapes, to remind one of God's words and presence. Many Sierra Leoneans also assert that the bumperstickers or decals they display, the style of clothes they wear, the tapes they play in their taxis, the pamphlets they distribute are intended for the outside gaze—of Americans, Christians, non-Sierra Leonean Muslims in general—and that they contribute a special set of categories by which presence is inscribed. Utilized in such a context, the inscriptions cry out in multivocal tones: I am a Muslim. I am a Sierra Leonean Muslim. I am here, like it or not! I am here, whether I like it or not!

The essence of these assertions was expressed to me one time by another taxi driver with whom I often rode. I once asked Ahmadu how his customers reacted to the Islamic objects in his cab. He replied:

I used to worry what people would think. Americans are so concerned with these things. They think you are a terrorist if you are playing a Qur'an tape! But I got tired of trying to play down the fact that I was a Muslim so that my customers wouldn't be afraid. I am a Muslim and I want people to know it. If you are afraid to get in my cab because the word of God is coming from my speakers then that says something about you. Americans need to start worrying about what we think of them!

These objects make concrete a series of qualified identifying statements that challenge the dislocating aspects of the transnational experience and the ways the host society perceives that experience. As Prosterman (1995:197) has pointed out in another context, place is marked and controlled by the reordering of elements, by "taking elements from one place and reemphasizing them or recombining [them]." This engenders a set of emotions and ideas that consciously construct and convey a world in which place is not only imbued with personal significance but is reordered to convey a series of messages that both communicates the multiple dislocations and differences of my informants' lives and, as Swedenburg (1992:570) contends, "offers dreams of collectivity."

Taxi Cabs and Hot Dog Stands: Interstices

How Sierra Leonean Muslim men and women differentiate objects to be displayed and how they determine where to place them illustrate the ways they constantly negotiate a social space that is ambiguously defined. These objects are, in essence, a site in which Islam is negotiated according to their owners' own subject positions. Those owners choose and utilize objects in order to make social statements about themselves, how they want others to see them and, ultimately, how they see others (Spooner 1986:225). In so doing, they create a community space in the site between actual location (Washington, D.C.), homeland (Sierra Leone), and global imagings (Islam) that reflects the way in which "disjunct and different cultural forms" (Öncü 1995:53) comprise complex domains of experience in which Islam has been constructed as the "thread that binds."

These objects, imbued with a deeply religious meaning that is characterized through "a direct association with acts of worship . . . or more commonly, their bearing of sacred images or writing, often only a single word, 'Allah' or 'Muhammad'" (Starrett 1995:53), construct a frame of reference through which experience is mediated. In her discussion of the Latino Festival in Washington, D.C., Cadaval (1991:206) points to the ways that participants decorate their food-vending stands (*kioskos* in Spanish) in order to highlight and intensify the "continuous cultural bargaining" that takes place between and within various national ethnic groups. The kioskos, she relates, physically define boundaries, bridging the gap between the private world of home and the public world of neighborhood. As a consequence, a "new aesthetic" emerges from "multiple interacting codes drawn from national and regional identity, tourism, political ideology, language, cultural background, and immigrant status" (206–7). Coombe and Stoller (1994:254) note a similar phenomenon occurring among West African street vendors in New York's Harlem: "A Songhay vendor in Harlem, for example, negotiates with other West African traders using Islamic precepts of propriety, he expresses his sense of entitlement to local business associations, and arbitrates terms of supply with Asian wholesalers in Chinatown. He also masters a new vernacular . . . to articulate solidarity with local residents."

Likewise, how my informants decorate their taxis and food stands, serves to reflect the ways they bridge the gap between various, sometimes competing modes of reference, and thus define their place in the community. But unlike Cadaval's kioskos, my informants' taxis/stands serve not only as physical boundaries between the private and public worlds of home and community, but as bridges between the multiple worlds of here (Washington, D.C.), there (Sierra Leone) and everywhere (Islam).

Heading toward the Islamic Center, I ask Aminata if she needs me to bring her anything.

Yes, yes. I need some more stickers. You know, the ones with Qur'an on them. I need all the help I can get! Business is down.

Does she want any particular verse?

No. Just the ones in Arabic, and maybe some in English. This way Americans know I am a Muslim.

Will it help business if Americans know she is a Muslim?

I think so, yes. They will know I am a religious woman. They will feel that the food here is better than at other stands.

Aminata's stand, a metal two-wheeled cart that may be towed by an automobile, sits on a corner in the heart of the District, a few blocks from several large hotel chains, one block from a high school, and directly in front of the headquarters of a prominent private foundation. Aminata often rearranges and redecorates her stand to accommodate her customers, most of whom work or study nearby, but who also include Sierra Leonean taxi drivers. Proud of her stand, Aminata often points out to her regulars a new plastic flower arrangement or display of potato chips, her brightly colored soda cooler overflowing with sparkling ice and soft drinks, or a new poster taped to the stand to liven up the plain metal exterior.

Her most prized possessions are the various Islamic objects that cover that exterior. There are two openings in a hot dog stand, the rear door and the front window, facing the sidewalk, through which food is sold. For Aminata's, each holds a special significance and each is the site of multiple Islamic objects. A large "Sabrett Kosher Hot Dog" sign and a series of stickers emblazoned with Qur'anic verses surround the window through which food is passed out, money taken in, and conversations held with customers. Directly in the center is a sticker with the Fatiha. The rear of the cart, the door through which food is brought in and where taxi drivers stop to chat when they do not want to park, is covered with similar stickers. Other than the Fatiha, Aminata, who does not read Arabic, is unsure what the stickers say; it is enough that they are Qur'anic verses.

For Aminata, the stickers that surround her front and rear doors serve as protective devices. During my fieldwork the rear-door stickers protected her from a very specific threat: the food vendor on the opposite corner. Aminata often accused this woman, an Ethiopian, of "throwing bad things" at her, of trying to poison her food and steal her customers. I arrived one day at her stand to find her in a terrible mood. When I asked her what was bothering her, Aminata informed me:

My business is down, Sister. That woman across the way, she is telling people bad things about my food. My best customer from [the foundation] was over there eating! She's taking the rice from my belly! She is making my food sour!

I asked her to elaborate.

Sometimes she comes to the back of her stand and stares at my stand. One day I saw her spit and then walk back to the front of her stand. She is throwing *juju*[1] things at my stand! My food tastes sour to people now.

The stickers at the front window act to protect her from more general threats.

Aminata also describes the religious stickers as a means of identifying herself to her patrons. When I asked her why she displayed no religious stickers on the closed sides of the cart, she responded, "it isn't necessary." However, the sides are not bare. They hold a series of advertisements for the products she sells (potato chips, sour gum balls, other snack foods), a very large Washington Redskins poster, and other "Skins" paraphernalia. Why the poster? It pleases her customers. Her profession of loyalty to the home team will, she believes, help her keep current customers and attract new patrons.

The conscious placement of all these "advertisements" frames Aminata in a particularly telling way. Customer windows are small; approaching, all one can see of the vendor is her head and upper body. The window gives the impression of a portrait, and in the case of Aminata the motif in which she chooses to frame herself is Islam. It produces a halo effect that is meant to communicate a number of things. Aminata believes strongly that if her customers know she is a Muslim they will "trust that I won't put bad things in the food." When I pressed her to describe these bad things, she responded in a whisper:

These juju things that some people believe will make customers come back again! These are bad things, and Americans do not like this sort of thing. I saw a TV show where Americans were saying that they believe these things come from the devil.[2] Maybe they do! I want them to know that I am a good Muslim woman. I don't deal with the devil.

Through religious stickers Aminata constructs and controls her interactions with her customers. She feels that the Islamic motif of her decorations beckons the potential customer by engaging in what she believes is a familiar and important social norm, that the food she serves is ritually pure (Sabrett's kosher hot dogs), free of "devilish" substances ("juju things"), and served by a "good Muslim" (pious) woman. This, she often told me, is the key to a successful business.

Aminata's decorations also allow her to stake her place in a broader world. By bringing together disparate cultural elements (global Islam, Sierra Leone, kosher hot dogs, the Christian-right and American football) an aesthetic emerges that points to her vending stand as representative of the cultural border on which Sierra Leoneans live. Competing social worlds are bridged, constructing in the hot dog stand a domain in which imagined movement is crystallized and the "time-out-of time, moving back and forth" (Cadaval 1991:207) between there, here, and everywhere, is encapsulated and made still.

The stand, then, is rooted. In this sense it is the opposite of the taxi, which moves continually through the city many hours a day. Indeed, movement is problematic for food vendors, who often express their need to stay in one place. Finding the ideal spot often takes time, perhaps several tries. For Aminata, the ideal spot is a street corner where

she can count on a steady stream of regular customers whom she generally knows by name or at least by sight. Most of her customers are from
the offices and the school nearby. Consequently, there are frequently
periods of the work day when she has little business. Her busy periods
are during the traditional office coffee break (10:00 A.M.), the lunch
hour (12 noon), and after school (around 3:00 P.M.).

For other vendors, the thought of lag time during the work day is
unacceptable. Mariama's stand sits in the heart of the federal district, in
front of a large drug store and just across the street from a Metro stop.
Her customers are people on the move, in transit between appointments, work, and home, and include many tourists. For Mariama, there
is no lunch hour per se, although at noon there is usually a line in front
of her stand extending halfway down the block. When I visited her at
mid-day, I would find myself working beside her, usually handling the
soda cooler. Unlike Aminata, Mariama rarely has time for leisurely discussions with her customers. "You can't make money if you are always
chatting with customers," she explained. For her, such chats means that
business is down, and at such times she is generally in a bad mood, not
receptive to small talk.

Taxi drivers, on the other hand, describe their identity as embedded
in actual movement. Taxis move throughout the city, following the flow
of ever-anonymous customers. As such, they represent moveable "sites
of inscription." Yet, despite the often random flow of their trafficking,
many taxi drivers with whom I rode attempted to reduce that random-
ness by following a particular circuit. There are neighborhoods that they
avoid because they are afraid of crime. Many drivers will make a point
to stay proximate to the Islamic Center around the times that prayers
are called, so that they can stop to fulfill their religious obligation in the
mosque. And many would make a point of visiting hot dog stands run
by Sierra Leonean friends and acquaintances. In doing so, they play a
very conscious role of "town criers," carrying news of the community,
exchanging gossip, and, not least, distributing religious objects and
imparting religious advice and instruction.

With only rare exceptions, "cabbies" are men (my informants tell me
there is one female Sierra Leonean taxi driver, but I never met anyone
who actually knew her). They move freely about the city. They often
emphasize the importance of that freedom in terms of their enhanced
ability to fulfill prayer obligations, and they express disdain for sitting in
one place, or being tied to a stationary workplace or rigid schedule. One
informant expressed it this way:

Driving a cab has its problems, but I am free to do as I please. If I want to start
work at noon I can. I can go to the mosque for prayer when I want, eat when I
want. No one can tell me what to do.

For many of these men, their taxis have become an important frame of reference through which their religious identity can be expressed and validated. The flow of religious identity into the workplace is still a fairly uncommon practice in America, and ignorance of basic Muslim ritual remains widespread. "Sunday is for religion," the manager of a local convenience store told one informant who had asked for Fridays off to attend the required communal prayer, typically bracketing off the public, secular workspace from the American-defined private realm of religion. In their resistance to such bounded categories of meaning, these taxi drivers blur the lines that seem so deeply etched into the American psyche. For them, their taxis come to embody an emergent Muslim identity set within and against a series of conflicting cultural discourses.

Moreover, in their resistance to dominant American understandings of the place of religion, these taxi drivers have come to view themselves as the disseminators of Islam. This is illustrated by the ways they decorate—inscribe—their taxis with religious markers, by their proffering of religious pamphlets to perfect strangers, on-the-job da'wa, and services they render fellow Muslims, such as giving free transport to the Islamic Center.

On their way to Friday communal prayer, many taxi drivers look for fellow congregants heading down Massachusetts Avenue, and offer them rides. Muslims who have been in the area for a time know this, so they wait on corners or near bus stops hoping to spot a passing Muslim-driven taxi. One Friday, when I was waiting at a bus stop about ten blocks from the Center, Mustafa drove by, pulled over, and offered me a lift. As I hopped in the front seat, several other men and women who were on their way to the mosque squeezed into the back. Mustafa pulled up in front of the Center to let his passengers off before parking down the block. Everyone hopped out of the cab except me. I would accompany Mustafa and walk back with him. A young Kuwaiti man, new to the community, reached for his wallet and offered to pay. Mustafa laughed, and we explained the situation to him. Again—and in a far more positive way than the story that opens this chapter—Mustafa's taxi had become a vehicle to enact piety. Identity had been inscribed onto place through action as well as by means of decorative symbols.

This active inscription of identity is also illustrated by the relationship that Sierra Leonean taxi drivers have with Sierra Leonean food vendors, most of whom are women. The women, too, often tell tales of dissatisfaction with working for Americans. Like other transnational women elsewhere in North America (see Colen 1986, 1990; Romero 1992), many had previously worked in nursing homes or as child care providers in the homes of upper-middle class families. My food vendor informants often explained that they preferred the confinement of their own hot dog stand to working in someone else's home, where they were often prohibited from practicing their religion. One informant, who had been caring for a two-year-old child, had been told by the parents, both lawyers, that she could not offer her five daily prayers when in their home.

I quit! I am required to pray no matter where I am. They won't let you pray and they pay very little! I make more as a hot dog seller, and I am not alone. Here I can talk to people and my friends can stop by for a chat; I can offer my prayers and I can do what I want.

Unlike taxi drivers, who often claim to be working for less money than they had made in other occupations, food vendors often earn more than Sierra Leonean women who work in health and child care. This is especially true for those who found themselves working in the private service sector, often without formal contract, where they were often taken advantage of in terms of wages and working conditions, and where, because of their transnational status, they often had no legal recourse. Vending food gives these women an opportunity to manage their own work lives, as well as to perform their religious duties.

As with taxi drivers, the freedom to fulfill religious obligations is often a guiding factor in their decision to become food vendors. As Isha, a woman I got to know late in my fieldwork, explained,

Even though I am not able to go to prayers at the mosque, I can pray here without interruption.

Holding up her prayer rug for me to see, she continued:

When the weather is warm I place my prayer rug down on the ground near the stand and pray. If someone needs help they will wait. No one can tell me not to pray. When the weather is bad I sit in the stand and pray.

For Aminata, who may have long intervals without many customers, finding time to offer prayer is rarely a problem. If she is busy with a customer when the prayer is called, she can make up the prayer later, when she is not otherwise engaged, preferably before the next prayer is called. For Mariama, who is constantly busy, prayers can be made up at home. Likewise, accommodations are made for the ritual ablutions required before prayer. Many vendors keep a jug of water for this purpose in their stands, while others lock up their stand and go to perform ablution in nearby public restrooms. Aminata has arranged with the foundation near which her stand sits to use their restroom facilities.

Thus, like taxi drivers, food vendors resist the imposition of bounded sacred/secular realms. However, unlike taxi drivers, food vendors do not see themselves as disseminators of the word of God. Rather, they see themselves as receivers of the messages taxi drivers bring. Taxi drivers remind food vendors when it is time for prayer and when holidays are to begin and end. The drivers also bring with them a variety of religious objects, Qur'ans, pamphlets, calendars, stickers, and posters. Some vendors prepare "African" food that they sell to taxi drivers on the side.[3] A great deal of banter takes place during these stops, punctuated by joking and laughter. At the same time, these stops often involve lengthy discussions of Friday sermons, which food vendors are generally unable to attend, and extended discussions of "proper" practice. During such discussions, tensions within the community may emerge.

On one occasion, I witnessed a dispute between a taxi driver and a food vendor concerning the upcoming celebration of the Prophet's birthday.

Taxi driver: It is haram [forbidden] to celebrate the Prophet's birthday!
Vendor: Why? We do it at home [in Sierra Leone]! Are you saying we are not good Muslims at home?
Taxi driver: They told me this at the mosque. We make many mistakes at home, but we can change this here [in the United States].
Vendor: I like to celebrate the Prophet's birthday! We do it quiet here. We sit and recite Qur'an and ask the Imam questions. I have learned a lot this way.
Taxi driver: What have you learned that you can't learn from the pamphlets and books I bring you?

The dispute went on in this fashion for nearly an hour, the question of celebrating the Prophet's birthday remaining unresolved.

Nevertheless, despite the controversial nature of some of the messages imparted, food vendors view taxi drivers as having more expertise then they do in matters of religion. As in Sierra Leone and in many other Muslim societies, men have greater access to the formal institutions of religion and the authorities therein. The women I work with are free to attend prayers and classes at the Islamic Center, but their work schedule often precludes this. Consequently, they often turn to the drivers for religious advice. One informant described the taxi drivers as her salvation:

I have learned more about Islam because of these cab drivers. They stop by and tell me what is going on at the mosque. They bring me books and remind me when Ramadan is to start and when the Id [al-Fitr] prayer is. I didn't even know that you could get a Qur'an in English until Mustafa gave me one. When I am not busy I sit here and read the Qur'an now. Islam is much more a part of my life since I have the stand.

Taxi drivers move in a world that is often alien to the food vendors, the world of global Islam. They gain access to that world at the Islamic Center and then bring that world, translated through the "texts" they carry and the way they interpret and explain those texts, back to the food vendors. The vendors embrace the objects/texts, but the extent to which they accept the meanings conveyed by the male carriers of those objects/texts is debatable. Likewise, the extent to which the taxi drivers find themselves caught between their understanding of the Islam of "home" and the emergent global Islam of the Muslim diaspora is constantly being negotiated.

The Social Life of Commodities

Appadurai (1986:3) reminds us that "commodities, like persons, have social lives." By focusing on the "things that are exchanged, rather than simply on the forms or functions of that exchange," we can better understand the link between exchange and value, which is, "politics, construed broadly." He proposes that we define the "commodity situation in the social life of any 'thing'" as the "situation in which its exhangeability (past, present, or future) for some other thing is its socially relevant feature" (13). Above all, he insists, that we look beyond production or purchase cost, material value, to the real meaning of the commodity: its social relevance. By extension, we might add social utilization. This is why the new mass-marketing of Islamic merchandise, whether hi-tech or more traditional, is so intriguing.

For Sierra Leonean Muslims in Washington, D.C., Islam, as produced and disseminated through the objects food vendors and taxi drivers carry, use, dispense, and display, constitutes the social life of such commodities. Rooted in a multiplicity of complex historical processes, the notion of a global Islam, a unified voice speaking for all Muslims, challenges the heterogenous realities of the transnational world my informants inhabit. Appadurai has described the contemporary transnational world as a "deterritorialized border on which lifestyles are brought into comparison on a number of different levels, creating intensified, sometimes critical, sometimes romantic self-reflections" (1990:11). Located at the crossroads of a multiplicity of shared spaces, Sierra Leoneans mediate the cross-cuttings of location, carefully etching onto their spatial context a transnational, deterritorialized Muslim identity. But we cannot stop there. It is the reterritorialization of space, the (re)construction of identity in the American context, that is of primary significance. This space defies easy compartmentalization, giving the present significance and forming "imaginative frames of description, narration [and] recognition" (Fischer and Abedi 1990:255) that ultimately challenge both territorialized and global definitions of identity.

To observe the ways Muslim Sierra Leoneans in the United States negotiate their lives is to look at the ways the fragmented spaces in which they live are encoded with meaning and are ultimately communicated. Whether physical or imagined, borders are encoded symbolically with powerful statements that suggest a multiplicity of referential alternatives to understanding one's position on those borders. It is the struggle between multiple understandings of Islam, the fluctuations between similarity and difference, and the continual negotiations of these understandings that give transnational social space its fluidity. Increasingly, the struggle for and negotiation of identity is being expressed in the social life of religious commodities. The spread of such commodities in all realms of society, and for members of all "imagined communities," ensures that the sites on which transnationals fix their inscriptions of identity will become ever more familiar. If the messages are not always decipherable, the formats are certainly becoming increasingly conventional—and recognizable. Sierra Leoneans in the United States speak to American society at large in its own "language," utilizing its own symbols, often the most mundane, and "writing" on many of its most viewed sites. Moreover, the politics becomes ever more broadly construed as the discussion goes beyond the rostrum of the mosque pulpit and the more traditional print and recording media to be increasingly played out on the car bumper, the taxi dashboard, or the window frame of the all-American hot dog stand.

Chapter 6
Mapping Women's Displacement and Difference

On September 11, 1995, an article entitled "INS Debates Female Mutilation as Basis for Asylum" appeared in the Metro section of the *Washington Post*. The article begins with a graphic, sensationalist depiction of what can only be fathomed by general readers as ritual torture:

The two African women, both from Sierra Leone, endured almost identical ordeals at the hands of secret tribal societies: they were abducted, gagged and bound; their sexual organs were partly cut away with a knife; and they were forced to swear they would never reveal what [had] been done to them or face death by witchcraft.

Both women, the article reveals, had recently gone to U.S. federal court seeking political asylum. Each grounded her case in recent Immigration Naturalization Services (INS) guidelines that accepted sexual abuse as possible grounds for asylum. The INS contested both claims, and two different judges had rendered diametrically opposite rulings. In Arlington, Virginia, one ruled that the woman who appeared before the bench—both were given pseudonyms in the article—had suffered "an atrocious form of persecution" and granted her asylum. In Baltimore, Maryland, a second judge flatly denied the other woman asylum. Rejecting the characterizations of "female circumcision" as genital mutilation imposed on an unwilling victim, Judge John F. Gossart, Jr., according to the reporter, ruled that the woman "could choose to support the practice, which he called important for maintaining tribal unity."

These two contrasting court rulings were handed down, the article noted, at a time "when female genital mutilation has captured the West's attention." In this respect, at least, the reporter was on target. The article appeared at the same time that delegates to the United Nations Fourth World Conference on Women were meeting in Beijing.

At the gathering, which received wide coverage in the American press, activists pressed for declarations equating sexual abuse, female circumcision included in this category, with violations of human rights.[1] Press coverage of the Beijing conference combined with a particular American focus on female circumcision—a focus that, arguably, overshadowed coverage of, for example, the systematic rape of Bosnian women—helped foster popular depictions of the "plight" of African and Muslim women that are, at once, narrowly bounded and sweeping in their generalities.

In conjunction with the sensationalist descriptions of "female genital mutilation"—by now popularly rendered as FGM—the symbolic images drawn upon by both the *Washington Post* reporter and the judges presiding over these particular cases construct women's lives in ways many Sierra Leonean women find deeply disturbing. The specter of "darkest Africa," characterized by static images of tribes, secret societies, witchcraft, the bush (or even jungle), still dominates popular American perceptions of a diverse and multi-faceted continent, creating an authoritative telling that strips away the uniqueness of millions of people's lives. This telling, these characterizations, now reified in the words of reporter, judges, and asylum seekers, become the basis upon which the perceptions of people who my informants meet daily are based.

To further confound matters, female circumcision is often posed in the context of Islamic religious practice. To cite only one example, in an essay about circumcision in Egypt (December 27, 1995), *Washington Post* columnist Judy Mann accused the "Islamic establishment" of putting pressure on the Egyptian government to retract a series of recent reforms concerning the practice. This "establishment" is never identified, but the implication of orthodox approval of circumcision, in Egypt and the Islamic world as a whole, is clearly erroneous. Even more so is Mann's simplistic concluding reference to the conflict between "the fundamentalists and the reformers." In fact, the common presumption that circumcision is an Islamic practice is challenged continually by Egyptian feminists and other opponents of the practice, who argue precisely the opposite, pointing out, for example, that circumcision also occurs in Egyptian Coptic communities (*Al-Ahram Weekly*, March 7–13 1996; *Washington Post*, August 28, 1994). Many "fundamentalists" who stand outside the "Islamic establishment" in Egypt and throughout the Muslim world also argue that circumcision is not religiously prescribed and is even un-Islamic. If circumcision must be categorized in general terms—ignoring the very different cultural meanings it entails in different places—it is better described as an African rather than an Islamic practice.

Nonetheless, the exotic, ever powerful Oriental-Islamic imagery persists, clouding reasoned discourse. In an earlier decision concerning a Jordanian woman who had been cruelly abused by her husband, Judge Paul Nejelski—the same judge who granted asylum to the Sierra Leonean woman in Arlington—wrote (according to the *Washington Post*, June 3, 1995) "that the woman had been persecuted because she sought her own identity and espoused Western values. . . . Also, she was among a group of women who refused to live in a 'harem' at the mercy of their husbands, their society and their government." In one catch-phrase the judge established a clear link between sexual abuse and embedded popular images of the cloistered Oriental woman. Given the generalized popular perceptions of Muslim women in need of being "saved" (Abu-Lughod 2002), as well as the prominent coverage of the debate about female circumcision in Egypt (e.g. *Washington Post*, August 28, 1994), it is not surprising that female circumcision is commonly equated with Islamic religious practice.[2]

The Sierra Leonean women I know have run headlong into such characterizations of Muslim and African women. Such constructions of difference, defined from without, have led many of these women to reflect anew on who they are. Viewed fundamentally as mutilated by "the undertow of tradition" (*Washington Post*, August 28, 1994), these women feel marginalized by American women, feminists in particular, "othered" by others' perceptions of specific signifiers of their female identities. Regularly confronted with American constructions of African-Muslim gendered identities (generally the oppressed-veiled-clitoridectimized-"genitally mutilated" other), as well as the multiple discourses of translocal Islam, a multiplicity of tensions arise that continually challenge any single understanding of what it means to be a Sierra Leonean Muslim woman living in America. The response of many of these women, in turn, challenges notions of a universalized female subject who is often essentialized within socially constructed categories of race, class, sexuality, religion, ethnicity, and cultural affiliation.

What do the experiences of these women tell us about the relationship between displacement and the construction of gendered identity? How do these women inscribe presence, contesting the categories "us" and "them," as well as popular American and feminist critiques of their lives that assume that all women cohere in a singular, homogenous female identity defined within socially constructed categories of womanhood? These women's voices subject to critical revision any notion that human experience is bounded by such simple cultural constructions. Rather, identity constructed within a transnational space becomes the site in which notions of place, defined in terms of gendered identity, are negotiated.

This chapter will address ways in which Sierra Leonean Muslim women living in Washington, D.C. negotiate and represent the multiple discourses of their transnational experience. I hope to demonstrate that for these women identity, in particular Muslim identity, is reconfigured in terms of the ambiguous link between place and self. The question of transnational identity is clearly centered on the ways all Sierra Leonean women negotiate and represent the multiple discourses of the cultural spaces they simultaneously occupy. Relocation challenges these women to question key assumptions about certainties tied to their home culture. Confronted with the often contradictory discourses of the multiple positionings of their lives, Sierra Leonean women are compelled to reflect on who they are and what it means to be Muslim women living abroad. Their stories reveal the precarious and multiple meanings of lives lived on the borders of transnational experience.

To Initiate or Not to Initiate?

In the wake of press coverage dealing with the plight of African women confronting "female genital mutilation"—with an increasing focus on the United States (e.g. *Washington Post,* February 23, 1994)—Sierra Leonean women began to reflect openly about the practice. That it had been two members from their own community who had played such a central role in publicizing the controversy in the D.C. area gave the matter special immediacy. Confronted with American constructions of their gendered identity, Sierra Leonean women considered the ways stereotypical cultural representations had, many felt, become tools that could be utilized to attain desired, and otherwise unobtainable, ends—in this case, citizenship or green card residency. But at what cost to self and community?

The dynamic is incredibly complex, as it touches upon issues of power and powerlessness vis-à-vis the dominant culture, as well as upon self-image, group identity, and the image presented to the dominant "other." On the surface, one might look at the Sierra Leonean women seeking asylum, at least the woman who won residency, as having successfully played the system, using an image of powerlessness ("female genital mutilation") in order to assert ultimate power (asylum), perhaps—as some of my informants suspected—to fool the system. But the issue cuts much deeper. If it did not, the Sierra Leonean women with whom I discussed the case might simply have applauded these women for "putting on the man," manipulating a growing discussion of female circumcision to attain the brass ring of a green card. These women would be viewed as tricksters, perhaps envied for their shrewdness. But this is not the discourse that ensued. In conjunction with a degree of sympathy, even respect for a perceived cleverness, my informants also

expressed anger at the ways these two women played into negative perceptions of who they are, in effect reifying popular media images,
thereby lending greater credence to a discourse that simplifies and seeks
to criminalize a complex ritual process without discussing broader
meanings. And in a world view in which *bundu*[3] is still highly secretive,
these women also decry what they perceive to be the revealing of very
private secrets.

Khadi called me one afternoon to tell me about the reaction in the
Sierra Leonean community to the press coverage and, more specifically,
her personal reaction. Outraged that the women in the news stories
would reveal ritual secrets, she accused them of feigning their expressed
fears for their daughters' safety. One paragraph from the September 11
Post article particularly infuriated her.

Can you imagine? They want to pretend that they won't initiate their daughters!
Listen to this! This woman in Hyattsville [Maryland] told the reporter what happened to her in the *bundu* bush—in front of her thirteen-year-old daughter!
Here, listen to the paragraph, I will read it: "Last week, the woman, who lives in
Hyattsville, repeated her story for a reporter while the woman's thirteen-year-old
daughter squirmed in a chair, covering her ears. The woman asked that neither
be identified and said she feared that the girl and her two younger sisters also
would be mutilated if they were forced to return to Sierra Leone."

Khadi let out a long "tssss. . . .," underscoring her disapproval.

In fact, prior to the outbreak of civil war Sierra Leonean parents frequently sent their American-born children home to be initiated into
secret societies. According to my informants, this common practice
often created a series of tensions for these women and their daughters,
challenging key assumptions about homeland and how to maintain links
to traditional culture. For many Sierra Leonean women, Khadi among
them, the debate has centered on the ambivalent feelings many mothers
harbor about sending their daughters back to Sierra Leone for initiation. Recalling both positive and negative personal experiences of the
ritual, they often find themselves pulled in two directions.

Khadi's ambivalence about whether to have her own daughter initiated clues us in to the complexities of the debate. She often expressed
to me her frustration at American perceptions that men played a significant role in the initiation of women into *bundu* society. In her own
experience, with both her father and her husband, the decision concerning initiation of girls was left strictly to the mother. Indeed, her
father did not want his daughters initiated. A devout Muslim, he
deemed *bundu* un-Islamic. But when his wife insisted, he bowed to her
argument that uninitiated daughters would be unmarriageable. However, he warned the women in charge of the ritual that if anything hap-

pened to his daughters he would drag them before a court in Freetown. Khadi's traces her ambivalence to her own traumatic initiation experience:

I was initiated, but almost died because I almost bled to death. I think I had what you call a near-death experience. I saw lights like on a disco ball. I saw light-skinned people dancing around, happy and dressed in gold. I wanted to step into the light and could not. They took me from the *bundu* bush so I never learned all the secrets. My father was furious that I almost died. They told him it was my own fault. They said I had eyes, that I could see beyond, and that their powers got tangled with mine and I almost died. It is well known that they are witches. They are more powerful then me, so I almost died. I did have eyes before I went into the bush. They killed my ability to see beyond.

Like many Sierra Leonean women with American-born daughters, Khadi had long considered the ramifications of not having a daughter initiated. When I got to know her, Fatmata had turned twelve, and pressure was beginning to mount for Khadi to decide one way or the other. She wavered, unable to make up her mind. When Sierra Leonean women in the community raised the subject she would either ignore them or divert the discussion to another topic. When she turned to her husband for advice, his usual response was, "It's up to you. That is women's business." The appearance of the recent court cases and the fact that they involved Sierra Leonean Muslim women only complicated matters for Khadi.[4] Her response to the *Washington Post* articles was influenced by her own personal dilemma, now being played out in a public arena that is not her own.

I asked Khadi if she knew who the two women were and why she thought they had opted for this course to seek asylum. She responded:

I think I know one of them, but the other I am not sure about. Americans are fools! They do not know when they are being taken. They listen to Alice Walker, you know this one who wrote a book and made a movie.[5] I read the book and saw the movie. It really made me angry! These women [referring back to the two women in the article] are clever. All this discussion about our traditions, saying we mutilate our daughters! It's a ploy to stay here! Of course I can't blame them, home is so horrible now. All the killing, the war.

Khadi's anger, like that of other Sierra Leonean women, at the popular debate among Western feminists concerning female circumcision is a direct challenge to the essentialized depiction of African women, what Dorinne Kondo has in another context called "a kind of symbolic violence [influencing] not only how we are treated, by others, but also how we think of ourselves" (1996:49). About the time that the cases of the two Sierra Leonean women came to court, the INS had distributed to U.S. asylum officers an "alert" describing "female circumcision" as "extremely painful, with 'serious, often fatal consequences . . . including [being] viewed as someone who 'deserves to be killed'" (*Washington Post*, September 11, 1995). This discourse, made increasingly public by the prevalence of such dramatic cases, empowered by authoritative and monologic certainty, potentially opens a door for Sierra Leonean women to challenge preconceived notions of African womanhood in the West, generating, "an arena of ideology at war" (Bruner and Gorfain 1984:56). In their analysis of the construction of the Masada story, Edward Bruner and Phyllis Gorfain describe how authoritative voices attempt to fix meaning and stabilize order, while voices that challenge and question established meanings deconstruct that authority. In the case of Sierra Leonean women, the "once told tale" of the physically, mentally, and spiritually oppressed African woman is challenged by the multivocal representations that are a way to challenge evolving stereotypes.

Khadi was the first Sierra Leonean woman to talk to me openly about her initiation into bundu, and about female circumcision in particular. Like so many other Sierra Leonean women, she confronts the remaking of her world in terms of the Western constructions of Third World women on a daily basis. Faced with the ambiguous, powerless, sometimes volatile representations of themselves, Khadi and my other informants search for ways to represent themselves that subvert established understandings, turning them on their heads, creating a dissident telling of the assumed "other" status that they occupy. For the women with whom I work, challenging the African-Muslim women tales of the American imagination is no easy task. The choices they make in representing themselves as Muslim women, in lifestyle and relationships with family and friends, clue us in to the ways in which they negotiate the complex web of contradictions that they face daily.

Of the many Sierra Leonean women I spoke with, three stand out for the ways in which they represent the mediated realities of transnational women's lives. Embedded in their stories is the wish to define themselves in their own terms, challenging discourses that ultimately reduce them to "any prefigured definition of their identity and reality" (Ong 1996:356). As Bruner and Gorfain note, stories are always "told in a dynamic chorus of styles which voice the social and ideological positions they represent" (1984:57). Hence, stories can be seen as dialogic, that is, as an interactive process in which listeners and tellers actively engage in interpretation, making the story meaningful to their present context (60).

In retelling three women's stories I hope to capture the way in which their lives are interconnected, and at the same time to give voice to their individual experiences. In so doing, I hope to show that their lives are multiply inscribed and therefore can not be contained in essentializing terms. As such, I argue that the lives of these women should be understood outside of the gendered categories that are defined in terms of the cultural, national, and geographical spaces of Sierra Leone, and in terms of the way in which everyday consciousness and practices are defined by the struggle between two cultural understandings. Their stories point to the ways in which they seek different forms of accommodation to give meaning to lives lived simultaneously in two places. As such, these women's lives are not separate or disconnected from each other, but are given meaning only in reference to each other.

Arrivals and Departures

In a political and social atmosphere of growing hostility to immigration, both legal and illegal—an atmosphere in which the romantic archetype has changed from the refugee seizing the unique opportunities to build a better life in America, to one in which the alien deprives "native" Americans of scarce resources, jobs, and social services and in which, after 9/11, many are perceived as terrorist threats—Sierra Leoneans do daily battle with a set of images that bear little resemblance to their personal American experience.[6]

Khadi, Sadatu, and Aminata arrived in the United States at different times and with different aspirations. They came at different ages, single and married, with and without spouses. They belong to different ethnic groups, have different educational backgrounds, and have had very different experiences, both successes and failures, in their encounter with the American dream. Despite this, their stories all contain a similar thread. The transnational experience has led each in her own way to question key assumptions about her culture, and about gendered identity in particular. However, at the same time that these women question the gendered categorizations within their own culture, they resist the imposition of Western definitions. Their shared experience is one of a lessening of the disjuncture between the gendered worlds of home and abroad, and one of an evolving interrelationship in which the two perspectives are internalized dialogically, creating a hybridized sense of identity (Bakhtin 1981; Ong 1996). Their stories speak clearly to this predicament.

Khadi

A successful social service professional, Khadi has lived in the United States for about twenty-five years. She came originally to attend university and to join her husband, who had arrived one year earlier. Pregnant with her first child and saddled with financial problems, she immediately took a job as a waitress. She spent the first nine years of her stay in America working full time in a restaurant, attending school part time, and relying on Sierra Leonean friends to help her with her children. At the time that I met her she was attending school full time, working toward a masters degree in education. She was determined that her education would one day allow her to return home and change what in the past had seemed to her the unquestionable realities of being a woman in Sierra Leone.

I want to go back home and start a center for high school girls who get pregnant and cannot finish school. In Sierra Leone they will not let you finish school if you get pregnant. I used to be very judgmental of those girls when I was in high school. I have changed my attitude. Things change in America.

Like many Sierra Leonean women, Khadi often struggles with the idea of "going home," a dilemma that marks and defines the emotional borders of the transnational experience. The comings and goings of friends and relatives between the United States and Sierra Leone often elicited a discussion of deep-seated feelings about their experiences, and clearly illustrates the ambiguous nature of that experience. Several days before the arrival of her sister's husband from Sierra Leone, Khadi expressed to me her dismay:

My brother-in-law, who will be coming in a few days, is a real dilemma for me. They expect that it will all be wonderful in the U.S., when in reality life is very difficult here. Cab driving is slavery [Ahmed, her husband, is a taxi driver], but Ahmed doesn't think so. He says it gives him freedom to go to the mosque. I am less free and feeling very depressed. My father-in-law is coming as well. So now I can't go to school full-time. With all these people coming I will have to cook all of the time. I hate cooking! I cannot stay in the kitchen more than two hours! Sierra Leonean women feel you have to slave in order to satisfy your husband. [One day] I roasted chicken, corn, and potatoes, and a Sierra Leonean woman said to me, "Is this all you are cooking for your husband?" If I go home [to Sierra Leone] I will be constantly criticized.

Khadi acknowledges that she has changed as a result of being in the United States, and for many of the women I work with this is a disturbing, at times even frightening turn of events. Khadi would often express her fears by criticizing her husband. She once described him to me as "too nationalist" because he considers "everything American bad and everything Sierra Leonean good." And she would often wonder if returning to Sierra Leone, which was Ahmed's dream, even as the civil war spread, was a good idea:

If Ahmed wants to go back to Sierra Leone, I must go. But the country is hopeless now. I don't know if it will change. But this [American] society is full of problems. I am not sure my children are being raised properly.

Her dilemma reflects a tangle of emotions in which the critical connections between family, marriage, and motherhood embody the complexities of transnational spaces. In telling her stories she would often focus on how she negotiated family claims to her time and emotions. The conflict expressed in these stories gives voice to an alternative perspective that is for many transnational women a means by which they can express the conflict between their personal desires, the expectations of their families, and the constant negotiation of home and abroad.

Shortly after her brother-in-law's arrival, Khadi's father-in-law came for a long visit, creating a situation in which she further questioned many of her assumptions about herself, particularly the assumption that she is a willing participant in what she began to define as an oppressive situation: the unquestionable authority of a woman's husband and his relatives. We spoke on the phone several days after the "old man" (as she always referred to him) had arrived.

The old man has arrived and he is running me ragged! He knocks on my bedroom door at 5:30 am to wake us for prayers! I lied to him this morning and told him I was bleeding.[7] I do not know what I will do after this week. I can't have my period again until December, after he goes.[8] I am constantly cooking all the time because people are always visiting him. I can't do this! I have the children, work, school, and now the demands of this old man!

At the time Khadi tried various alternative religious practices to contest her husband's, and now his father's, demands on her time. She told me, for example, that she often prayed silently in bed in order to avoid getting up for the dawn prayer. But according to her husband, Islam prescribes a particular form of ritual prayer that cannot be altered unless, as Ahmed insisted, "you are a cripple."[9]

Khadi and Ahmed fought often about religion. Ahmed is devoted to strict practice, which Khadi disputes. His father's arrival on the scene served to give authority to Ahmed's assertions about proper practice. The "old man" was an elder. "You can't defy an old man in our culture, and especially not your father-in-law," Khadi told me. Moreover, he was also a village notable, someone to whom disputants turned to help settle claims. Nevertheless, Khadi continued to fight with Ahmed, and to find ways to avoid the "old man's" insistence that the household should conform to his sense of proper religious regimen.

Several days after our first conversation about the matter, Khadi continued to express dismay at the religious demands placed upon the household by her husband, bolstered by his father's presence:

I went to pick up the kids' report cards from school and their teachers said they were coming to school too tired. It's the old man's fault because he makes them get up at 5:30 in the morning for the first prayer and makes them stay up for the 11:00 P.M. prayer! That old man is a bully and doesn't understand! He can take naps during the day, we cannot. It is not like back home. You cannot stop for prayers and naps in school or at work. And I do not like his attitude toward women! I never questioned this attitude back home, but now I hate it. Look what he did: I was late for work so I did not serve him breakfast. The rice and sauce were on the stove. He refused to serve himself and didn't eat until I came home to serve him at 3:00 in the afternoon!

The children's poor performance at school outraged Khadi, and she had raised the issue with Ahmed.

Ahmed and I have fought about this business of the children. I wish I would have raised my children to question authority and then they would have told the old man that this prayer business was too much for them.

As our conversation continued, she vocalized the conflict inherent for many transnational women whose lives have changed in unexpected directions:

I think I have a dysfunctional family. Not in terms of America or Sierra Leone, but in terms of progress. Ahmed and I have progressed differently. Ahmed believes in "God-dai"[10] He even told me he was not upset about the way his father treated his mother when he was growing up. He treated her very badly. Ahmed believes he received a lot of blessings because his mother suffered for him. Can you imagine? He told me, "Blessed men get fool-women." Meaning women who are fools, empty headed and do what ever they are told! I asked him, "What about me?" and he said, "You got clever because I did things to lose those blessings!" I don't know what things he did!

For Khadi, migration to the United States has created a set of conditions by which she feels confident to challenge prefigured definitions of identity. Her reaction to the comings and goings of her family conveys an emerging agency centered on the struggle to articulate her changing gendered identity. As such, she articulates a sense of self that spans borders, raising questions that revolve around the mediation and breakdown of boundaries.

Sadatu

Sadatu is a former model and singer who is presently working as a nurse's aide in a senior citizens' home in northern Virginia. She arrived in the United States about twenty-three years ago, as a teenager, to live with an aunt and attend high school in New Jersey. Describing herself as an "innocent teenager" she found herself suddenly immersed in urban America:

I found myself living in the projects in Jersey City! I was clueless to what that meant. I grew up in the village with my grandmother. I hardly even went to Free-town! I expected America to be different, but I cannot remember what it is I expected. By the time I finished high school I was speaking black English and behaving like an American! People constantly criticize me for this. Especially because I speak English with my daughter, not Krio. But I know how to take care of myself. My aunt's man tried to lay his hands on me. My aunt tried to blame me when I told her to tell him to get off me. I got out of there and went to California to be a model and singer. I cut one album of songs that were inspired by the traditional Mandingo songs I heard growing up. I stopped singing and modeling when I got married and came to live here [in Washington, D.C.].

Like Khadi, Sadatu often laments the conflicts inherent in living in two worlds. But unlike Khadi, Sadatu came of age in the United States. Consequently, her conflicts center less on becoming more American and more on a struggle to be Sierra Leonean. Nevertheless, Sadatu's two worlds are interrelated, and her feelings, like Khadi's, often find voice as she reflects on the comings and goings of husbands, friends and relatives.

Sadatu met Mustafa at a party in Maryland given by her cousins. She was in the area to promote the album of Sierra Leonean songs that she had just recently recorded in California. According to Sadatu, she and Mustafa were attracted instantly to each other and began to date. At the time (she was nineteen, he thirty-eight), Mustafa had not yet become a "born-again" Muslim. As Sadatu tells it, she found the thought of marrying an "older" man attractive. "Older men mean security," she told me. They decided to get married and to hold the ceremony in Sierra Leone. When I met them they had been married for four years and had a two-year-old daughter.

When Mustafa introduced me to Sadatu, she was giving him trouble about arrangements for a trip home that he had planned. He insisted that while he was gone she should stay with his brother Abdul and his wife. Sadatu refused; she wanted to stay alone with their daughter in their apartment. I agreed to meet with her. My intent was to hear her side of the story, but I quickly found myself caught up in mediating a complex family squabble. I asked Sadatu why she did not want to move in with Mustafa's brother.

I wish Mustafa would realize I can take care of myself. Damn, I lived in the projects [in Jersey City]! I will not live with that woman! I like Mustafa's brother, but his wife is a witch! She will put stuff in the food and kill me, my daughter, and this baby I am carrying! I had a miscarriage last September. The baby was Down's syndrome. Abdul's wife said I did something wrong during intercourse and that was why the baby was sick. Then she said that I made the baby sick because when I was pregnant I went to a good friend's funeral. According to tradition, you are not supposed to see a dead body when you are pregnant. I don't believe that stuff! She is a back-scratching witch! When I had the miscarriage, she said to me, "I hope you learned your lesson." She will put stuff in the food if I go to live with her! She does that juju stuff. She is really a witch! Watch out for her! Talk to Mustafa for me. Tell him I would rather have a roommate here in our place.

Sadatu's response illustrates the way in which disjunctive subject positions, simultaneously expressed, de-center a singular cultural orientation. In rejecting one traditional belief (dead bodies can hurt unborn babies) and by accepting another (witchcraft), she attempts different forms of accommodation that mediate between two categories of experience. Equally compelling is her assertion that she can "take care of herself." This is a direct challenge to her other assertion, that Mustafa was an attractive marriage partner because of his age, and was therefore better able to care for her properly. The meanings of her discourse may appear unstable and varied, but they are not. They reflect the way in which categories of experience lay side by side, neither conflicting nor agreeing with one another, but instead constructing new sets of categories that incorporate the dual voices of home and abroad.

I agreed to talk to Mustafa, and I ultimately convinced him that Sadatu was capable of taking care of herself. Mustafa was to be gone for several months. Sadatu and I convinced him that he should leave enough money in the bank in Washington to cover her rent and other relevant expenses. Mustafa later confided to me that he was not convinced Sadatu was able to manage the money.

She still has a taste for clothes and makeup and that California life she led. She will spend it all on clothes. She turns my lights off when she is like this! If she keeps it up I will take another wife!

Mustafa left for Sierra Leone, asking his brother and me to watch out for Sadatu.

A month after Mustafa's departure, Sadatu phoned me. She complained that Mustafa had not left enough money for her and her daughter to live on, and that the small salary she was making at the nursing home was not enough. Pregnant, she felt all alone. And now Mustafa's sister had arrived from Sierra Leone bringing a tape-recorded message that contained bad news. Screaming at the top of her lungs in both Krio and English, she told me,

When Mustafa comes back to the States I am going to leave him! He took a second wife!

I was surprised to hear this outburst because several months before this incident Sadatu had told me that she would happily accept co-wives. I reminded her of our conversation and asked her what had changed her mind. She replied,

I will be a good first wife. I will not treat her the way my mother was treated by my father's first wife. I will accept my husband taking another wife. My mother was a second wife. She was a market woman and very independent. I want to be like that. Mustafa wants, and will take, another wife. He wants ten children and I will only have four. So I will accept other wives when we return home. I am not angry because he took a wife. I am angry because he told me on a tape and not face to face.

Sadatu seemed to be recanting her initial threat to leave Mustafa. But she then reasserted that she would not put up with a second wife:

I am not going to go home and sit with one foot on the oven!

When I asked her what she meant, she replied:

I mean I am not going to be a full-time wife and just cook and cook. I am going to take care of my own business. When he called me from Sierra Leone last night I told him that I will leave him and that I will start seeing other men. In fact I told him I was already seeing another man! He was really mad [she laughed]! Can you imagine that he believes I will do this, as pregnant as I am![11] Already people are calling me up saying he was on the phone all night asking everyone who I was seeing! I told him I was not having sex with the man I am seeing because I am pregnant. But I told him I am seeing a man who will care for me. If we were home I would accept the traditional way [polygamy], but we are here. Back home, sometimes the first wife finds the second wife. And the husband should at least ask if you approve of the second wife. You really do not have a choice. You either accept or leave. Most women just accept.

Her anger bubbled up again.

I will make him suffer! I am not in the village anymore! When you travel you change. Mustafa has been in the U.S. for twenty years—he should have changed! He told me that he just wants a second wife because of religion.[12] Bullshit! This is not enough! I will make him suffer!

Although in the past Sadatu had been willing—in theory at least—to let Mustafa take a second wife, this was conditional on their being in Sierra Leone. She had never agreed to it while they still lived in the United States.

Implicit in Sadatu's condition is the mapping of a boundary, one that she has drawn for herself between past (Sierra Leone), present (United States), and a possible future (Sierra Leone). Neatly categorized, the negotiation of the border appeared easy. But Mustafa's actions blurred the border she had created, allowing one world to flow into the other, creating, in the same way that Khadi's father-in-law's visit had, a meshing of two worlds along with the messy conflicts of that encounter. This incident not only illustrates the range of possible commitments to family that these women are often asked to make, but the tensions inherent in those decisions and the way in which their responses play themselves out across boundaries. The boundaries that Sadatu had constructed are negotiable only on her own terms. In taking a second wife, Mustafa had ultimately destabalized not only Sadatu's borders, but her need to create a space in which she could enact her womanhood on her own terms.

Aminata

Aminata arrived in the United States six years before I met her, hoping to pave the way for her five children and her husband. Like many of the Sierra Leonean women I met, she is a food vendor. Monday through Friday she sells hot dogs on a corner in downtown Washington, hoping to earn enough money to send home to help her family to come to the United States. Shortly after arriving in the United States, like many other Sierra Leonean women who vend food, Aminata rented a stand and began working toward eventual ownership.

She was able to attain this goal in 1991, the year of my initial field work. However facing the daily onslaught of living expenses in the Washington area, she continued to see herself as "working for nothing." In addition, the difficulties her husband faced in getting a visa were a constant irritation to her.

I thought it would be easy. I would make money and my husband, then my children would come. My husband cannot get a visa, my children are growing up without me, and I am sure he uses my sweat [the money she sends home] on other women!

As with Khadi and Sadatu, the comings and goings of significant others give voice to the difficult negotiations of life lived across boundaries. However, unlike Sadatu and Khadi, Aminata's struggles center on her family's inability actually to travel to the United States.

Her dilemma plays itself out in the relationships she has had with men.

My husband and children are in Sierra Leone. I have tried for two and half years to be good about sex, but I cannot help myself because a lot of men are chasing me. I have feelings.

Finally succumbing to her desires, Aminata took a lover.

Suliman is a Muslim, but when I first met him he drank. I hated it because the smell made me sick, and when he kissed me I felt I could not get the smell off

of me. Finally I convinced him that it was bad. Muslims should not drink. Now
he prays five times a day. Now when I miss a prayer he reminds me to make it
up. Yes, we sleep together. It is a problem, but I told you I cannot help myself.
After you sleep with a man [any man, including your husband] you must wash
your hair, sheets, and everything you touch. I could not keep up with work and
all the cleaning up. So now, Monday through Friday we do not sleep together.
Just on the weekends when I have more time to clean up.

For Aminata, adding the ritually required post-sex cleaning to her
already demanding daily routine proved impractical.

In Washington, D.C., street food vendors rise between 3:00 and 4:00
A.M. to prepare for the day's work. Their preparation consists of hauling
their stand to "their" places, firing up the steam table, preparing coffee,
and purchasing buns, all before the morning rush, which starts at 6:30
A.M. They leave "their" corners around 5:00 P.M. After the long process
of packing up, they haul their carts to one of the many storage garages
outside the District, where they may spend up to four hours packing
food into containers, draining the water from the steam tables, and
scrubbing down the cart with disinfectant. Then they finally return
home, usually by 10 P.M., to spend the rest of the evening preparing
food for the following day, especially the condiments and homemade
chili that Americans love to put on hot dogs. Amid all this work, they
have little time to spend with their families. In general, the work day of
a food vendor does not end until after midnight, and my informants
understandably often complain of exhaustion.

Many of the vendors I know hire older Sierra Leonean women to care
for their children during the week. These latter women are often
friends' mothers who have come from Sierra Leone to visit. Accordingly,
the arrangement lasts only as long as the woman is in the States, which
is usually a year or less. The vendor then must find someone else to help
out with household duties. When possible, food vendors with children
try to bring their own mothers over to help them. To many this is obviously preferable because they do not have to pay their mothers and feel
that their children are in the best hands.

For Khadi, Sadatu, and Aminata the arrivals and departures of loved
ones heighten the dilemma of living between two worlds and provide
occasions for expressing their feelings of frustration. Their utterances,
laced with references to Islamic religious practice, give voice to the
changing nature of their Muslim identity. Islam, and the dilemma of
practice in a foreign context, is a significant part of the changing realities of their lives. Khadi now questions things that in the past, having
been brought up in a strict Muslim home, she would have thought
unquestionable. Sadatu, also brought up in a strict Muslim home, had
abandoned her religion upon arrival in the United States. Only after

meeting Mustafa did she find herself turning to Islam, but not without difficulties. Aminata's relationship with Islam has, by her own account, remained constant. She never turned from her religion after her arrival in the States, but instead sees herself as refining her practice.

Islam: One Path

I met Khadi, Sadatu, and Aminata for the first time during the month of Ramadan, in 1991. Ramadan is a time of religious introspection for many Muslims, and each of these women proved willing to discuss openly her understanding of Islam, how she saw herself as a Muslim, and how her understanding of her Muslim identity came into play in her daily life. In their struggles to recreate the Ramadan traditions of home, Khadi, Sadatu, and Aminata each reflected on the difficulties of being Muslim in the United States.

Khadi

I first spoke to Khadi over the telephone. I had just met her husband, Ahmed, several days earlier at the Islamic Center, and was following up with a phone call. I introduced myself to Khadi, hoping that her husband had told her about me and the research I was doing. She affirmed that he had mentioned me and had said that I was interested in Islam, but offered little else. I explained my project in greater detail, and she seemed intrigued. I asked her if we could meet at some point. She hesitated, and then said,

Yes, I would like to meet you. But you should know that Ahmed and I have very different views about Islam. I am not fasting this Ramadan, and Ahmed is upset with me. Every time I fast I feel sick. I work full-time and go to school. I have children to take care of and no one to help me. I don't have the time to be sick. I think Islam is important and my children are being brought up to be good Muslims. But this is difficult here.

For Khadi, the general disjunctures that emerge in a non-Muslim society are often expressed in her feelings about child-rearing. Deeply disturbed by the lack of religious instruction in the American public school system, particularly the lack of prayer, Khadi and Ahmed had decided to send their three children to Catholic school. Believing that any prayer was better than none, Khadi was unconcerned that her children were being instructed in the belief system of another faith.

I send my kids to Catholic school. Prayer and religion should be left to the family, but this is difficult to achieve here. This society is filled with problems because they took prayer out of the schools. This is why I send my kids to Catholic school. I believe children should be in a religious environment.

For Khadi and Ahmed there is no inherent conflict in Muslim children attending a non-Muslim parochial school. They are raising their children as Muslims, convinced that the children who abandon Islam are those whose parents only give lip service to religion. When speaking of their own children, they often told me that the key to keeping children on the right path, both generally speaking and for Islam in particular, is to instill a sense of pride in who they are. All their children are devout Muslims. Khadi recently told me, with evident satisfaction, that her son Ali, who is now twenty-six years old, has assumed the role of leading the evening prayers at home. She also told me that all three of her children now fast for the entire month of Ramadan.

Khadi admits that her husband has been the guiding force in teaching her children to practice correctly. At the same time, she feels that her resistance to Ahmed's claims on her religious life, as illustrated above in her reaction to her father-in-law's visit, taught her children that the meaning of Islam did not reside in "merely practices, but in the soul." Between her and Ahmed's differing visions, she told me, "these kids were given a full picture of what Islam really is."

The difficulty of practicing Islam is a frequent topic of discussion for many of the women with whom I work. This difficulty, often expressed in terms of family relationships, commonly centers on the daily conflicts they encounter while living in a non-Muslim society. Caught between a "traditional" Sierra Leonean understanding of the role of the wife, and her own changed understanding based in her American experience, Khadi often centers her discussion of Islam and Muslim identity on her relationship with her husband. Comparing their upbringings and finding fault with Ahmed's understanding of what a good Muslim should be, Khadi often points to their different ethnic backgrounds:

My mother is Fula and my father was Mandingo. Even though you really are a member of your father's tribe, you still are connected to your mother's people. I am Fula more then anything—at least that is how I feel. Ahmed is Kano, so my children are considered Kano. Kano people do not have a lot of Muslim identity, like the Fula do. The Kano, Limba, and Mende have a different notion of religion, not like the Fula, Mandingo, and Susu. For the Kano, their religion is very outward and this is how they give it inner meaning. They converted very late and feel the need to express themselves as Muslims in a very outward way, making sure that everyone knows. They derive their spirituality from practice.[13] The Fula have been Muslim a long time and are confident in their belief. We are more realistic and do not need to express it outwardly. We feel it inside all of the time, and our everyday behavior reflects this. We derive our spirituality from within.

Khadi and Ahmed were married in Sierra Leone soon after she graduated from high school. Their parents approved of the marriage, Khadi told me, because they both came from "good Muslim families." When I asked her if there was any conflict because Ahmed was Kano, she said, "No. Most Sierra Leonean Muslims will marry another Muslim from another tribe; it is only a problem when you marry a Christian." At the same time, Khadi would often invoke their ethnic difference and the Fula's deep historical links to Islam in order to challenge Ahmed's assertions that she was practicing incorrectly. However, I never heard her actually say this to his face.

I did often hear other Sierra Leoneans make similar distinctions between various ethnic groups. They would often say that the Fula, Mandingo, and Susu were "better Muslims" because they were "one hundred percent Muslim," meaning that few among them had been converted by Christian missionaries back home, while other ethnic groups in the region had succumbed to the lure of the Church. I had also heard such assertions in Sierra Leone. For example, many Susu people I met, both in Sierra Leone and Washington, claimed that the only Susu man ever to have converted to Christianity had done so with the sole purpose of gaining funding for a school in his village.[14]

Nevertheless, Ahmed insisted constantly that Khadi begin practicing Islam the way he thought proper, particularly with regard to prayer. As Khadi put it:

I pray [silently] in my bed every night. Ahmed says this is unacceptable because I am not a cripple. He has given me a year to make up my mind about prayer.

"What will he do if you don't?" I asked.

I don't know, but he could order me to pray. I suppose he wants me to pray so the path is consistent with the children's.

In fact, Khadi would often tell me that she was powerless in such matters when her husband put his foot down.

I have no choice. If he wants me to pray in his way, I must. If he wants me to go home, even if the country is hopeless, I must go. I behave this way for the sake of the children. I do not want them to lose their culture. In the presence of the kids, Ahmed is in charge.

Khadi's assertion that she does not want her children to "lose their culture," refers to her belief that ultimately a husband/father must make decisions to which wives and children must defer. This directly contradicts her assertion noted in the above section that she wishes that she had raised her children to question authority. In this case and others, Khadi's discourse centers on accommodation, but her actions contain at least a hint of resistance against the patriarchy by which her marriage is in theory defined.

This is seen most clearly in the different ways that Khadi acted in front of her husband compared to how she behaved when he was not around. When Ahmed would express opinions about family life, Islam, and similar topics, Khadi would often remain silent, seemingly communicating agreement. In her private statements, however, she angrily rejected her husband's claims on her life. One evening, when we were all discussing issues of marriage and children, Ahmed voiced his belief that a man's value rests in his having many children and that multiple marriages are a valid means to achieve this end. Khadi sat silent throughout. When he left us alone, Khadi turned to me with fire in her eyes:

I have never accepted multiple marriages! I have always been against this and Ahmed knows it. He wouldn't dare! My mother was a first wife. She married her cousin. It was not a good thing. The other wives always laid their problems on my mother. She was the scapegoat.[15] And this business about children! He is trying to shame me because I do not want any more. My three are enough!

Khadi proceeded to tell me the story of her last pregnancy. Whispering, she described what was a significant turning point in her relationship with her husband. Soon after Ahmed left for one of his many trips "back home,"[16] Khadi called him and told him that she was five weeks pregnant. She was in her sixth month of pregnancy when he returned, only to be summoned by his father within two months of being back in the U.S. and told to return to Sierra Leone.

This really made me mad! When I went into labor, Ahmed's uncle took me to the hospital and just left me there! My children call him grandfather. He is like a father-in-law to me so it would have been wrong for him to stay. He returned after I had the baby and picked me up. I forgot to tell him to shop for food. So three days after I gave birth I had to go shopping! If Ahmed was here or we were back home I never would have had to do this.

"Back home," according to Khadi, the community looks after a new mother. Her relatives and neighbors cook for her and help with daily chores such as going to the market.[17]

Still deeply angry ten years later, Khadi finds it hard to forgive Ahmed for leaving her alone at such a difficult time. In Sierra Leone, as she recently told me, a Muslim woman is "dead for forty days after she gives birth. The dangers are great and you should not pass the threshold until the forty days are up."[18] For Sierra Leonean women in the United States, forty days of seclusion is generally impossible. So she has subsequently refused to let herself be put in that situation again:

I went on the pill a year ago. I am afraid of getting pregnant. I keep telling him [Ahmed] when we go home we will have another child. All he can say is that we will be too old.

She gave me a knowing smile.

Khadi's discourse illustrates two culturally and seemingly contradictory tellings of her experience. On the one hand it would appear that she gives into her husband when she states that she must listen to him to instill appropriately the "cultural values" (Sierra Leonean) in her children; at the same time, Khadi resists her husband's assertions through a variety of actions, that are reflective of a growing ideology that revolves around issues of gendered identity in a transnational context. Khadi's sense of self is mediated through the dual worlds in which she resides. Her discourse reflects the way in which two sets of values can sit side by side without any seeming contradiction. The link between these two perspectives resides not in the contradictions, but rather in the way in which neither perspective can wholly determine transnational gendered identity. As such, the disjunctures of Khadi's life, her religious life in particular, point to the ambivalence that she feels—and that women in similar circumstances feel—when reflecting on their lives.

Sadatu

Like Khadi, Sadatu also feels disjunctures in her religious life. But unlike Khadi, Sadatu often discusses her struggle to be a "better Muslim." Her husband Mustafa, like Ahmed, has demanded that she change her behavior to suit his understanding of religious propriety. But unlike Khadi, Sadatu struggles to appease her husband, wanting desperately to please him. Her struggle is to remake herself into the perfect Muslim woman, as defined by the pamphlets and books that Mustafa brings home from the Islamic Center (see Chapters 4 and 5). Fearing she is unable to meet these standards, Sadatu feels deeply guilty. Her discourse frequently centers on what her husband demands of her.

Mustafa wants me to be Islamically proper. He told me to stop modeling and singing. He said these things lead to pornography. I think maybe he is right. I never thought about practicing my religion in America until I met him. I try to pray five times a day, but it is hard. My heart and soul are not always into it. I often pretend, just going through the motions. I do feel guilty about this.

A young, stylish woman, Sadatu gave up a successful modeling career to find herself now married to a man who, two years into their marriage, had turned to Islam in ways that she had not anticipated.

On Laylat al-Qadr the entire Qur'an is recited at the mosque.[19] That night Sadatu, Mustafa, Ami, their two-year-old daughter, and I went to the Islamic Center. The recitation would last all night, so the worshipers arrived carrying food, pillows, and blankets. During the drive to the Center Mustafa talked on and on about the blessings we would receive for spending the whole night at the mosque. Sadatu was sullen. She later complained to me that she had to be at work at the nursing home early the next morning; Mustafa, as a taxi driver, could begin work any time he liked. She questioned the practicality of a night spent in the mosque. Nevertheless, she agreed to stay and try to remain awake.

I should stay. I have many sins to wipe away. If you stay up the whole night your sins are washed way. It is easier to do this in Sierra Leone. People do not just stay in the mosque the whole night. People wander around going in and out of the mosque where the Qur'an is being recited. You go to people's homes and visit and eat. It is different here, and Mustafa says you get more blessings this way than the way we do it back home.

By midnight the prayers and lectures preceding the reading were over. The imam announced that recitation of the Qur'an would begin at 2:00 A.M. Sadatu began to fade. It was a brisk April night, but the heat in the Center was turned up beyond comfort. Sadatu suggested to me that we open the basement doors. When Sadatu and I approached the doors we were immediately taken to task by a group of Moroccan women who protested that men might look in on us. Sadatu lost her cool.

These women sit in a circle and every time someone walks in the room they scratch each other and say something about that person. If men look in, it is because they are not good Muslims! They should not be in the mosque and have such thoughts on their minds! I want to go home. I am so tired and my daughter should not have to be around these women and their back-scratching ways. You never know about these type of women.[20]

Asleep in my arms, two-year-old Ami stirred and moaned. Sadatu grew tense.

I want to go home now, and I am going up to the men's section to tell Mustafa. Don't let those witches look at my baby! Turn your back to them and hold her closer. Keep saying the Fatiha.

By 1:00 A.M. Sadatu, Ami, and I were on our way back to their apartment. After dropping us off, Mustafa returned to the mosque. As soon as he left us, Sadatu lamented:

I know I should have stayed there, but I am so sick of the back-biting in the mosque. Mustafa tells me I should ignore these women, that I am there to pray, to get blessings.

This incident highlights Sadatu's daily struggles to come to terms with her husband's expectations while at the same time negotiating the multiple interactions inevitable in Center culture. Feeling put upon at times, Sadatu nevertheless endeavors to impose a strict set of rules on herself, constantly seeking ways to prove to Mustafa, and to herself, that she is indeed on the way to being "Islamically proper." This often results in an alternating series of resistances and accommodations.

One afternoon Sadatu called me to ask if I wanted to go to Pentagon City, one of the largest upscale shopping malls in the Washington metropolitan area. I agreed to meet her at the food court there, and hurried to catch the Metro. I found Sadatu dressed as she used to dress when she was a model. I told her she looked beautiful. She smiled.

These are clothes from my past. Mustafa told me to get rid of this stuff, but I put it in the back of a closet. He never goes in there.

She suggested that we go into one of the fancier department stores to get "make-overs." I declined the make-over, but told her I would go in to keep her company. Afterward, we went back to the food court. As we talked, sipping cold soft drinks, I noticed Sadatu's face, which had been bright and happy, suddenly drop. "What's wrong?" I asked. "That," she replied. "Look over there." I turned, to see several women sitting in a nearby booth who were dressed in hijab. "I shouldn't be wearing these clothes," Sadatu continued. "Mustafa's right. I am showing myself off and this is haram." She wanted to return to her apartment so she could change into "proper" attire.

As Sadatu struggles with conflicting desires to please her husband or herself, she focuses on categories of the permissible and forbidden.[21] The night before Id al-Fitr, the feast marking the end of Ramadan, she and I spent the evening preparing a lavish meal that would be served the following morning after prayers. Describing various feast day foods to me, Sadatu explained that she now serves her family only halal meat.

We [Sadatu, Mustafa, and Ami] just started eating halal meat a month ago. Before that we just bought meat at the Safeway [a grocery chain in the area]. I feel better about this meat. It is clean. Safeway meat floats when you boil it, and it makes you feel bloated. Halal meat makes you feel light, and it does not float when you boil it.

An obvious sign of Muslim identity, halal meat becomes a rallying symbol for many Muslims living in the diaspora. For Sadatu, it has become what Ruth Mandel (1989:41) has appropriately identified for Turkish migrants living in West Germany, a "form of resistance against the prevailing norms of an alien society, a society commonly perceived as dangerous, infidel and immoral." For Sadatu, halal meat serves as a symbol to contest not only the alien society in which she is attempting to be a good Muslim, but also the internalized alien society within herself, one whose voice echoes throughout her discourse, making it difficult to live up to her husband's aspirations.

Food, like other cultural idioms, is multivalent. Its meanings emerge only within particular contexts. In the case of transnationals, whatever "traditional" food, and ways of serving and eating eat it, form a link with the past that helps to ease tensions inherent in dual systems of meaning. More specifically, because foodways "provide a whole area of performance in which statements of identity can be made—in preparing, eating, serving, forbidding, and talking about food" (Kalčik 1985:54; also see Brown and Mussell 1985)—the ways that transnational women utilize them to devise strategies to express gendered identity illustrates the duality of the subject positions they hold. In Sadatu's new-found insistence that her family eat properly slaughtered meat, she is displaying her willingness to accede to her husband's wishes and communicating her need to be identified as a "good Muslim woman."[22]

Aminata

I was introduced to Aminata by a male informant who knew I wanted to meet women who actively practice Islam. My first impression of her was of a hard-working, independent woman deeply devoted to her religion. I met her for the first time at her street-corner hot dog stand located in the heart of the Washington, D.C. business district. I explained my research interests, and she offered me a hot dog. Not particularly hungry, but not wishing to refuse her offer, I hesitated. Aminata immediately pointed to the "Sabrett Kosher Hotdog" sign displayed prominently on her stand, then to her Ethiopian competitor across the street, and assured me I had no cause to worry.

I only serve clean meat at this stand. I am not like some of these other Muslim women who ignore Islam. Her food [pointing again to her competitor] is dirty! Her hot dogs have pork in them, and besides, she is not Sierra Leonean. So don't buy things from her.

For Muslim food vendors in particular, halal meat is a symbol by which they contest the broader cultural context in which to sell their product. Many of the hot dog vendors in and around the District display a multiplicity of signs to indicate that their food is symbolically "clean." Like Aminata, some display Sabrett placards, while others have handmade signs stating outright that they serve only halal meat. The assertion, in English, is often framed in Qur'anic verse. Aminata has chosen to display a familiar brand name to indicate that her hot dogs are kosher, an acceptable alternative to the very limited and expensive halal products, including beef hot dogs, sold at Muslim-owned meat markets that are now mostly found in northern Virginia.[23]

Busy during the lunch rush with her customers, mostly business men and women and high school students, Aminata spends much of the rest of her day gossiping with Sierra Leonean taxi drivers, who cruise by frequently, chatting with her customers—or "my anthropologist," as she often referred to me—and cherishing her newly purchased stand. Halal meat, like the many Islamic decorations that cover the exterior of her stand, publicly asserts the food vendor's identity (see Chapter 5). For Aminata these also serve as a sacred boundary between her public and private life.

As stated earlier in this chapter, Aminata often lamented her inability to control her sexual urges, and she struggled to keep this aspect of her private life separate from her public life. In this way the guilt that she would sometimes express to me could be lessened.

I am a young woman. Why shouldn't I have a boyfriend? It is really haram to sleep with a man other than your husband. I feel guilty. I even have Suliman working on helping me get my husband over here! I think if we succeed, God might forgive us. If my husband was here I would never have a boyfriend.

"Do you think your husband is being faithful?" I asked. She laughed bitterly.

No. I told you before he is probably using the money I send on other women! That is part of the reason I will not give up Suliman. If he [her husband] comes here he will probably try to send for his other woman and dump me! Then I will have no one! I am grateful to Suliman. He is very good to me, and I have been very good for him. America turned him [away] from Islam. After meeting me he does not drink any more, and he now prays five times a day. God will forgive me because I have made him a good Muslim again.

Still, she and Suliman would avoid each other during the work week, especially at religious/sacred events, maintaining a boundary between their public and private worlds that allowed each to preserve a valued public purity. For example, on the day of the Id al-Fitr prayer, Aminata arrived at the mosque late.

I needed a ride to the mosque and had to call a lot of people before I could get someone to pick me up. I could not ride in the same car as Suliman, even though there were other people taking a ride with him. I would not remain pure for prayer if we were in the same car.

For Aminata, the boundary between purity and pollution allows her to negotiate the complex web of contradictions in which she finds herself entangled by taking on a lover, neatly placing a public and private life on two sides of an imagined margin.

One day, however, the boundary suddenly collapsed, leaving Aminata to trudge through the mire of contradictions that the dissolution of imagined boundaries can create. She called me late one night in tears:

My belly has not had rice on it in days! I cannot eat. Suliman has taken a new woman! Do you remember the day you helped me move to my new apartment and he borrowed your car? He went and picked that woman up! He lied to us! He did not call me for days after I moved. When I called him and he finally answered the phone he said he was sick. I know this is not true. When he finally came over to see me all he wanted was sex, but I would not give him any! He got mad and ripped my underwear and forced me! Then he confessed that he had a girlfriend.

When I suggested that she avoid seeing him in the future, she seemed baffled.

I need him for rides to work [everyday]. You know I cannot drive.[24] He helps me haul the stand to my place.

The next time I saw Aminata was at her stand. Knowing that I was deeply troubled by the turn in her relationship with Suliman, she greeted me with an announcement:

I told him to go! I am going to really work hard to bring my husband now. I told him [Suliman] that when my husband comes he will give me the best love. It made him angry! He said I was just saying that because I was jealous of the other woman.

However, several days later Aminata phoned me and asked me to hurry over to her apartment. When I arrived, she greeted me at the door wailing and angry.

I went to the Giant [a grocery chain in the area] and when I was returning I saw Suliman in his car with the other woman! I knew they were going to his apartment! I followed them to his apartment and started banging on the door! They did not answer. I knew they were in there! I heard her talking on the phone. I kept banging! I knew they wanted to do something [have sex], but I was not going to let him lay down with dogs in his apartment!

For several days afterward Suliman tried to phone Aminata, but she refused to answer his calls. He asked his niece, who was staying with Aminata at the time, to beg her to please talk to him. Aminata told me that she would not speak to him until he decided between her and his other woman.

People are telling me that I am being taken advantage of. That I am acting cheap because I tell him that I love him and that I will do anything for him. I am going to be tough.

Nevertheless, while realizing that she could not marry Suliman and recognizing that her behavior was not in line with what she understood to be proper, Aminata continued to lament losing Suliman, and to wish that everything could be as before.

For several years after I completed my field work I lost touch with Aminata. Then I phoned one Ramadan (January 1996), to see how she was doing. Excited to hear my voice, she immediately caught me up on her good news: her husband had been in the States for three years now, and in the past year she had given birth to a baby girl! Not only that, but her husband had arrived during Id al-Fitr. For many Muslims this day is a fitting time to start life anew. For Aminata, as she related it to me, this was to be the step that would perfect her religious practice. No longer would she be committing unacceptable acts. When I asked her what had happened with Suliman, she sighed:

You know how much I loved him! [But] he wanted to marry someone else. I was killing myself, staying up all night watching his apartment! Finally my husband came and it was over. When I told Suliman that my husband had arrived, he was shocked. He didn't believe me and called me a liar!

Laughing heartily, she said, "I finally gave him what he deserves!"

(De)essentializing Women's Lives

In telling these three women's stories I hope to counter essentialized definitions of Sierra Leonean womanhood, challenging popular Western representations that reduce Third World-African-Muslim women to the role of quintessential victims. These stories reveal the ways in which identities emerge in the context of changing locales, breaking down the boundaries of an imagined, singular other. Reflecting on their lives in relation to the de-territorialized realities of their world, I believe that these women are empowered by "the liminal spaces between cultures and societies [that] represent new imaginations about power and about the self" (Ong 1996:367).

Khadi's, Sadatu's, and Aminata's stories each reflect an emerging sense of self as transnational women. The moral ambivalences that seem to be a part of all three stories reflect the way in which such women can reflect on their lives through a series of different locales (Sierra Leone and the United States). As such, "they articulate a transnational, translational subjectivity that has developed through the mediation and dissolution of boundaries" (Ong 1996:366). All three stories reveal the emergence of gendered identities that bridge the gap between homeland and abroad, constructing identities that are embedded in the fluctuation between accommodation and resistance to the demands placed on their lives by others, particularly in terms of their relationship to Islam. Khadi's identity is remade in terms of her resistance to her husband's demands about proper Islamic practice, and the way in which she builds that resistance into a set of positive assertions about herself. In contrast, Sadatu's need to be more properly Muslim remakes her sense of self in terms of the ways in which she struggles to accommodate her husband. As such, her identity resides in a continual battle within her self. Aminata's need to be properly Muslim is challenged by her relationship with her lover from whom she bounds off her public world. For these women, gendered identity as filtered through Muslim identity is a site of struggle in which the localities of their lives become intertwined in complex ways.

It is not always a struggle in which they will prevail. Myriad pressures—from family, husbands, children, the Sierra Leonean and broader African and Muslim communities—push and pull them in different ways. As transnationals, not quite ever here or there, home or abroad, the pressures on them are even more complex. "Tradition" means different things and is played out in different ways in America and Sierra Leone. Hence the common assertion that certain behaviors or practices, such as multiple marriages or obedience to husbands, would be more palatable "back home" but are unacceptable "here." The same can be said for newly acquired attitudes, whether rooted in classic American ideals of "liberation" or "freedom," or the new religious understandings generated by translocal Islam and practiced in particular ways by a multiethnic congregation at the Islamic Center. For the transnational there are no easy answers. Against the common perception of the "melting pot," for these women—as in many cases for their men—the American transnational experience has fostered concurrent desires to change their lives and to retain their traditions.

Whichever way they are pulled at a given moment or in the face of a given set of circumstances, it should be noted, above all, that these women struggle actively with their own lives. This chapter began with a discussion of female circumcision, not only because the ongoing discussion about African-Muslim, and at times Sierra Leonean women posits a mirror by which these women view themselves in the reflection of the American "other," but also because the popular characterization of them as the ultimate victims of sexual aggression—genital mutilation—is so much at odds with any personal understanding of their own reality. The complexities of initiation into secret women's societies aside, the obvious conclusion is that the lives of Sierra Leonean Muslim women, like those of women everywhere, are far richer than that depicted by narrow-focused critics of particular cultural traditions, however well-intentioned. The future of Sierra Leonean ritual practice of bundu will, ultimately, rest with the women who have been initiated into its secrets. For Sierra Leonean women in the United States it is but one of many traditions that will have to be negotiated in the context of their very fluid Sierra Leonean/Muslim/American identities. Its fundamental importance may be that for women who debate whether or not to send their daughters "home" for initiation, and for those who have decided definitively one way or the other, it points to what is in many ways the most profound and vexing question facing transnational parents, mothers and fathers: how to raise children in America who will carry on an identity that for the parents remains rooted firmly in an attachment to "homeland" and to a religion that remains alien to American cultural consciousness.

Chapter 7
"We Owe Our Children the Pride": The Imagined Geography of a Muslim Homeland

"What is your name?" I asked a seven-year-old girl who sat down beside me at the home of Amir and Sama. "Amy, my name is Amy." Her father, Amir's first cousin, who was sitting near by, smiled. Sama, Amir's wife, who overheard this exchange from the kitchen, stomped out and loudly proclaimed to the child: "Your name is Amie, Aminata! You are Sierra Leonean, not American!"

The child stared blankly, ignoring Sama. Staring back, silent and seething, Sama turned on the child's father: "What are you doing? Why do you let your child take on this American name? How will she know who she is?" For Sama, as well as for other Sierra Leoneans living far from home, names, particularly of children born and raised in America, have come to symbolize boundaries of a community based in an imagined homeland. A significant identity marker, the "Americanization" of Sierra Leonean Muslim names by children is not taken lightly by most parents. Changing a name to "sound American," one parent told me, "is to erase our existence."

To transnational Sierra Leonean parents, American-born children, perhaps more than any other aspect of their lives, signify the ambiguity of borders between homeland and diaspora. Inscribed by their parents with the "imagined geography" of homeland, children become the terrain on which boundaries between "there" and "here" are crossed and recrossed. Parents recreate Sierra Leone for their children—and in their children—juxtaposing their African homeland with their understanding of the American experience. In so doing they weave a complex fabric of multiple identities. Through ritual events, educational experiences (both secular and religious), and the construction of everyday life, parents create for themselves—and for their children—emotionally powerful experiences that encapsulate and have come to represent the experience of lives lived away from home.

In some ways viewing their own children as strangers, parents struggle to make those children familiar. They lament that their children, neither fully Sierra Leonean nor fully American, and not properly Muslim, do not know who they—or their parents—are. But how do parents imagine their children as Sierra Leoneans, as Muslims, as Americans? In what ways do parents recast their transnational experience, contesting and/ or complying with that experience, to form an authoritative telling of lives lived across multiple localities?

Central to the lives of many parents is the notion of an "authentic" Sierra Leonean Muslim culture. This notion, articulated in a number of ways, is centered on the parents' powerful, romanticized, and deeply nostalgic telling of homeland—a homeland that is, for many of my informants, entwined with Islam. But whose Islam? This question becomes increasingly complex when one looks at the ways notions of religious and cultural authenticity are cast. Parents often lament the "Americanization" of children and work to offset the process. In a multiplicity of ways, in particular through ceremony and ritual, they draw a set of boundaries for their children that reflect a collective identity and, so they hope, protect their children from a variety of outside forces (Cohen 1985:48). A complex process of compliance and resistance to the "melting pot," community boundaries are drawn, affirmed, reinforced, and contested in a series of assertions anchored in symbolic/ritual statements of "authenticity" by which Sierra Leonean parents construct for their children an authoritative telling centered on an imagined, Muslim homeland.

This Muslim homeland, as Ruth Mandel has observed among Turks living in Germany, assumes "the authority of a legitimate and even desirable 'centre' in contrast to an increasingly 'peripheral'" homeland (1990:154). Geography, in this sense, becomes an ideological center around which transnational lives revolve, a "guiding orientation, to be negotiated amidst a host of contradictions" (155), embedded in the "essentialized nostalgia" (Bruner 1996a:159) of homeland that parents inscribe in their children's lives. To their parents, American-born Sierra Leonean children represent transition, a metaphorical border zone in which parents gaze into a (re)created Sierra Leone, a Sierra Leone imbued with their own desire for "the uncontaminated [pre-immigration] past, the so-called pure culture" (161) of home. However, this "pure" culture of past, recalled experience, what Bruner has in another context characterized as a "disembodied, decontextualized, sanitized, hypothetical Other" (161), becomes in the (re)telling an embodied, contextualized, desanitized, and reified Familiar. In their attempt to map Sierra Leone onto the American landscape of their children's lives, parents construct a bounded and imagined stable homeland in which they desire their children to remain, one that will, they hope, insure the future of the community.

On the other hand, to Sierra Leonean children born and raised in the United States, the adults of the community serve as the mediating force in which the realities of cultural encounter are explored. These children, for their part, often describe themselves as simultaneously Sierra Leonean, Muslim, and American. In naming themselves, they more comfortably blur boundaries that their parents struggle to maintain in their own and in their children's lives.

Name changing by children is indeed often an attempt to challenge, or at least to blur, the boundaries that parents create for them. In staring blankly at Sama, and ultimately ignoring her, Amy/Amie challenged her aunt's attempt to essentialize her experience, and to ignore the cross-cultural realities of her Sierra Leonean-American experience. Equally challenged, parents increasingly turn to ceremonies and rituals that they think will instill a sense of communal belonging in their children.

Naming Children Properly

Recall the naming ceremony described in Chapter 3 in which the American Thanksgiving either enhanced or collided with transplanted local (ethnic-religious) custom. That particular ceremony was held in a private home, the garden apartment of the proud parents. The presiding imam, a Saudi-trained Sierra Leonean newly arrived in the States, scolded the small assembly not for this particular ceremony, but for others he had attended—or at least heard about—in which alcohol had been served, and in which the ritual practice had been improper, not, as he put it, "as the Arabs do." His critique cuts to the heart of the ongoing dilemmas in which Sierra Leonean parents all too often find themselves from the very out set. How should they publically name their children.

Abbas, a cab driver who has one child, related to me his understanding of how naming ceremonies have changed in America. His emphasis on Islamic aspects of the naming process is deeply reflective of how important that aspect is to the emerging Sierra Leonean-Muslim-American identity.

Abu Bakr is my real name. This is my Muslim name [the name he was given at his naming ceremony as an infant]. On the seventh day after the baby is born we have a naming ceremony. This is when the child goes out for the first time. In the U.S. this is impractical because you have the baby in the hospital and you must bring the baby home. So the baby travels before the naming ceremony. So here you have the naming ceremony long after the baby has been out and about.

Abbas places special emphasis on the transformation of the ritual in the American context:

In Sierra Leone, naming ceremony parties are not a big deal, but in the U.S. they have big parties at night. I do not think that these big parties are proper. We are supposed to be naming the child, letting the child know that he is Muslim—Sierra Leonean, too—but a Muslim. This is what it means to be a Muslim.

For Abbas, who recognizes that it is impossible to (re)create Sierra Leonean naming ceremonies in the United States, the search for authenticity is still important. Clearly that search lies in the realm of Islam. In his assertion that "big parties are not proper," he searches for authenticity in his version of purity of ritual practice. His discourse, particularly in relation to the children of the community, is what Stewart and Shaw (1994:8) have labeled "anti-syncretic," a discourse that involves "the erasure of elements deemed alien from particular religious and ritual forms." However, this is not a one-way process: erasure in the case of Sierra Leoneans in the United States is often qualified, and is in many instances contested.

For the vast majority of my informants there is a consciousness that the imagined pure forms of the pre-traveled past, while discussed and desired, are not so easily attained. Nevertheless, they consistently remain a goal. As Stewart and Shaw put it (8), "Selected forms may be identified as foreign and extirpated, or alternatively recast and retained through claims that they have always really been 'ours,' thereby deleting former religious synthesis from authorized cultural memory." The process of the continual recasting of imagined traditional forms, particularly in the development of an essentialized Sierra Leonean homeland as connected to Islam, is especially apparent in the way in which Sierra Leoneans present Sierra Leone to their children.

The "Big Party"

I arrive at a Day's Inn located in the District. It is 6:00 P.M. Saturday evening. I am early; the party will not really start until 9:00 P.M. with the actual naming around 10:00 P.M.. This particular hotel is one of my informants' favorites. I have attended many such ceremonies in its reception hall and have been told it is an ideal spot for a "big party." Relatively inexpensive to rent, it is also centrally located. Two Sierra Leonean imams, Alhaji Sisay and Alhaji Foday, will preside over this ceremony.[1] Alhaji Sisay is an artist—he paints beautiful landscapes of Sierra Leonean settings—who has arrived recently in this country. By virtue of his age, piety, and ability to dispense wisdom in acceptable ways, he has taken on the role of a leading imam in the community. The other, younger imam, Alhaji Foday, has been in this country for many years. College educated in Saudi Arabia, he completed a Ph.D. in political science from an American university. I had met him fairly early in my fieldwork and attended a variety of functions at which he presided, including weddings, divorces, and memorial services. It was he who invited me to this particular naming ceremony.

This naming ceremony is for a little girl who is, much to my surprise at the time, already a toddler, perhaps two years old. I am told that it took her parents many years to save up enough money for this party. Tables line the periphery of the room, each overflowing with Sierra Leonean foods that women in the community have prepared. Five chairs sit in the center of the room. In front of the chairs, a white cloth is spread out on the floor. Sitting on the white cloth is a bowl of "rice flour" (rice flour, sugar, and water mixed together) with kola nuts stuck in it, next to it a bowl of water and several loaves of bread. I am told that this is the "sacrifice."[2]

The ceremony begins. Alhaji Sisay, Alhaji Foday, the child's parents, and the girl's "godmother"[3] sit in the chairs in the center of the room. The child who is to be named sits in her godmother's lap. Alhaji Foday, microphone in hand, begins to speak to the crowd of several hundred. He begins the ceremony in English, explaining:

I will speak in English. We are obliged to do this out of respect for each other. No [indigenous African] language should dominate. We are in America and should all speak English.

Then, in Arabic, he recites the Fatiha, the opening sura of the Qur'an, which is always used to begin any action in the life of a pious Muslim.

This imam's alternating and self-conscious use of English and Arabic is telling. In their discussion of "anti-syncretism," Stewart and Shaw (1994:7) assert that "agents concerned with the defence of religious boundaries . . . [are] frequently bound up with the construction of 'authenticity,' which in turn is linked to notions of 'purity.'" They add, however, that the "assumption that assertions of purity speak out naturally and transcendentally as assertions of authenticity" is questionable. Stewart and Shaw go on to say that "authenticity or originality," while not dependent on purity, nevertheless can be claimed as unique: "both putatively pure *and* putatively syncretic traditions can be 'authentic' if people claim these traditions are unique, and uniquely their historical possession." By using both English and Arabic, Alhaji Foday links the historical present to the imagined past. In his assertion that English, which is the dominant language of both the present site and of the colonial past, unites the assembly, he is negotiating and redefining the boundaries of practice and ideology—boundaries defined by transnational experience. At the same time, his use of Arabic, the sacred language of Islam, authenticates his assertions. While English positions the participants in the historical present, Arabic globalizes and hence lends a sacred power to their experience. No sooner does Alhaji Foday position his audience than he deterritorializes the event.[4]

Alhaji Sisay is then introduced. Taking an opposite stance—and complicating matters for those present—the second imam begins his oration by announcing, "I will speak in Krio, but I ask your forgiveness." By his assertion, Alhaji Sisay, who is fluent in English, immediately contests his counterpart's positioning of the event. His deliberate use of Krio—an indigenous language that all present understand—signals to the participants that this is, above all, a Sierra Leonean event. By situating the naming ceremony in a "local" geographic space, Alhaji Sisay reterritorializes the ritual, challenging the assumption that global discourses of experience are appropriate for the naming of a Sierra Leonean child. At the same time, he too, punctuates his assertion with Qur'anic recitation, giving a power to his words that is based in a universal language and the sacred language of Islam.

Alhaji Sisay now switches his focus to the question of appropriate Muslim—and Sierra Leonean Muslim—behavior, here underscoring the first imam's assertions of global Muslim practice. He admonishes the assembly:

I notice that there is a back room here and maybe there is beer there. We are Muslims, and alcohol is evil.

Suddenly he shifts his tone, from reprimand to empathy:

We need blessings, many more, living here in the U.S. with its evil influences. We need to start this child out on the right path.

He has now qualified his assertion of global Islamic discourse, reminding the participants that they are in fact in a foreign context and therefore must work hard to set the child being named on the right path. That path connects Islam both to the larger Muslim world and to notions of traditional indigenous practice. Alhaji Sisay next recites several passages from the Qur'an. The crowd punctuate the recitation by holding their hands out, palms turned up to the ceiling, and saying "amin" (amen). The recitation finished, we raise our hands to our faces and wash the Qur'an over ourselves.[5]

Now Alhaji Foday rises and, to my surprise, introduces me to the assembly:

She will write a Ph.D. and will help us. She has been to Sierra Leone, and now she is here with us. She knows us well. People will know we are here because of this woman.

The crowd stares. Some smile; those sitting close by want to talk to me. People begin passing me scraps of paper with their phone numbers. As I collect the notes I wonder exactly what kind of role the imam has cast me in.

Alhaji Foday now moves on to more pressing business:

Why are we at this naming ceremony? To keep us away from the evils of this country, as well as to give us the bounty of this country. We can achieve this through regular prayer. We should keep our behavior within the bounds of Islam and our culture. It will keep us honest. You should take the best of America, especially education, and take it back to Sierra Leone. Do not back-bite each other! It is not good, it is a disgrace! Let us set this child on the right path.

With his statement, Alhaji Foday has reified Alhaji Sisay's repositioning of the event within a Sierra Leonean context. He underscores this by reminding the participants that there is more than an evil Other against which they need to protect themselves.

With more Qur'anic recitation, Alhaji Foday blesses the parents, the child, and her godmother. We are told to silently recite the Fatiha, palms raised to the ceiling. Silently, we implore God to set the child on the right path. Again we wash our faces with our prayers. Opening statements over, the ceremony as such can now begin.

Alhaji Foday holds the child, who stares silently out at the crowd. She appears unperturbed by being the center of attention. The imam silently whispers into the little girl's ear the adhan along with her names and their meanings. He asks the parents if they have agreed on the names, then instructs them how they should raise their child:

This child should be taught that women have power, but man is the head of the household.

Loudly, with emotion, he announces the baby's name, Isatu, to the assembly. The imam recites her name over and over, and as he does so people race up to throw bills of various denominations onto the child and her parents. Money flies like confetti.[6] I ask the woman next to me why people are throwing money. She responds:

The money is being thrown, given, as a sign of respect toward the parents. It is to let them know that we are glad that the child is here among us. In Sierra Leone they kill a sheep when the baby's name is first called out. In America the meat is brought in, cut up, and passed out in little plastic bags.

Alhaji Foday ends the ceremony by thanking the parents and reciting the Fatiha three times. Afterward, I notice little plastic bags of meat being distributed. The imams receive their portions first. The bread and the bowl of rice flour are also passed around. Guests take a bit of rice flour in order to share in the blessings. I am told that the kola nuts are offered only to the most important guests. I ask about the meat: are we supposed to cook and eat it when we return home? A woman answers:

Yes, yes of course. That meat has many blessings. If you eat it you will have those blessings.

Do I have to cook it a special way?

No, cook it any way you like. But eat it, because it has many blessings.

This big party was one of the more elaborate naming ceremonies I attended. Guests came attired in their finest traditional outfits, the women in bright, multi-colored African cloth and elaborate head scarves, the men in flowing, elaborately embroidered but sedately colored gowns and matching headgear. There was an undercurrent of conspicuous consumption: the ceremony in a rented hall, the gifts bestowed on the child, the party-like atmosphere. This party was larger than others I attended, but the basic elements were familiar.

In some quarters dissenting voices have begun to question the propriety of the naming ceremony as party. It is not enough, some now said, to merely denounce the alcohol in the back room and to insist upon a more timely event, in keeping with religious precept. Indeed, at the time of my fieldwork, a new discourse about naming ceremonies was beginning to emerge. This discourse centered on the movement toward a more "traditional" interpretation of Islam among a particular group of my informants who began to challenge the ways naming ceremonies are often celebrated. As I noted in Chapter 3, several informants told me that the trend toward elaborate parties has created a situation in which children are named very late, a frightening prospect.

I attended one naming ceremony that clearly struck me as transitional, one in which the dissenting voices suddenly grew louder. The child being named was close to a year old, well beyond the seven-day time limit for naming. The ceremony took place in the back yard of the parents' suburban Maryland home, a modest split-level in a working-class neighborhood. The imams—the same two as in the previous example—and the male and female elders of the Sierra Leonenan community sat with the parents and godmother under a yellow and white rented tent. The atmosphere was party-like, although the venue was less elaborate than the rented hall. What was different was how the emerging discourse about naming was expressed in the imams' sermon, as well as in several speeches delivered by elders. Imam Foday began the ceremony by criticizing implicitly the procrastination in naming children:

When a child is born, after seven days you are to call the adhan in both his ears and name him. This is our obligation to the child. How will this child know who he is until we name him? How will he know he is a Muslim?

The child was then named. The basic ritual elements were the same as at the big party. But afterward an elder stood to admonish the crowd:

I am very upset with all of you! You come to name a child and you hide beer in a room so we will not see it! We are Muslims, we are Sierra Leonean! What do other Muslims think of us when we behave this way! Do we deserve to be members of the Muslim community with this behavior? Our imam [Alhaji Foday] is always there for you. His sister Zaynab died and only a few of you came to recite the Qur'an, yet here he is for you! You are not even listening to me now!

The crowd by now grew restless, and some began to eat. The male elders, angry, stood up and threatened to leave. The hosts placated them and asked the crowd to behave for their child's sake. The imams and elders then recited the Qur'an. The ceremony now over, the party began.

The naming ceremony described in Chapter 3 represents a full-fledged expression of the new discourse. The child being named was three weeks old, two weeks beyond the theoretical seven-day limit but in fact one of the youngest babies I saw named during my fieldwork. An imam I had never met, who had arrived recently from Sierra Leone, presided over this ceremony. He began the ceremony with a sermon, to which the crowd listened intently. His sermon praised the Arabs for their "proper" practice, and implored us to follow their example and practice Islam correctly. "If you practice as the Arabs do," he declared, "then you will reap the same benefits." Most important, "Your children will be trained properly and have the tools not to give in to the evils of America." The sermon included stern admonitions about the impropriety of other naming ceremonies, especially those punctuated by the presence of alcohol. Money was thrown, but in a much less flamboyant manner. There was no sacrifice, no rice flour or kola nuts. This, I was told by an informant, was the proper way to name a child: "This child will be brought up properly, for she has been named properly. She will know who she is because her parents have put her feet on the right path." Naming a child is the way in which parents insure that their children embark on the "right path." Keeping them on that path, especially after they enter the American school system, is a much more complex problem.

The Fullah Islamic School

The Fullah Progressive Union Islamic and Cultural Center,[7] more popularly known as the Fullah Islamic School, opened its doors in 1989 (two years before my initial fieldwork) in response to a growing sense among adults in the community that their children, born and now raised in the United States, are losing their Sierra Leonean Muslim identity. When I attended regularly, in the winter and spring of 1991, the school held classes once a week, on Sunday. The founders hoped eventually to turn the venture into a full-time school. Classes were held in an old elementary school building in Maryland that was now owned by an individual who rented out space to tenants. The Fullah School organizers never told me how much rent they pay, but indicated it was formidable. Even so, the landlord was unwilling to give them a key to the building. He sometimes forgets to show up, leaving them no choice but to hold classes outdoors on the playground.[8] In such cases, inclement weather could force them to cancel the week's lesson. On one occasion, when the director of the Washington, D.C. Islamic Center came to observe the school in action, he arrived to find teachers and children locked out of the building. He told me he was deeply moved by their determination to hold classes outside, and stayed to lead prayers following the lessons.

I attended classes regularly for the majority of my initial fieldwork period, and spoke extensively with the chairman of the school, one of the founders. Muhammad has been in the United States for twenty years. When I asked him what compelled the Fullah Union to organize a school, he replied:

We used to send our children to the MCC [Muslim Community Center] in Silver Springs [Maryland], but we felt the program was not good enough for our children because they emphasized Pakistani culture. We decided our kids needed something else. They needed Sierra Leonean culture as well as Islam.

This statement clearly reflects growing feelings among Sierra Leonean adults throughout the D.C. area who question those community members who have openly rejected Sierra Leonean interpretations of Islam, calling themselves "born-again" Muslims. The school was initially established for Fullah children only. However, in response to the desire of Sierra Leonean parents from other ethnic groups to participate—others who were also dissatisfied with the globalized discourse on Islam—the school opened its doors to the Sierra Leonean Muslim community at large after its first semester of operation. Muhammad continued:

Originally we started the school just for the FPU members because we were afraid that if a non-member's child got hurt they would sue us. Our lawyers said to bring others in after one semester and to ask parents to sign a release form.

This sounded difficult because at home such a form would be insulting and frightening. But we had to ask people, even though this was such a foreign thing.

Whatever discomfort may have been entailed, parents agreed to sign the forms without much argument. Reflecting on this, Muhammad expressed the dilemma for many Sierra Leonean Muslim parents who had stayed on in the United States longer they anticipated:

We did not think much about it [Islam and Sierra Leonean identity] when our kids were small. Those of us who have older children, when we first had children we did not think about those things. We thought we would go to school [college] in the U.S. and go home [to Sierra Leone], but this did not happen. We do not want our children to become alien to the culture in their own house. Africans in general, not just Sierra Leoneans, are guilty of letting their kids lose their culture. Look at the Jews and the Spanish—they really push their culture.

Will the children eventually return to Sierra Leone?

I know some parents believe that their children will return to Sierra Leone, but those of us here will not force our children to go home. But we want them to know where they came from.

When I asked Muhammad about the ultimate goal of the school, his response was telling. Initially focusing on the problem of language, his discourse blossomed into a broad critique of the Sierra Leonean community in the United States, particularly the way adults in the community practice Islam, and turning to larger questions of religious and ethnic Muslim identity.

Our kids are losing Krio and Fullah. We want to remedy this. Some of the kids are not receptive. The problem is at the homes of these kids. We tell parents to pray and participate. If the children see their parents praying they will also pray. This is also a school for adults. We want parents to stay and discuss community business, bring them into the development of the school. We tell them we are not babysitters. The kids that are the biggest challenge are the twelve-year-olds. The little ones are easy. They have not been greatly influenced by American society. These older ones resist us. We want to teach these kids what it is to be a Muslim, to have pride in this. We want them not to be ashamed of their Muslimness or that they have to pray five time a day. Pride in being a Muslim and a Sierra Leonean is a big issue for us. Our main goal is to have a community of Sierra Leonean Muslims, a masjid [mosque], a center to teach our kids, and to have this all housed in one place. In this way we may be able to subsidize the living expenses of some of our people, such as an imam and his family.

Has the school been successful in achieving its goals?

It has worked to some extent. Five years ago you would find a Christmas tree in every Sierra Leonean household. This bothered me, so I went to the members

of the FPU and said we should give presents on Id al-Fitr. I then arranged a pic-
nic for all members, telling them to save their Christmas presents and give them
then. There are no Christmas trees in any house any more. Now we truly celebrate Ramadan.[9]

While the school has been successful in changing attitudes among
parents, the financial challenge of keeping the school open has been
substantial. Participants in the school often feel ignored by the larger
Muslim community in the metropolitan area. When I asked Muhammad
to identify the greatest obstacles to achieving their goals, he stated:

Renting space for all of this is very difficult. We want to put the Center in a house
that we own. Money is hard; we need $100,000 to buy a house. We would have
the mosque in the basement and the school upstairs. In having a place that is
ours we can really give a sense of community to our kids. We can start a youth
league. This is the only way our kids can get to know one another. If we have our
own place we can celebrate birthdays, holidays, etc. This is why we need a Center; we do not want to lose our sense of community. We want our kids to be
proud to be Muslim. But it is hard to get help to achieve this. Leaders in the
[larger] Muslim community have their minds in other places, not on Islam. Our
kids, the community as a whole, are bombarded with tele-evangelists. They can
lose their pride.

While Muhammad spoke to numerous hurdles facing Sierra Leonean
parents, he felt the biggest obstacle lay within the community itself:

The Sierra Leonean community, which is part of the Muslim community in D.C.,
and hence the U.S. and the world, must be proud. We must educate the community—ignorance is our biggest problem. In 1972, Sierra Leoneans did not know
where the mosque [Islamic Center] was; today Sierra Leoneans are seen at mas-
jids all over D.C.

What accounted for this change?

As we get older and wiser we turn to religion. We know our center will turn people back to Islam. Young people building families will not have the problems we
had. Years ago those of us who had children had nowhere to turn. We are making a place for families to turn. We owe our children the pride.

Muhammad's words, which echo the feelings of many parents, point
to the multiplicity of levels on which transnational Muslim parents are
challenged. Many Sierra Leonean parents have asked themselves, how
can they counter the "evil," outside forces of the alien nation in which
their children are being raised. For many, the Fullah Islamic school
offers an answer.

Organization

The school's organization is deeply reflective of the processes by which
founders and participating parents have come to challenge their present

cultural context. That challenge manifests itself in the construction of an alternative context in which children—at least so they hope—can absorb what parents believe to be appropriate understandings of Sierra Leonean identity. As we have seen so far in the construction of naming ceremonies, how Sierra Leonean Muslims living in the diaspora render their world intelligible lies within the realm of an emerging American Islam—an American Islam that, in the case of the organizers of the school, is a negotiable construct. This negotiation ultimately clues children in to what their parents perceive as an appropriate framework of meaning.

The school is composed of three grades. The three classes meet in one room that is divided by flimsy movable dividers that do little to contain sound. The classroom is vintage public school, circa 1950s, and shows its age. The building is still used during the week, though by whom is not clear. The cinder block walls are covered with pictures of prominent African Americans—and Fullah School teachers told me they were disappointed that because they did not own the property they were unable to inscribe the walls with their own identity.

First Grade

In all classes the ages of students, boys and girls, vary. This is especially true for the beginners. Children as young as four attend alongside several adults, but the average age of the students is between seven and ten years old. The criterion for registration in this class, not unlike traditional Qur'anic schools in the Islamic world, is the level of Islamic knowledge. The assumption is that the students in the first grade class know little or nothing about being a Muslim. Instruction is in English, the primary language of all the American-born students.

The teacher, Sharif, a graduate student working toward a Ph.D. in urban planning, stands silently in front of the students, waiting for them to quiet themselves. Mild-mannered and encouraging, he begins the lesson by reminding them that it is their responsibility to remember to bring notebooks, pencils, and the assigned text to class at all times. Taking personal responsibility for even the smallest actions, he tells them, "helps us to be more responsible Muslims." Emphasizing the importance of homework, he proceeds to verbally test the students' recall of Arabic letters.

A primary concern of the school is that the children learn to read Arabic, a skill that is not familiar to Sierra Leonean parents who attended Qur'anic school in Sierra Leone. Back home, the emphasis was on memorization. In the Fullah school, as one parent told me, "These children should be able to read the Qur'an and know what it means, not just to

Figure 7. Students at Fullah Progressive Union Islamic School, 1992.
Photograph by the author.

make sounds." The teacher agrees. He tells me after class that his primary goal for the beginning class is to "get the children to recognize the letters." Sound and context will be emphasized in the next grade. By then he expects them to be able to recognize Arabic words, making possible the more complex task of reading and understanding the Qur'an. Sharif begins the test by writing an Arabic character on the blackboard. The children shout out "jimm!" and are praised. Flash cards are produced and more letters reviewed.

Pleased with their progress, Sharif moves on to the day's lesson. "Why are we Muslims? he asks the class. Who is Allah?" He then turns to the blackboard and draws a diagram:

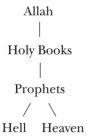

Pointing to the diagram, he answers his own questions: "Allah sends holy books to Prophets, and if you follow you go to heaven. If not, you go to hell."

The children listen intently, some writing his words down in their notebooks. The younger ones fidget, possibly unable to understand, some not yet writing. The teacher proceeds:

What is Islam? It is a way of life. It tells how to live our lives. To follow the five pillars of faith.

On the blackboard he lists the five pillars, then turns silently, observes the class for a moment, and asks the students to recite the Fatiha. The students recite in Arabic. Sharif now writes an English translation, then the Arabic, and finally an English transliteration side-by-side on the blackboard. The students are expected to copy all three versions into their notebooks. The central placement of the English translation the board is telling. In many classes in this country the Arabic would surely occupy the center, and in some cases the English translation would not appear. After class I asked Sharif why he translated the passage.

We want these kids to understand. Sounds without meaning are irrelevant. You see, this is why the Islamic Center in D.C. and the MCC here in Maryland don't work for our kids. They just learn the Arabic. How are our kids going to really be Muslims in this society if they do not understand what it all means?

The recitation of the Fatiha leads to a discussion about prayer. Sharif lists the optimal prayer times for a Muslim on the board, then adds a new diagram. He tells the students:

We pray five times a day. This is a pillar of faith and required of all Muslims.

He then has the children read out loud from a diagram of prayer times in the shape of a clock that he has drawn on the blackboard. Having started to explain the five pillars of faith, Sharif now proceeds to define and explain the other four:

Zakat is giving charity. It is your duty to give this charity. You must fast during Ramadan. You abstain from food from dawn until sunset. You must perform Hajj, but only if you can afford to go to Mecca. If you go, the male will be called a hajji and the female hajja. Most important of all is the Shahada, the declaration of faith. Let's recite it.

The students recite in Arabic. "La illahi illa Allah, wa Muhammad Rasul Allah [There is no God but God, and Muhammad is the Prophet of God]." Asked for the meaning, they then recite in English, following which Sharif dismisses the class. The students are allowed a recess before they will be called back to participate, along with the other children and adults present, in the midday prayer. They bolt from their desks, bursting through the door in one fell swoop.

Second Grade

The intermediate class consists primarily of children between the ages of ten and fourteen. To be in this class a student must have either passed the beginning level or demonstrated a knowledge of the basic tenets of Islam and the Arabic alphabet. The focus of the class, based on the books used, is *ibadat*, acts of worship.

School has begun and the teacher has not yet arrived. The children sit, chattering and fidgeting in their seats. Yusuf enters in a flurry, apologizing to the children as he hurries to the head of the class. He is wearing a suit and tie, an outfit that is not the usual garb of the teachers in this school, who generally wear pants and top made from the multi-colored cotton fabrics worn all over West Africa. Yusuf appears extremely uncomfortable. Pulling at his tie, he is aware that the children are surprised by his outfit, never having seen him dressed this way. He feels compelled to explain:

Sometimes humans are late, as I was today. This is acceptable. I am dressed this way today because I did not have time to go home to change into the clothes I wear to teach. But these Western clothes do not make me less of a Muslim. You can still dress like a Muslim using Western clothes. Okay?

The children nod in approval. He begins the session with a question: "What is the Shahada?" The students yell out, loudly and with passion: "The declaration of faith!" The teacher next asks: "Why and how do we say it?" The students recite the Shahada in Arabic.

The class then stands. The students recite the Fatiha, then proclaim, "Allahu Akbar" (God is most great). Yusuf writes the Shahada on the board in transliteration and asks the children to say it. He erases the board and asks them to say it again. He then tests each student individually, asking each to repeat the invocation in front of the whole class. When several students are unable to say it from memory, he grows angry:

You will not go any further in this school until you can say this from memory! The Shahada should always be on your lips!

He makes the children repeat the passage ten additional times, then goes on to discuss its meaning:

What does the Shahada mean? It refers to almighty God and His oneness and His attributes. It tells us that the Holy Qur'an is the book of God and all its contents are the words of God. That Muhammad, peace be upon Him, is the Messenger of God and His chosen prophet, the last of all prophets, and that we must follow the Prophet's teachings.

Embedded in many lessons in this school is a discussion of Christian beliefs. Many of these Sierra Leonean children attend Catholic school during the week, a choice their parents make because they believe that any religious school environment is superior to a nonreligious one. Many of the parents had attended Christian schools in Sierra Leone. However, as one parent told me, while they had not lost their Muslim faith or been converted to Christianity, they had seen other Muslim children in Christian schools abandon Islam for Christianity in Sierra Leone. Fearing that children who attended Catholic school in the United States would be under even greater pressure, not only at school but by the predominately non-Muslim society in which they live, the committee that fashioned the curriculum for the Fullah School felt they should incorporate some discussion of Christianity, particularly the Trinity.

The Christian concept of the Trinity is seen by Muslims as antithetical to their most basic belief, *tawhid*, the oneness of God. The abundance of books addressing the issue that are available on the shelves of libraries

and bookstores in Islamic Centers throughout the United States points
to the degree to which Muslim religious discourse has engaged the issue.
Likewise, the Trinity is woven through the curriculum of religious
instruction in classes held at these centers for adults and children. At
the Fullah Islamic School the Trinity was addressed at all class levels
nearly every week, directly and indirectly.

The teacher of the intermediate class would begin every class session
with a discussion about the oneness of God.

Teacher: There is no God except the almighty God! Who knows what the Trinity
means?
Student A: There are other religions in the world, such as the Christian religion,
and they believe that God is son, spirit, and father. We do not believe this. God
is just one. He does not have a mom and dad.
Teacher: Good! Are there any questions?
Student B: Are we supposed to be afraid of dying?
Teacher: It depends on what you do in this life. If you do not do what you are
supposed to do, you should be afraid.

The teacher turns the lesson back to the oneness of God.

Teacher: Who is One?
Children: (all together) Allah!
Teacher: Describe God to me!
Children (all together): He has no mother and father and no one speaks to
Him! He is One! He has no kids!

The class then stand, recite the Fatiha, and proclaim: "Allahu Akbar!"

The teacher ends the class by imploring the students to memorize the
Shahada and to internalize its meaning. "Know it by heart next Sunday," he says, then dismisses the class for recess. The students bolt out
the door. They, too, will return after the parents' meeting for noonday
prayers.

Third Grade

The average age of the students in this class ranges from fifteen to seventeen years. These students are expected to be able to read and write in
Arabic. The emphasis in this class is on hadith, prayer, issues of cleanli-
ness, Qur'anic study, and more advanced Arabic. The teacher, Ali,
begins his lecture by imploring the students not to simply memorize the
Qur'an:

Today we will read Sura Three, "Al-Lahab"[10] [The Flame]. You should have read
it since our last class. Some of you asked before class if you were supposed to
have memorized it. Memorizing the Qur'an is important, but more important is

that you recognize what you are reading, that you know the meaning and understand it.

Asking the students to open their books and repeat after him, Ali recites the sura. He then asks individual students to recite various sections. As they do, he corrects their pronunciation. Satisfied that his students are well versed in reading Arabic, he proceeds to explain the passage:

The fire of hell is the only fire strong enough to melt rock, and a volcano gives us only a glimpse of what the temperature of hell is like.

Seemingly baffled by what the teacher is saying, one student raises his hand and asks:

But what about the sun? It's hot enough to melt rock!

Implicit in this student's question is what the school director, in his explanation to me of the school's goals, called its "biggest challenge." The teacher stands silent, eyes cast down. Then he responds:

Yes, the sun is hot, but this is not the point of the sura. Even the sun can only give us a glimpse of what hell-fire is like.

The student looks skeptical, as do many of his classmates. They have accumulated a store of scientific knowledge that comes with education in the United States, knowledge that their parents and many of the teachers at this school may not have, or about which they may not feel confident. I often heard parents and teachers lament that this particular age group is "a difficult group to teach." Much of that difficulty lies in constant questioning by the students in the classroom. Calm and reserved in front of the class, the teacher would often feel frustrated, unable, as he once told me, "to reach past the walls of their American upbringing."

The teacher completes his discussion of the sura, then asks the students to take out a sheet of paper. He dictates Qur'anic verse in Arabic, which the students are expected to transcribe. Once this task is completed, the students are given a recess. Unlike the little ones, they do not burst from the room. Instead, they form groups and chat, hoping to be able to stay for the parents' meeting. But they are asked to go outside by their teacher, who runs the meeting and an adult education class.

Adult Meeting/Class

While the children play outside, the adults present gather for a combined meeting and study session. The meeting serves to remind parents of their obligation to raise their children as good Muslims, as well as serving as a sounding board for parental concerns. It is also a forum in which adults who are unsure of their Islamic knowledge can freely ask questions. Ali, the senior class teacher, begins the meeting by asking the group to recite the Fatiha. Still troubled by the challenge raised by his teenage student, the instructor begins:

Muslims have no choice. We cannot veer from God. We are in a world full of criticism. Islam should never be forced, those who will tell it is are liars. But if you are antagonized you can fight for your religion. You can only do things with non-Muslims as long as they [the actions] do not contradict your beliefs.

He reminds parents of their responsibilities:

Parents must participate in the school because it is very difficult to teach kids in this country. We want parents to work with their kids at home. Do not dump your kids and go away. Do not let them come to school without notebooks. No matter how much you know, there is always something more to learn. We are not just here to study Islam, but culture and language. It is our primary goal to pass on our religion and culture to our kids because there are too many bad influences in the U.S.

Affirmative nods from the group punctuate Ali's opening statement. He reminds the adults that they are never too old to learn:

No matter how much we know, we need to learn more. We need to ask ourselves, "What is the meaning of Islam?" We should be able to answer this, to pass this basic knowledge to our children. This school can only serve as part of the learning process. You must continue it at home.

He stands silent for a moment, surveying the class. His statements begin to take on a sermon-like quality:

What is the meaning of Islam? What does the word actually mean? Absolute obedience! Following the five pillars of faith! Never, never use intermediaries between yourself and God!

Someone in the audience raises his hand, turning the discussion to issues of practice:

You tell us to be absolutely obedient. It is difficult sometimes, because living in this country you are never sure if you are making a mistake. For example, can we eat the meat slaughtered here, the meat you buy in the market?

Ali responds:

We can eat the food slaughtered by Christians and Jews because the slaughter is in the name of God. But it is better to eat meat slaughtered by Muslim hands.

But while it is essential that we eat meat that is halal, it is more important that we do not consume anything that is haram. We must never eat pork or drink alcohol! This is why a Muslim woman must never marry a non-Muslim man. In serving her husband she may have to do things that break the laws of Islam, like serve him alcohol or pork.

Another member of the audience raises the issue of prayer:

For some of us, praying five times a day is possible, but for some of us it is not. We go to work and have nowhere clean to pray. Or people there ridicule us, or do not allow us to pray. What shall we do?

Ali responds:

You must say your five daily prayers. It is one of the pillars of faith, and you are obligated to do so. Bring a prayer rug with you and you will always have a clean place to pray. Ignore the ridicule of others. You get fifty blessings, ten for each prayer, when you complete your five daily prayers. You must do this for your children. If they do not see you pray, they will wonder why they should. Prayer is good.

He then describes prayer, focusing on the actual physical act:

You must first raise your hands in surrender to Allah. This movement is recommended, not obligatory.

An adult student suddenly interrupts:

But I was taught in Sierra Leone that this movement is obligatory!

The teacher responds:

The people who taught you did not know this. They taught what they knew.

Pausing for effect, he continues:

You then hold your hands in front of your chest. You do this so you do not make unnecessary movements. You should not scratch or itch, but if something bites you, you can protect yourself.

Another adult now interjects:

Itching is nature!

The teacher, growing impatient, responds:

Yes, but scratching an itch gives you pleasure and therefore distracts your prayers. Reading the Fatiha is mandatory when you are standing with hands across your chest or at your sides. Reciting loud or quiet is *sunna* [tradition of the Prophet].

Someone else raises a parallel question:

In Sierra Leone we crush our heads on the floor when praying to make a mark so people will respect you.

Teacher:

This is nonsense because the prophet never had a mark on his head.

The adults, becoming angry, retort:

But this is tradition! We have been taught that this is the right way!

The teacher, remaining calm, reiterates that "This is nonsense." By now there is marked tension in the air.

The confrontation is telling. In the teacher's attempt to challenge "local" interpretations of Islam, he is disrupting the way these Sierra Leoneans are weaving global and local interpretations of Islam for their children and themselves in an attempt to create a sense of continuity. This weave is a challenge to the disjunctures these men and women feel in relation to Islamic institutions that do not recognize their particular interpretations of Islam as valid. As such, the teacher becomes at once a sounding board for their concerns and a target for their frustrations. Ali ends the meeting, also clearly frustrated, reminding the adults present that they must help to gather the children for noon prayers.

Graduation

Graduation is held this year (1991) on Father's Day in a Maryland community center. The room in which the ceremony will take place is packed with people when I arrive, most dressed in traditional costume. As at other celebrations, most women wear various styles of clothing made from the same patterned African cloth. The atmosphere is festive. The room is decorated with colorful paper streamers and balloons. A recording of the Qur'an plays loudly in the corner. Set before rows of chairs is a dais at which the speakers will be seated. The ceremony, due to begin at 1:00 P.M., does not get underway until around 3:00. No one, myself included, is surprised. At last, the assembly sit and the speakers are introduced. The first speaker is the chairman of the Fullah Progressive Union. He reminds the parents, children, and teachers why they have gathered:

This school is sowing the seeds of our culture in our children. The two children who are graduating are leaders and role models that the younger children should look up to.

Throughout his remarks, the audience shouts "amin" and applaud.

The next speaker is Yusuf, the second grade teacher. He too addresses the role of the school and its importance:

This school will prevent us from tearing the fabric of our families apart. We must not tear this fabric because it will tear our nation and culture apart. To prevent this we have established this school. We teach Islam, recitation, sunna, hadith, *shari'a* [law], prayer. We started this school with fifteen children and now we have thirty-five in the senior class! We need this school to rescue us from the abandonment of our religion and culture!

Then Ali, the third grade teacher and main force behind the creation of the school's curriculum, rises. He speaks specifically to the parents present:

In 1984, when I arrived [in America], we were more concerned with parties, but now things have changed. We have become aware that we are Muslim and from Muslim families. Parents must participate so that they can help children study. Islam is on the move in the United States! So stand on your two feet and walk together strong! We teach the children Qur'an, tawhid, shari'a, the Arabic language, because the best way to understand the Qur'an is to learn Arabic. Arabic math because math comes from the Arabs. Islamic history because we are part of it. We teach them how to behave toward their parents.

He then presents the two graduates, a young man and woman, with gifts from the school. Each receives a Qur'an, prayer beads, and a prayer rug. In addition, the young woman receives a scarf and the young man a prayer cap. As Ali presents each of their gifts, he instructs them and the audience:

Here is a Qur'an. You should read and recite every day. Women should not touch it when they are menstruating. You must always wash before you touch the Qur'an. This prayer rug will always give you a clean place to pray, wherever you are. These head covers, a scarf for the woman and a cap for the man, are to cover yourselves. You must both always cover yourselves [at all times].

They are then handed the prayer beads and their certificates, and each is asked to make a speech.

Jennaba, the young woman, goes first. She is the pride of the community. An award-winning public high school student, she has recently been accepted at an Ivy League school on a full scholarship. She has decided, however, to attend the University of Maryland. When I asked her why she had made that decision, she told me that she wanted to stay

Figure 8. Graduation ceremony, Fullah Progressive Union Islamic School, 1992.
Photograph by the author.

close to her parents. To live apart from them was, she felt, improper. As
she told me this, her parents looked on with enormous pride. This kind
of child, they told me, is the result of proper upbringing. And the Fullah
School had helped them to achieve this goal. Jennaba's speech is full of
praise for her parents, the school, and Islam, and disdain for the way in
which American children, particularly girls, are brought up. Short and
to the point, her remarks convey beautifully the goals articulated by the
school's founders and the parents who have elected to send their children:

I was watching the Oprah Winfrey Show the other day. The girls Oprah was
interviewing had dropped out of school for their boyfriends! Where were their
parents? Their parents should have disciplined their children from the beginning, not waited until they were fourteen years old. My parents steered me correctly. I am profoundly grateful. You, as parents and community members, must
teach and guide the young ones in our community. Thank you all.

Said, the young male graduate, deeply shy, quietly and briefly thanks
everyone for helping him become what he is today:

I want to thank my parents and the community members who created this
school. It is because of you all that I am what I am today. Thank you.

Figure 9. Children reciting Qur'an at Fullah Progressive Union School graduation ceremony. Photograph by the author.

The parents of these graduates speak next. Ibrahim's mother is first:

I wish all the fathers in the audience a Happy Father's Day! I want to thank the FPU for their concern about our childrens' Islamic education. We all left home in search of education, but our children are faced with negative forces. These children are our pride and future. If these two can make it so can all the other children in this community. We must give them the life that we did not have. Thank You.

Jennaba's father, president of the Fullah Progressive Union, speaks next. He places all of Jennaba's high school academic awards, some forty in all, on display and proceeds to point to and describe each of them to the audience. He then implores all parents to guide their children on the right path so that some day they too will be standing where he is. The ceremony ends with prayers and Qur'anic recitation. This done, all head for the table of food that has been set up on the right side of the room. Every family has contributed a dish.

"What Are Our Kids Thinking?"

For Sierra Leoneans living in Washington, D.C., creating a place (homeland) has become the metaphor through which they construct a world that they so desire their children to be a part of. As such, like all metaphors, disparate domains of meaning are connected and made one, stitched together carefully so that the seams do not show. Through ritual, celebration, and the emergence of a school, a sense of homeland is constructed and authenticated. The meaning of being a Sierra Leonean living in America is enacted in the way in which this metaphor is represented in the lives of this community, providing a sense of collective and individual identity. Hence, the foundation that these men, women, and children are constructing forms the beginnings of a new piece of the American fabric: Sierra Leonean-Muslim-American.

In one respect the common chorus of parents—we came here to get educated, to better ourselves, and to enhance our lives—echoes that of millions of earlier migrants to American shores. Yet, like many predecessors who never quite pulled up roots back home before embarking on the journey, and who always felt that some day, somehow they would return, these Sierra Leonean parents find themselves living a series of disjunctures. Neither here nor there, they are not quite sure where they really want to be. They feel—at least at present—that they cannot go home. Civil war has ravaged their homeland. But even if they could return and fit back in, would it be fair to relocate their children now?

One solution is to bring "home" here, to map Sierra Leone onto their community, to instill a sense of cultural, ethnic, national, and religious pride in their American-born children. Many of these children will embrace some, perhaps much, of what is imparted. Others, of course, will not. In struggling with their own American-born, Sierra Leonean-mapped identities, these children, like the children of other immigrants, migrants, and transnationals before them, will invariably see things differently from their parents. Some may even hold their parents up to a degree of ridicule (see Mandell 1995 for images of Arab American children playfully imitating their immigrant relatives, and otherwise rebelling). Frustration, even shame will enter the picture, as it does at times enter their parents' experiences, albeit in different ways.

Several years after I left the field I received a call from Khadi. She called to check in with me and to wish me a happy holiday ('Id al-Adha). In the course of trading news, Khadi told me she was deeply disturbed by a recent incident involving her children that had, as she related, suddenly made her fear that all her efforts, as well as the efforts of other Sierra Leonean parents, to imbue her/their children with a bounded sense of community rooted in Sierra Leonean identity had foundered. Her lament about the state of the children in the community revolved around two very different, but in her eyes related events.

Khadi began by filling me in on the "scandal" surrounding Hawa, a young American-born Sierra Leonean woman, with whom I had spoken a great deal when I was doing fieldwork in the community. She was now twenty-one and a high school graduate, but had recently become an unwed mother. She kept the child and is living with the baby's father in the District of Columbia, but she refused to marry him. Along with the rest of the community, Khadi is convinced that none of this would have happened if the young woman had stayed within the bounds of her community and if her parents had arranged for their daughter to marry a Sierra Leonean man. I asked Khadi how Hawa was managing, given not only the difficulties and complexities of being a young unwed mother, but the obvious community disapproval. Khadi's answer summarized both her own personal exasperation and that of the entire community:

That child infuriates me! I am like a mother to her [Khadi and Hawa's mother are very good friends]. As soon as I knew she was pregnant I told her not to worry. We can have a small quiet [wedding] reception. This way she would not be shamed. She refused! She said she didn't want to marry the guy! Can you imagine? He took her virginity and she doesn't want to marry him! My mother always told me that virginity was the most important thing. Why pay a pound if you can have a cow for ten shillings!

"Is the father Sierra Leonean?" I asked.

Oh my God, No! He is African American. I know you think I am ethnocentric, JoAnn. But we are losing our kids! They are not marrying other Sierra Leonean children. Everyone in the community thought if we always brought the kids together they would be attracted to each other and eventually would want to marry each other. What happened? Recently I realized that a group of Sierra Leonean teenagers can be in a room together alone and no parent has to go in and turn the lights back on! We thought it was because we had taught them to respect their virginity, but it turns out to be our big mistake!

"What do you mean? What mistake did you make?" I asked. Suddenly the story shifted into a parallel source of aggravation.

I was at a naming ceremony with Ibrahim [her youngest son]. I was on one side of the room and he was on the other. I was watching him watch this cute little girl. He stared at her for forty-five minutes! I walked up to him and reminded him that staring is wrong, but told him that if he was interested I could arrange to have them get together.

"What do you mean by getting together? Do you mean an arranged marriage?" I asked.

Well, if they like each other, yes. But he jumped when I said this! He told me he was not interested and said to me, "Mommy, she's just a little girl with lipstick— she's only twelve!" I thought she was fifteen and argued with him. I decided to go over and talk with her mother, who, by the way, I had never met. Well, Ibrahim was right, she is only twelve! But most important, she is Jamaican and a

Christian. So that put an end to that. But it scared me, JoAnn. What are our kids thinking? Why aren't they attracted to each other?

Following this incident Khadi asked her children whether they would consider marrying any of the other children in the community with whom they had grown up. She was dumbstruck when they answered that this was impossible. But they, too, were baffled by the very question Khadi had raised. As she related it to me, they answered her query with a question of their own, one that now sent shockwaves through the community.

When I asked the kids if they were interested in anyone in the community, they put that face on. You know, the one they put on when you asked them what they thought about the sheep we had sacrificed when they were born. Total disgust, remember? Well that is the face they put on when I asked them who they might like to marry! They said, "Mommy, how can we be interested in people who are our family?"

Khadi was astounded to discover that her children—along with all the other children in the Sierra Leonean community—somehow thought they were biologically related to each other.

That's when I realized that all our children believe they are blood related because everyone is "auntie" and "uncle." We insist that they call all adults "auntie" and "uncle" out of respect. They think these are blood relatives, and so their children are cousins. In the States you do not marry cousins. Now I know why whenever I talk about my parents being cousins, they get a look of disgust on their faces!

Horrified by her discovery, Khadi notified other parents in the community about their children's perceptions of community kinship and the way it plays into their American socialization. At the time we spoke, the parents had decided to call a mass meeting to discuss the matter. Like Khadi, many must wonder if it is already too late. Will their kids "marry out," and if so, will they marry non-Muslims? "At least they must marry Muslims," Khadi concluded. But that prospect does not really comfort her. She is the first to admit that it is not what she envisioned for her kids.

If their children are, as most Sierra Leoneans assert, their future, what then does the future hold for this community? Should we assume that because the children have positioned everyone in the community as family and privilege American notions of kinship over those of Sierra Leone (the world of their fathers and mothers), that the cultural power of their center (America) will prevail over their parents' homeland, which will increasingly become to American-born children a distant periphery? Will Sierra Leonean children such as Ibrahim—who has embraced his religion, but who knows Sierra Leone only through his parents' and other community members' constructions of homeland, and who has obviously misconstrued the nature of relations within the community—marry out of the community because as Americans they perceive a marriage within the community as incestuous? Will this result in the dissolution of any sense of the community identity that their parents have worked so hard to promote?

The lives of transnationals are marked by accommodations to social mores, and civic and religious sensibilities that are foreign, as well as by a tug-of-war with rooted traditions of homeland that are never left behind. When confronted with the realization that they have not been successful in conveying to their children their strong sense of community boundaries, Sierra Leoneans will seek solutions to their dilemma. I can well imagine the conversations and arguments, the ideas and words that flew when the community sat down to discuss Khadi's discovery. Some, no doubt, attempt to draw thicker, more impenetrable boundaries between this community and all others. If the civil war in Sierra Leone has indeed ended, some may react by sending their children "back home" for formative education and socialization. But others will seek solutions by redrawing community boundaries to allow greater accommodation in a larger community of common interest. The Fullah School did this when it opened its doors to Sierra Leoneans of all ethnic backgrounds. And now Khadi suggests a similar, albeit broader accommodation, a willingness, if need be, to accept non-Sierra Leonean Muslims, as marriage partners for her children.

As Sierra Leoneans come to terms with the insertion, vis-à-vis their children, of cultural constructs that threaten to liquidate their sense of being, they redefine their own situation to enable the cultural bridge that they are building to their children's American lives, as well as the bridge they struggle to maintain to homeland, to accommodate the troubled waters below. What emerges is a transnational aesthetic, a form of accommodation that resists the ultimate incorporation of their children, and hence themselves, into the "melting pot." The transmission of identity from parent to child illustrates the complexity of the back-and-forth, here-there-and-everywhere cultural flows that are produced by transnational connections across and beyond national-religious-community borders.

The way in which the senior teacher at the Fullah School, Ali, finds himself caught in the cross-fire between parents and children is particularly illustrative. One minute his traditional hell-fire imagery of the afterlife is challenged by an American high-school science student, and he comes off as old-fashioned, naive. Soon after, he finds himself derided as an innovator, a usurper of tradition and purveyor of a foreign Islam, by parents who seek the comfort of a broad-based Muslim community, but grasp simultaneously at an Islam they can call their own, one that is recognizable, familiar, a piece of home. One moment the parents bemoan their children's aggressive interrogation of the teacher—while recognizing it as part of the education so many of them came to the United States to attain. The next they have the teacher's back to the wall as they pepper him with questions that he cannot answer to their approval.

In much the same way, the naming ceremony, in all its guises, has become a stage for both imparting tradition to a new generation and affirming self. But again, whose self, and which ritual format is more appropriate? The Sierra Leonean American "big party," with all its material overtones? Or the Sierra Leonean American "(re)invention of tradition" embodied in the more sedate affair, replete with admonitions to "practice as the Arabs" do, to model the all-important event less on traditions back home than on translocal Muslim sensibilities shaped by Sierra Leonean imams who have trained in Saudi Arabia—the perceived orthodox "center"—and by congregants of an American-based Islamic Center where Muslims from every nation gather and negotiate commonality and communality?

Finally there is Amie—Aminata—the seven-year-old Sierra Leonean American girl who told me her name was Amy, then silently stared down her outraged aunt. While they often do not see themselves in the same predicament as their parents, transnational children are in their own way caught between two worlds. But in their case, which world is really home? When Amie is old enough to be Amy freely, who will she be?

Notes

Chapter 1. Multiple Sites/Virtual Sitings: Ethnography in Transnational Contexts

1. The sources cited in this section should in no way be taken as comprehensive; the bibliographies contained in these books point to other sources. Still, one cannot help but note that the pool of scholars is as yet still relatively small.

2. The same holds true for studies of Muslims in Europe, where there is a growing literature on South Asians and Arabs, particularly North Africans, but little as yet on sub-Saharan Africans. A recent exception is Metcalf (1996); also see Ebin (1990, 1996); Johnson (2002).

3. My work and my assessment was completed before the events of 9/11/01. Since then the monitoring and counting of immigrant populations—although not yet West Africans—has undergone a serious reevaluation.

4. There are no official U.S. government statistics for the numbers of Sierra Leoneans residing in this country. The only available figures are for African immigrants as a whole until the late 1970s, when separate statistics for Egypt and Nigeria begin to appear. Thereafter, figures for Ethiopia and Ghana are added. The numbers for Africa as a whole are 1951–60: 16,600; 1961–70: 39,300; 1971–80: 91,500; 1981–90: 192,300; 1991–93: 91,000; 1994: 26,700. There are no available statistics beyond 1994. These figures obviously do not account for the numbers of people who do not hold official immigrant status—students, refugees, asylum seekers, long-term visitors, and undocumented immigrants, often referred to as illegal aliens (U.S. Bureau of Census 1977, 1996). At the time of writing, information from the 2000 census was not yet available.

5. The quota system based on national origin was initiated in rudimentary form in the 1921 Quota Act and revised and continued in the 1924 Immigration Act and the 1952 Immigration and Nationality Act. It imposed country-by-country quotas to control immigration to the United States from all countries of the world outside of the Western hemisphere. After 1924, when the system received its basic form, each country's quota was based on the number of persons of national origin who were in the United States in 1920. Hence, because the nation in 1920 was primarily British, Irish, and German, use of the 1920 national origins basis in assignment of country-by-country quotas heavily favored immigration to the United States of persons born in the British Isles and Germany, while sharply limiting immigration from the rest of Europe, Asia, Latin America, and Africa. An individual was required to seek entry to the United States under the quota of his country of birth, regardless of his or her country of citizenship or residence. Of the total number of immigrants who entered the United States

in fiscal 1965, 70 percent were from the British Isles or Germany. With the passing of HR 2580 into public law in 1965, the quota system was abolished. Instead of country-by-country quotas, an overall annual quota of 170,000 immigrants from outside the Western hemisphere was permitted. Applicants for entry into the United States would be evaluated on the basis of certain conditions applying to them as individuals, regardless of which non-Western hemisphere country they were born in (Congressional Quarterly 1965:459–82).

6. The legal document that allows non-citizens to reside and work permanently in the United States.

Chapter 2. Field of Dreams: The Anthropologist Far Away at Home

1. The names of all individuals in this book are pseudonyms.

2. That sense of nostalgia has become a central focus of my work (D'Alisera 1997; 1998), in which I explore the way imagined communities are often attached to imagined places, such as homeland. These imagined places are often powerful and unifying symbols that serve to construct collective identities in which displacement and deterritorialization shape the "hybridized subject" (Gupta and Ferguson 1992:18), creating an imagined territory in which transnationals can refashion a new sense of self. How place is imagined then is the key to exploring the relation between space, place and transnational identity.

3. While living in Cairo, a subsequent year of exposure to Egyptian romance films from the 1950s and early '60s in which the telephone loomed large—and familiar—has tempered this American-centered view. My basic dilemma, however, remained problematic at the time.

4. Recent writings on the telephone (e.g., Schwartz 1996) and other, newer technologies of personal communication (the Internet, for example; see Marcus 1996) have begun to pose original questions about how these devices are being utilized to further a sense of, even create, community in lieu of face-to-face contact. This is an avenue for research that I hope to pursue further in the future.

5. With the advent of affordable and accessible cellular technology, the phone can now be carried everywhere, at times with startling implications. A colleague who had visited a Sierra Leonean refugee camp in Guinea several years ago reports that many refugees communicated regularly with relatives in the United States via cell phones (Rosalind Shaw, personal communication 1998).

Chapter 3. Icons of Longing: Homeland and Memory

1. *Sierra Leone Today* was distributed widely among the Sierra Leonean community in the D.C. area throughout the period of my fieldwork (1991–93). As of 1994 it ceased publication, but it is due to be replaced in the future with a newspaper that, according to the former magazine editor, will be less expensive to publish. By cutting publication costs he hopes to reach an even wider audience outside the D.C. area. For a fuller discussion of the symbology of the cotton tree, see D'Alisera (2002).

2. The article was adapted from *Sierra Leonean Studies* 16 (1961):131–34). The article, however, was originally published for the first time in 1947 in a Freetown publication called *The Starlight Magazine*.

3. Khadi is referring to the classic "melting pot" narrative of immigrant America, an idea she found unacceptable. She often criticized other members

of the community for gauging the success of community members in terms of "their ability to melt in."

4. In 1989, while doing preliminary fieldwork in Sierra Leone, I was told by a Krio friend that the Cotton Tree stood for freedom. When I asked what he meant, he told me that after 1807 when Britain passed the Abolition Act, outlawing the slave trade for British subjects and charging the British navy with the responsibility of capturing slave vessels and freeing their human cargo, the men and women who became known as Recaptives or Liberated Africans (Alie 1990:66) were unshackled under the Cotton Tree. Whether or not this tale is true, it underlines Khadi's point that the tree holds specific meanings to the residents of Freetown, and in particular to the Krio population whose roots lie with those freed captives. (For more on the Krio, see Alie 1990; Cohen 1981; Fyle 1981; Kup 1975; Spitzer 1974; Wyse 1988, 1989.)

5. Connerton (1989) has suggested that memory is "sedimented, or amassed in the body" between two different types of social practice. The first type, an incorporating practice, are messages that are sent by means of current bodily practices. The sender and the receiver of the message must be present to sustain a particular activity. A smile or a handshake are examples of an incorporating practice. Inscribing practices, are devices that trap and hold information long after a human has ceased to be part of the process of informing. Photographs, print and electronic media are examples of this kind of practice (1989:72–73). These practices are not mutually exclusive, images, words and action work hand-in-hand to (re)enact the past.

6. "Ceremony" here reflects an indigenous category of description. The use of "ceremony" to denote what is, in the Turnerian sense, "ritual," is problematic. According to Turner (1964), ceremony confirms while ritual transforms from one state to another. In the unidirectional process, the ritual subject is separated from a stable state, made liminal and transformed. He/she emerges from the ritual changed, into a new stable state of being. However, for the transnational child, whose subject position at the start of the naming ritual is one of a liminality embedded in the imagined geographies of his/her parents' transnational experience, the naming ritual repositions the child not in a stable new status, but instead in a new state of liminality. The child's subject position is ultimately multi-liminal. The naming ceremony, despite its intended purpose, which is to reterritorialize the child in the imagined homeland of his/her parents, nevertheless deterritorializes the child in terms of his/her place of birth. Ultimately the child is multiply displaced, neither here nor there.

7. Sierra Leonean men who choose to participate in sports in the Washington, D.C. metropolitan area are overwhelmingly football fans, and more important Washington Redskins fans. Games are rarely missed, and this was the year that the Redskins would win the Superbowl. Baseball, the "national pastime," was of no interest to these men. Women, if interested in sports, would only express that interest in terms of the men they were involved with, although many of the women who were food vendors in the District displayed Redskins paraphernalia on their food carts because they said it pleased their customers and made for better business (D'Alisera 1997).

8. In the Sierra Leonean context one scholar has written that "sacrifice" refers to "strategies employed . . . to control the outcomes of spiritual and human action" and to "appease angry ancestors" (Ferme 1992:27). Of the many forms such sacrifices may take, the one I refer to involved the preparation of special foods and their placement in auspicious places at ceremonies. As Ferme

notes, what makes these actions sacrifices is "their ritual setting, with the offering of prayers and blessings" in a communal setting.

9. By 1995 I was told that a group of Imam Bashar's followers had formed in the District, where they met monthly and hold transcontinental conference calls with their spiritual leader in Freetown.

10. Women in the community often took me to task for being a "bad wife." "You are going to lose that man," they would tell me. "You don't pay enough attention to him. He is too good for you!" When I attended community events without him, they would often send me home with food and ginger beer, trying to cover my neglect. When they thought that I was being really neglectful, they would tease me by telling my husband directly, "Get rid of that one and we will find you a nice Sierra Leonean wife!"

Chapter 4. Spiritual Centers, Peripheral Identities: On the Sacred Border of American Islam

1. The holiday is in fact disputed in many parts of the Muslim world. But it is also widely celebrated, and has been since the twelfth century A.D./sixth century A.H. These celebrations, like those for other *mawlids* (saint's days), are often quite festive, involving street processions, the sale of special foods and holiday objects, and special prayers in the mosque.

Chapter 5. I ♥ Islam: Popular Religious Commodities and Sites of Inscription

1. According to John Nunley *juju* can be translated as "medicine"; however the term medicine as used in the Western context is too narrow. Instead, "Medicine composes a world view. It can be used for destruction, protection, good and bad luck, and healing—in brief, every aspect of living" (1987:61). My informants often used the concept of juju to describe its negative or destructive aspects, seeing themselves as targets of others ill will.

2. She was referring to the many Christian shows one can find on cable television in the area. In this case, she referred to a series of anti-witchcraft spots running at the time on Pat Robertson's *700 Club*.

3. The issue here is not one of "clean" food, because the hot dogs they sell, while rarely *halal*, are generally kosher, and therefore pork-free and ritually slaughtered. The matter is more simply one of taste preferences.

Chapter 6. Mapping Women's Displacement and Difference

1. The entire conference was clouded by controversy. Leading spokespersons for the American religious right argued that, due to Chinese government policies concerning birth control, the conference venue was inappropriate. Some human rights groups expressed concern about the setting as well. Most women's activists countered that it was important to attend the meeting precisely because of Chinese human rights violations. To hold the conference on Chinese soil, they argued, would constitute a moral victory. The First Lady, Hillary Clinton, led the American delegation, generating further controversy at home.

2. On the other hand, it should be no less disturbing that the judge in the second, Baltimore, case, feels free to speak in equally essentialist terms about Africans "maintaining tribal unity."

3. Part of a large complex of secret societies in the West African forest belt area, a region of Central West Atlantic Africa that includes Liberia, Sierra Leone, and parts of Guinea and the Ivory Coast (Bellman 1984). The majority of women that I worked with, both Christian and Muslim, have been initiated into bundu.

4. Fatmata is now twenty-three years old and has not been initiated. Khadi never made a definitive decision. In her own words, she "put it off until it did not seem to make sense. Fatmata is old enough to decide and I don't think she will do it. We never talk about it." Khadi's younger sister, who also lives in the Washington area, is outspoken in rejecting any notion of sending her two daughters, who are now nearing initiation age, back home to be initiated.

5. Khadi is referring to Alice Walker's 1993 book, *Warrior Marks: Female Genital Mutilation and the Sexual Blinding of Women*, and the video of the same name ("Warrior Marks," 1993) that was produced in conjunction with the book.

6. While it is true that the opposing images, immigrant-as-heroic and immigrant-as-threat, have alternated at various points in American history, Sierra Leoneans, like many of the immigrants of the past, arrive assuming that the "streets will be paved with gold" and that their efforts to "make it" will be appreciated. Their experiences often speak to a different reality, especially as the pendulum shifts.

7. According to Islamic law, a menstruating woman is prohibited from offering prayers, entering the mosque, touching the Qur'an, and generally participating in any religious activity. Sierra Leonean women with whom I work generally take this prohibition very seriously—in some cases, as with Khadi, to their advantage (see Lawrence 1988:117–36, for another case in which women utilize menstrual taboos to their advantage).

8. The original plan was for her father-in-law to return to Sierra Leone in December. In fact he stayed into the summer and expected Ahmed to return with him for a six-month stay in Sierra Leone.

9. Ahmed here took issue with Khadi's claim that an ablebodied person can fulfill the obligation of ritual prayer in other then the prescribed fashion. While there is provision in Islam for individual and spontaneous prayer (*du'a*), it is not to the exclusion of ritual prayer (Glassé 1989:317).

10. According to Khadi, God-dai is a Krio term that can mean a number of different things. It can mean, "God is there," in the sense of a warning or even a curse if someone harms you. If one is generally not doing well in life, it can mean, "God will provide."

11. She was six or seven months pregnant at the time of this conversation.

12. In Islamic law it is legal for a man to marry up to four wives, although the law certainly does not mandate polygyny. However, the legal statute of polygyny also requires fair treatment and equal support of all wives.

13. Some early agents of Islam in Sierra Leone promoted their religion through the Futa Jallon jihad, instigated by Fula traders in 1727. The jihad did contribute to the Islamization of northern Sierra Leone (the Susu, Limba, Yalunka, and Koranko). But conversion was not the primary aim of the jihad, and force was not the main instrument of Muslim expansion in Sierra Leone. The normal pattern was through peaceful means by long distance traders, missionaries, and teachers, most of whom were Mandingo (Alie 1990:43–46).

14. This man lived in the village where I had initially planned to do field

work. He ran a one-room school and worked very closely with the local imam, who ran the village Qur'anic school.

15. Khadi often mentioned that her mother was blamed by her three co-wives for any indiscretion her father may have committed, such as affairs with other women. Khadi attributed this to her mother's position as the first wife, and to the fact that this first marriage was an arranged cross-cousin marriage. She often said that her "other mothers" thought her mother had too many privileges as a first wife and relative. She told me that "they would often accuse her of going behind my father's back or denying them their share of money or food. If rice was missing they would blame my mother and say that she was being greedy because she was the first wife."

16. Until the civil war made it impossible, Ahmed returned to Sierra Leone at least once a year. When I asked him why, he responded by saying, "My father needs to consult with me about our properties. I am the eldest son, my mother is my father's first wife and cousin, and I will be responsible when he's gone. I need to keep up to date and know what is going on to protect myself." Over the years Ahmed's father has had a series of sets of four wives. The result is that Ahmed has thirty-two brothers and sisters, all with claims on their father's properties. Ahmed has always felt certain that if he stayed away too long his claims might diminish.

17. Much in this spirit, Ahmed and Khadi drove up to Pennsylvania from Maryland when I was confined to my bed with a difficult pregnancy, so that she could cook for my husband and help in any way that she could.

18. It is common practice throughout the Muslim world for women to be confined to their homes for forty days after birth. Khadi's allusions to "dangers" have remained just that. Neither she nor any of the other Sierra Leonean women I have asked has ever been willing to clarify for me what these dangers are.

19. The Night of Fate (sometimes translated as the Night of Power) during Ramadan that marks the beginning of the Prophet Muhammad's recitation of the Qur'an.

20. The relationship between Sierra Leonean women who actively participate in the Center and the Moroccan women is a complex one. Sierra Leonean women are often intimidated by the North Africans, whom they perceive as embodying a more accurate knowledge of Islam (see Chapter 4). Elder Moroccan women seat themselves where they had a domineering view of the room and they often take it upon themselves to correct the dress, attitude, and demeanor of other women. Sub-Saharan African women were often a target of their displeasure, as was I, because of my relationship with them.

21. In Islamic legal tradition, all actions are considered to fit into one of five categories: obligatory (*fard*), recommended (*mustahab*), neutral (*mubah*), discouraged (*makruh*), and forbidden (*haram*).

22. For examples on how women use food to mirror their desires in other contexts, see Williams (1985); Theophano (1991).

23. Kosher meat, like halal meat, is ritually slaughtered and contains no pork. The ritual slaughters in Jewish and Muslim traditions are virtually identical; both are supervised by a religious official, the process must be swift, and the blood must be completely drained from the dying animal. Before the spread of halal butchers in this country in recent years, many Muslims made do with kosher meat. Many Muslim food vendors continue to use kosher meat even though they may feel that halal meat is slaughtered more properly. As noted in Aminata's

case, the reason is often economic. Another reason relates to the familiarity of the product to non-Muslim customers, most of whom would not know what halal meat is, let alone be able to distinguish one Muslim brand of hot dogs from another.

24. Aminata had never learned to drive because, as she told me, "I always have someone to give me a ride, and the insurance for a car costs too much. Also, I would have to pay to park the car down here by the stand. I would lose my profits." However, several weeks after this incident she purchased a car and was taking driving lessons from one of her taxi driver friends.

Chapter 7. "We Owe Our Children the Pride": The Imagined Geography of a Muslim Homeland

1. Multiple imams frequently preside over such ceremonies (namings, forty-day memorials, weddings), and this tandem often worked the same event. As the following story indicates, they each reinforce different aspects of community identity, at times complementing each other, at times working at cross-purposes.

2. In the Sierra Leonean context one scholar has written that "sacrifice" refers to "strategies employed . . . to control the outcomes of spiritual and human action" and to "appease angry ancestors" (Ferme 1992:27). Of the many forms such sacrifices may take, the one I refer to involved the preparation of special foods and their placement in auspicious places at ceremonies. As Ferme notes, what makes these actions sacrifices is "their ritual setting, with the offering of prayers and blessings" in a communal setting.

3. "Godmother" is how people referred to her, and in most respects she fulfilled the role as generically defined: she would assume responsibility for the girl in her parents' absence.

4. Recall Mustafa's hostility to Arabic language pamphlets being distributed outside the Islamic Center in Chapter 4.

5. This is an act that all Muslims do in prayer, but the notion of washing ones self with the Qur'an is how my informants refer to it. This is not an act of washing away something, but rather an act of applying blessings. It is somewhat equivalent to the act of "drinking the Qur'an" that is found among many Muslim peoples. That is, the verses of the Qur'an are written on a board or paper and either they are immersed in water or water is poured over them, thereby creating an inky liquid that contains blessings and is then drunk, Allowing the participant to ingest blessings (see Osman el-Tom 1985).

6. The amount of money thrown is unknown to me—it would have been extremely rude to ask. However, I did ask what would happen to the money afterward and was told that it would go to pay for the expenses of the party.

7. The Fullah Progressive Union is a social organization for ethnic Fula from Sierra Leone to promote community solidarity and to provide assistance to community members. I am using the spelling Fullah instead of Fula because it is the way this group of people has decided to spell it.

8. This happened several times when I attended the school. I was never able to meet the owner. My informants told me that he was unavailable for an interview. So it was never clear to me why he refused to give them the key to the building. My informants also expressed concern about how I would write about the situation. They feared that they would lose their privileges if I named and criticized the owner.

9. It is traditional to give children presents, often money (*idiyah* or, more colloquially, *idi*) and new outfits, for the Id. Yet in the American context there is also a melding with, some would say an accommodation to, the Christmas and Hanukkah gift-giving to which the children are exposed. For a general discussion of Muslim responses to American holidays, especially non-Muslim religious holidays, see Haddad and Lummis (1987:91–96).

10. In the name of Allah, most benevolent, ever-merciful. Destroyed will be the hands of Abu Lahab, and he himself will perish. Of no avail shall be his wealth, nor what he has acquired. He will be roasted in the fire, and his wife, the portress of firewood, will have a strap of coir rope around her neck (al-Qur'an, translated by Ahmed Ali 1984).

References Cited

Abdul-Rauf, Muhammad. 1978. *History of the Islamic Center*. Washington, D.C.: Islamic Center.

Abusharaf, Rogaia Mustafa. 2002. *Wanderings: Sudanese Migrants and Exiles in North America*. Ithaca, N.Y.: Cornell University Press.

Abraham, Nabeel and Andrew Shryock. 2000. *Arab Detroit: From Margin to Mainstream*. Detroit: Wayne State University Press.

Abraham, Sameer Y. and Nabeel Abraham, eds. 1981. *The Arab World and Arab Americans: Understanding a Neglected Minority*. Detroit: Center for Urban Studies, Wayne State University.

———. 1983. *Arabs in the New World: Studies on Arab-American Communities*. Detroit: Wayne State University Press.

Abu-Lughod, Lila. 1991. Writing Against Culture. In *Recapturing Anthropology: Working in the Present*, ed. Richard Fox, 137–62. Santa Fe, N.M.: School of American Research.

———. 2002. Do Muslim Women Really Need Saving? Anthropological Reflections on Cultural Relativism and Its Others. *American Anthropologist* 104: 783–90.

Al-Ahram Weekly. 1996. An Everyday Nightmare. March 7–13.

Alie, Joe A. 1990. *A New History of Sierra Leone*. New York: St. Martin's Press.

Amit, Vered. 2000. *Constructing the Field: Ethnographic Fieldwork in the Contemporary World*. London: Routledge.

Anderson, Benedict. 1983. *Imagined Communities: Reflections on the Origin and Spread of Nationalism*. London: Verso.

Antoun, Richard. 1989. *Muslim Preacher in the Modern World*. Princeton, N.J.: Princeton University Press.

Appadurai, Arjun. 1986. Introduction: Commodities and the Politics of Value. In *The Social Life of Things: Commodities in Cultural Perspective*, ed. Arjun Appadurai, 3–65. Cambridge: Cambridge University Press.

———. 1988. Theory in Anthropology: Center and Periphery. *Comparative Studies in Society and History* 28, 1: 356–61.

———. 1990. Disjuncture and Difference in the Global Cultural Economy. *Public Culture* 2: 1–14.

———. 1991. Global Ethnoscapes: Notes and Queries for a Transnational Anthropology. In *Recapturing Anthropology: Working in the Present*, ed. Richard Fox, 191–210. Santa Fe, N.M.: School of American Research.

———. 1996. *Modernity at Large: Cultural Dimensions of Globalization*. Minneapolis: University of Minnesota Press.

Armstrong, Robert Plant. 1981. *The Powers of Presence: Consciousness, Myth, and Affecting Presence*. Philadelphia: University of Pennsylvania Press.

Aswad, Barbara C. and Barbara Bilgé, eds. 1996. *Family and Gender Among American Muslims: Issues Facing Middle Eastern Immigrants and Their Descendants.* Philadelphia: Temple University Press.

Austin, Joe. 1996. Rewriting New York City. In *Connected: Engagements with Media,* ed. George Marcus, 271–312. Chicago: University of Chicago Press.

Bakhtin, Mikhail M. 1981. *The Dialogic Imagination.* Austin: University of Texas Press.

Bammer, Angelika. 1994. Introduction. In *Displacements: Cultural Identities in Question,* ed. Angelika Bammer, xi–xx. Bloomington: Indiana University Press.

Basch, Linda, Nina Glick Schiller and Cristina Szanton Blanc. 1994. *Nations Unbound: Transnational Projects, Postcolonial Predicaments and Deterritorialized Nation-States.* Basel: Gordon and Breach.

Bellman, Beryl L. 1984. *The Language of Secrecy: Symbols and Metaphors in Poro Ritual.* New Brunswick, N.J.: Rutgers University Press.

Bhabba, Homi. 1994. *The Location of Culture.* New York: Routledge.

Blair, Betty. 1991. Iranian Immigrant Name Changes in Los Angeles. In *Creative Ethnicity: Symbols and Strategies of Contemporary Ethnic Life,* ed. Stephen Stern and John Allan Cicala, 122–36. Logan: Utah State University Press.

Bledsoe, Caroline and Kenneth Robey. 1986. Arabic Literacy and Secrecy Among the Mende of Sierra Leone. *Man* 21: 202–226.

Bodnar, John. 1985. *The Transplanted: A History of Immigrants in Urban America.* Bloomington: Indiana University Press.

Bourdieu, Pierre. 1977. *Outline of a Theory of Practice.* New York: Cambridge University Press.

Breytenbach, Breyten. 1991 The Long March from Hearth to Heart. *Social Research* 58, 1: 69–83.

Brown, Linda Keller and Kay Mussell. 1985. Introduction. In *Ethnic and Regional Foodways in the United States: The Performance of Group Identity,* ed. Linda Keller Brown and Kay Mussell, 3–18. Knoxville: University of Tennessee Press.

Bruner, Edward M. 1986. Experience and Its Expressions. In *The Anthropology of Experience,* ed. Victor Turner and Edward M. Bruner, 3–32. Urbana: University of Illinois Press.

———. 1996a. Tourism in the Balinese Borderzone. In *Displacement, Diaspora, and Geographies of Identities,* ed. Smadar Lavie and Ted Swedenburg, 157–80. Durham, N.C.: Duke University Press.

———. 1996b. Tourism in Ghana: The Representation of Slavery and the Return of the Black Diaspora. *American Anthropologist* 98: 290–304.

Bruner, Edward and Phyllis Gorfain. 1984. Dialogic Narration and the Paradoxes of Masada. In *Text, Play and Story: The Construction of Self and Society,* ed. Edward Bruner 56–79. Washington, D.C.: American Ethnological Society.

Cadaval, Olivia. 1991. Making a Place Home: The Latino Festival. In *Creative Ethnicity: Symbols and Strategies of Contemporary Ethnic Life,* ed. Stephen Stern and John Allan Cicala, 204–22. Logan: Utah State University Press.

Chidester, David and Edward T. Linenthal. 1995. Introduction. In *American Sacred Space,* ed. David Chidester and Edward T. Linenthal, 1–42. Bloomington: Indiana University Press.

Clifford, James. 1988. *The Predicament of Culture: Twentieth-Century Ethnography, Literature, and Art.* Cambridge, Mass.: Harvard University Press.

———. 1992. Travelling Cultures. In *Cultural Studies,* ed. Lawrence Grossberg, Cary Nelson, Paula Treicher, Linda Baughman, and John Macgregor Wise, 96–116. New York: Routledge.

————. 1997. *Routes: Travel and Translation in the Late Twentieth Century*. Cambridge, Mass: Harvard University Press.

Cohen, A. P. 1985. *The Symbolic Construction of Community*. Chichester: Ellis Horwood.

Cohen, Abner. 1981. *The Politics of Elite Culture: Explorations in the Dramaturgy of Power in Modern African Society*. Berkeley: University of California Press.

Colen, Shelle. 1986. "With Respect and Feelings": Voices of West Indian Childcare and Domestic Workers in New York City. In *All American Women: Lines That Divide, Ties That Bind*, ed. J. B. Cole, 46–70. New York: Free Press.

————. 1990. "Housekeeping" for the Green Card: West Indian Household Workers, the State and Stratified Production in New York. In *At Work in Homes: Domestic Workers in World Perspective*, ed. R. Sanjek and S. Colen, 89–118. Washington, D.C.: American Anthropological Society.

Coombe, Rosemary and Paul Stoller. 1994 "X Marks the Spot": The Ambiguities of African Trading in the Commerce of the Black Public Sphere. *Public Culture* 7: 249–74.

Congressional Quarterly. 1965 *Almanac, 89th Congress, 1st Session*, vol. 21. Washington, D.C.: Congressional Quarterly Service.

Connerton, Paul. 1989. *How Societies Remember*. Cambridge: Cambridge University Press.

Crane, Susan A. 2000. Introduction: Of Museums and Memory. In *Museums and Memory*, ed. Susan A. Crane, 1–16. Stanford, Calif.: Stanford University Press.

D'Alisera, JoAnn. 1997. The Transnational Search for Muslim Identity: Sierra Leoneans in America's Capital. Ph.D. dissertation, Department of Anthropology, University of Illinois, Urbana-Champaign.

————. 1998. Born in the USA: Naming Ceremonies of Infants Among Sierra Leoneans Living in the American Capital. *Anthropology Today* 14, 1:16–19.

————. 1999. Field of Dreams: The Anthropologist Far Away at Home. *Anthropology and Humanism* 24(1):5–19.

————. 2001. I ♥ Islam: Popular Religious Commodities, Sites of Inscription, and Transnational Sierra Leonean Identity. *Journal of Material Culture* 6, 1: 89–108.

————. 2002. Icons of Longing: Homeland and Memory in the Sierra Leonean Disapora. *PoLAR* 25, 2: 73–88.

D'Amico-Samuels, Deborah. 1991. Undoing Fieldwork: Personal, Political, Theoretical, and Methodological Implications. In *Decolonizing Anthropology*, ed. Faye Harrison, 68–87. Washington, D.C.: American Anthropological Association-Association of Black Anthropologists.

de Certeau, Michel. 1984. *The Practice of Everyday Life*. Berkeley: University of California Press.

Drewal, Margaret Thompson. 1992. *Yoruba Ritual: Performers, Play, and Agency*. Bloomington: Indiana University Press.

Ebin, Victoria. 1990. Commerçants et missionaires: Une confrérie musulmane sénégalaise à New York. *Hommes et migrations* 1132: 25–31

————. 1996. Making Room Versus Creating Space: The Construction of Spacial Categories by Itinerant Mouride Traders. In *Making Muslim Space in North America and Europe*, ed. Barbara Metcalf, 92–109. Berkeley: University of California Press.

Eickelman, Dale. 1982. The Study of Islam in Local Contexts. *Contributions to Asian Studies* 17: 1–16.

————. 1992. Mass Higher Education and the Religious Imagination in Contemporary Arab Society. *American Ethnologist* 19: 643–55.

Eickelman, Dale and James Piscatori. 1990. Social Theory in the Study of Muslim Societies. In *Muslim Travelers: Pilgrimage, Migration, and the Religious Imagination*, ed. Dale Eickelman and James Piscatori, 3–28. Berkeley: University of California Press.

Ferme, Mariane. 1992. "Hammocks Belong to Men, Stools to Women": Constructing and Contesting Gender Domains in a Mende Village (Sierra Leone, West Africa). Ph.D. Dissertation, University of Chicago.

————. 1994. What "Alhaji Airplane" Saw in Mecca, and What Happened When He Came Home: Ritual Transformation in a Mende Community (Sierra Leone). In *Syncretism/Anti-Syncretism: The Politics of Religious Synthesis*, ed. Charles Stewart and Rosalind Shaw, 27–44. London: Routledge.

Fischer, Michael and Mehdi Abedi. 1990. *Debating Muslims: Cultural Dialogues in Postmodernity and Tradition*. Madison: University of Wisconsin Press.

Foner, Nancy. 1987. *New Immigrants in New York*. New York: Columbia University Press.

————. 2000. *From Ellis Island to JFK: New York's Two Great Waves of Immigration*. New Haven, Conn.: Yale University; New York: Russell Sage Foundation.

————. 2001. *Islands in the City: West Indian Migration to New York*. Berkeley: University of California Press.

Forty, Adrian. 1999 Introduction. In *The Art of Forgetting*, ed. Adrian Forty and Susanne Küchler, 1–18. Oxford: Berg.

Fortier, Anne-Marie. 2000. *Migrant Belongings: Memory, Space, Identity*. Oxford: Berg.

Foucault, Michel. 1986. Of Other Spaces. *Diacritics: A Review of Contemporary Criticism* 16: 22–27.

Fox, Richard. 1991. Introduction: Working in the Present. In *Recapturing Anthropology: Working in the Present*, ed. Richard Fox, 1–17. Santa Fe, New Mexico: School of American Research.

Fyle, C. Magbaily. 1981 *The History of Sierra Leone: A Concise Introduction*. London: Evans.

Gaffney, Patrick D. 1994. *The Prophet's Pulpit: Islamic Preaching in Contemporary Egypt*. Berkeley: University of California Press.

Ganguly, Keya. 1992 Migrant Identities: Personal Memory and the Construction of Selfhood. *Cultural Studies* 6, 1: 27–50.

Geertz, Clifford. 1973. *The Interpretation of Cultures*. New York: Basic Books.

————. 1980. *Negara: The Theater State in Nineteenth-Century Bali*. Princeton, N.J.: Princeton University Press.

Giddens, Anthony. 1990. *The Consequences of Modernity*. Cambridge: Polity.

Gilroy, Paul. 1993. *The Black Atlantic: Modernity and Double Consciousness*. Cambridge, Mass.: Harvard University Press.

Glassé, Cyril. 1989. *The Concise Encyclopedia of Islam*. San Francisco: HarperCollins.

Gottlieb, Alma. 1992. *Under the Kapok Tree: Identity and Difference in Beng Thought*. Bloomington: Indiana University Press.

Gottlieb, Alma and Philip Graham. 1994. *Parallel Worlds: An Anthropologist and a Writer Encounter Africa*. Chicago: University of Chicago Press.

Greenblatt, Stephen. 1991. Resonance and Wonder. In *Exhibiting Cultures: The Poetics and Politics of Museum Display*, ed. Ivan Karp and Steven D. Lavine, 42–56. Washington, D.C.: Smithsonian Institution Press.

Gupta, Akhil and James Ferguson. 1992. Beyond "Culture": Space, Identity, and the Politics of Difference. *Cultural Anthropology* 7, 1: 6–23.

————. 1997a. *Anthropological Locations: Boundaries and Grounds of a Field Science.* Berkeley: University of California Press.

————. 1997b. *Culture, Power, Place: Explorations in Critical Anthropology.* Durham, N.C.: Duke University Press.

————. 1997c. "The Field" as Site, Method, and Location in Anthropology. In *Anthropological Locations: Boundaries and Grounds of a Field Science,* ed. Akhil Gupta and James Ferguson, 1–46. Berkeley: University of California Press.

Haddad, Yvonne Yazbeck, ed. 1991. *The Muslims in America.* New York: Oxford University Press.

Haddad, Yvonne Yazbeck and John Esposito. 2000. *Muslims on the Americanization Path?* New York: Oxford University Press.

Haddad, Yvonne Yazbeck and Adair T. Lummis. 1987. *Islamic Values in the United States: A Comparative Study.* New York: Oxford University Press.

Haddad, Yvonne Yazbeck and Jane Idleman Smith. 1994. *Muslim Communities in North America.* Albany: State University of New York Press.

Handler, Richard. 1985. On Dialogue and Destructive Analysis: Problems in Narrating Nationalism and Ethnicity. *Journal of Anthropological Research* 41: 171–82.

Hannerz, Ulf. 1996. *Transnational Connections: Culture, People, Place.* London: Routledge.

Hastrup, Kirsten and Karen Fog Olwig. 1997. Introduction. In *Siting Culture: The Shifting Anthropological Object,* ed. Karen Fog Olwig and Kirsten Hastrup, 1–16. London: Routledge.

Hobsbawm, Eric. 1991. Exile: A Keynote Address. *Social Research* 58, 1: 65–68.

Holtzman, Jon D. 2000. *Nuer Journeys, Nuer Lives: Sudanese Refugees in Minnesota.* Boston: Allyn and Bacon.

Jansen, Stef. 1998 Homeless at Home: Narratives of Post-Yugoslav Identities. In *Migrants of Identity: Perceptions of Home in a World Movement,* ed. Nigel Rapport and Andrew Dawson, 85–110. Oxford: Berg.

Johnson, Michelle Cecilia. 2002. "Being Mandinga, Being Muslim: Transnational Debates on Personhood and Religious Identity in Guinea-Bissau and Portugal." Ph.D. dissertation, University of Illinois, Urbana-Champaign.

Kalčik, Susan. 1985. Ethnic Foodways in America: Symbol and Performance of Identity. In *Ethnic and Regional Foodways in the United States: The Performance of Group Identity,* ed. Linda Keller Brown and May Mussel, 37–65. Knoxville: University of Tennessee Press.

Karp, Ivan. 1991. Culture and Representation. In *Exhibiting Cultures: The Poetics and Politics of Museum Display,* ed. Ivan Karp and Steven D. Lavine, 11–24. Washington, D.C.: Smithsonian Institution Press.

Khouj, Abdullah Muhammad. 1991. *Handbook of Fasting.* Washington, D.C.: Islamic Center.

Kondo, Dorinne. 1996. Bad Girls: Theater, Women of Color, and the Politics of Representation. In *Women Writing Culture,* ed. Ruth Behar and Deborah Gordon, 49–64. Berkeley: University Of California Press.

Kup, A. P. 1975 *Sierra Leone: A Concise History.* New York: St. Martin's Press.

Laitin, David. 1986. *Hegemony and Culture: Politics and Religious Change Among the Yoruba.* Chicago: University of Chicago Press.

Lambek, Michael. 1990. Certain Knowledge, Contestable Authority: Power and Practice on the Islamic Periphery. *American Ethnologist* 17: 23–40.

Launay, Robert. 1990. Pedigrees and Paradigms: Scholarly Credentials Among the Dyula of the Northern Ivory Coast. In *Muslim Travellers: Pilgrimage, Migration, and the Religious Imagination,* ed. Dale Eickelman and James Piscatori, 175–99. Berkeley: University of California Press.

Lavie, Smadar and Ted Swedenburg. 1996. Introduction. In *Displacement, Diaspora, and Geographies of Identity,* ed. Smadar Lavie and Ted Swedenburg, 1–26. Durham, N.C.: Duke University Press.

Lawrence, Denise L. 1988. Menstrual Politics: Women and Pigs in Rural Portugal. In *Blood Magic: The Anthropology of Menstruation,* ed. Thomas Buckley and Alma Gottlieb, 117–36. Berkeley: University of California Press.

MacGaffey, Janet and Rémy Bazenguissa-Ganga. 2000. *Congo-Paris: Transnational Traders on the Margins of the Law.* Bloomington: Indiana University Press.

Mahler, Sarah. 1995. *American Dreaming: Immigrant Life on the Margins.* Princeton, N.J.: Princeton University Press.

Malkki, Liisa H. 1992. National Geographic: The Rooting of Peoples and the Territorialization of National Identity Among Scholars and Refugees. *Cultural Anthropology* 7, 1: 24–44.

Mandel, Ruth. 1990. Shifting Centres, Emerging Identities: Turkey and Germany in the Lives of the Turkish *Gastarbeiter.* In *Muslim Travellers: Pilgrimage, Migration, and the Religious Imagination,* ed. Dale Eickelman and James Piscatori, 53–174. Berkeley: University of California Press.

———. 1989 Turkish Headscarves and the "Foreign Problem": Constructing Difference Through Emblems of Identity. *New German Critique* 46: 27–46.

Mandell, Joan. 1995. *Arabs in Detroit.* Video. ACCESS and Olive Branch Productions.

Marcus, George. 1986. Contemporary Problems of Ethnography in the Modern World System. In *Writing Culture: The Poetics and Politics of Ethnography,* ed. James Clifford and George Marcus, 165–93. Berkeley: University of California Press.

———. 1995. Ethnography in/of the World System: The Emergence of Multi-Sited Ethnography. *Annual Review of Anthropology* 24: 95–117.

———. 1996. *Connected: Engagements with Media.* Chicago: University of Chicago Press.

McGown, Rima Berns. 1999. *Muslims in the Diaspora: The Somali Communities of London and Toronto.* Toronto: University of Toronto Press.

McDannell, Colleen. 1995. *Material Christianity: Religion and Popular Culture in America.* New Haven, Conn.: Yale University Press.

Metcalf, Barbara Daly, ed. 1996. *Making Muslim Space in North America and Europe.* Berkeley: University of California Press.

Myerhoff, Barbara. 1978. *Number Our Days.* New York: Simon and Schuster.

Naff, Alixa. 1985. *Becoming American: The Early Arab Immigrant Experience.* Carbondale: Southern Illinois University Press.

Naficy, Hamid. 1991. The Poetics and Practice of Iranian Nostalgia in Exile. *Diaspora* 1: 285–302.

———. 1993. *The Making of Exile Culture: Iranian Television in Los Angeles.* Minneapolis: University of Minnesota Press.

Needham, Rodney. 1981. *Circumstantial Deliveries.* Berkeley: University of California Press.

Nielsen, Jørgen S. 1992. *Muslims in Western Europe.* Edinburgh: Edinburgh University Press.

Nora, Pierre. 1989. Between Memory and History: Les lieux de mémoire. *Representations* 26: 7–25.

Nunley, John W. 1987. *Moving with the Face of the Devil: Art and Politics in Urban West Africa.* Urbana: University of Illinois Press.

Nyang, Sulayman S. 1999. *Islam in the United States of America.* Chicago: ABC International Group, Inc.

Okely, J. 1984. Fieldwork in the Home Counties. *RAIN* 61: 4–6.

Olwig, Karen Fog and Kirsten Hastrup. 1997. *Siting Culture: The Shifting Anthropological Object.* London: Routledge.

Öncü, Ayşe. 1995. Packaging Islam: Cultural Politics on the Landscape of Turkish Commercial Television. *Public Culture* 8: 51–71.

Ong, Aihwa. 1996. Women Out of China: Travelling Tales and Travelling Theories in Postcolonial Feminism. In *Women Writing Culture*, ed. Ruth Behar and Deborah Gordon, 350–72. Berkeley: University of California Press.

Ortner, Sherry. 1973. On Key Symbols. *American Anthropologist* 75: 1338–46.

———. 1997. Fieldwork in the Postcommunity. *Anthropology and Humanism* 22,1: 61–80.

Osman el-Tom, Abdullahi. 1985. Drinking the Koran: The Meaning of Koranic Verses in Berti Erasure. *Africa* 55: 414–31.

Ossman, Susan. 1994. *Picturing Casablanca.* Berkeley: University of California Press.

Passaro, Joanne. 1997. "You Can't Take the Subway to the Field!": Village Epistemologies in the Global Village. In *Anthropological locations: Boundaries and Grounds of a Field Science*, ed. Akhil Gupta and James Ferguson, 147–62. Berkeley: University of California Press.

Prosterman, Leslie. 1995. *Ordinary Life, Festival Days: Aesthetics in the Miswestern County Fair.* Washington, D.C.: Smithsonian Institution Press.

Al-Qur'an: A Contemporary Translation. 1984. Trans. Ahmed Ali. Princeton N.J.: Princeton University Press.

Rapport, Nigel and Andrew Dawson. 1998. Home and Movement: A Polemic. In *Migrants of Identity: Perceptions of Home in a World Movement*, ed. Nigel Rapport and Andrew Dawson, 19–38. Oxford: Berg.

Romero, Mary. 1992. *Maid in America.* New York: Routledge.

Rosaldo, Renato, 1988. Ideology, Place, and People Without Culture. *Cultural Anthropology.* 3,1: 77–87.

———. 1989 *Culture and Truth: The Remaking of Social Annalysis.* Boston: Beacon Press.

Rouse, Roger. 1991. Mexican Migration and the Social Space of Postmodernism. *Diaspora* 1, 11: 8–23.

Al-Sawwaf, Muhammad. 1977. *The Muslim Book of Prayer.* Mecca, Saudi Arabia.

Schiller, Nina Glick and Georges Eugene Fouron. 2001. *Georges Woke Up Laughing: Long Distance Nationalism and the Search for Home.* Durham, N.C.: Duke University Press.

Schwartz, Lynne Sharon. 1996. Only Connect? In *Tolstoy's Dictaphone: Technology and the Muse*, ed. Sven Birkerts, 28–146. St. Paul, Minn.: Graywolf Press.

Slyomovics, Susan. 1998. *The Object of Memory: Arab and Jew Narrate the Palestinian Village.* Philadelphia: University Pennsylvania Press.

Smith, Jane I. 2000. *Islam in America.* New York: Columbia University Press.

Spitzer, Leo. 1974. *The Creoles of Sierra Leone: Responses to Colonialism, 1870–1945.* Madison: University of Wisconsin Press.

Spooner, Brian. 1986. Weavers and Dealers: The Authenticity of an Oriental Carpet. In *The Social Life of Things: Commodities in Cultural Perspective*, ed. Arjun Appadurai, 195–235. Cambridge: Cambridge University Press.

Starret, Gregory. 1995. The Political Economy of Religious Commodities in Cairo. *American Anthropologist* 97: 51–58.

Stern, Stephen. 1991. Introduction. In *Creative Ethnicity: Symbols and Strategies of Contemporary Ethnic Life*, ed. Stephen Stern and John Alan Cicala, xi–xx. Logan: Utah State University Press.

Stewart, Charles and Rosalind Shaw. 1994. Introduction: Problematizing Syncretism. In *Sycretism/Anti-syncretism: The Politics of Religious Synthesis*, ed. Charles Stewart and Rosalind Shaw, 1–26. London: Routledge.

Stewart, Susan. 1984. *On Longing: Narratives of the Miniature, the Gigantic, the Souvenir, the Collection*. Baltimore: John Hopkins University Press.

Stokes, Martin, ed. 1994. *Ethnicity, Identity, and Music*. Oxford: Berg.

Stoller, Paul. 1995. *Embodying Colonial Memories: Spirit Possession, Power, and the Hauka in West Africa*. New York: Routledge.

———. 1996. Spaces, Places, and Fields: the Politics of West African Trading in New York City's Informal Economy. *American Anthropologist* 98: 776–88.

———. 1997. Globalizing Method: The Problems of Doing Ethnography in Transnational Spaces, *Anthropology and Humanism* 22,1: 81–94.

———. 2002. *Money Has No Smell: The Africanization of New York City*. Chicago: University of Chicago Press.

Strathern, Marilyn. 1987. The Limits of Auto-Anthropology. In *Anthropology at Home*, ed. Anthony Jackson, 16–37. ASA Monograph 25. London: Tavistock Publications.

Swedenburg, Ted. 1992. Seeing Double: Palestinian/American Histories of the Kufiya. *Michigan Quarterly Review* 31: 557–77.

———. 1995. *Memories of Revolt: The 1936–1939 Rebellion and the Palestinian National Past*. Minneapolis: University of Minnesota Press.

Tapper, Nancy. 1990. *Ziyaret*: Gender, Movement, and Exchange in a Turkish Community. In *Muslim Travellers: Pilgrimage, Migration, and the Religious Imagination*, ed. Dale Eickelman and James Piscatori, 236–55. Berkeley: University of California Press.

Theophano, Janet. 1991. "I gave him cake": An Interpretation of Two Italian-American Weddings. In *Creative Ethnicity: Symbols and Strategies of Contemporary Ethnic Life*, ed. Stephen Stern and John Allan Cicala, 44–54. Logan: Utah State University Press.

Trinh, T. Minh-ha. 1994. Other Than Myself/My Other Self. In *Travellers' Tales: Narratives of Home and Displacement*, ed. George Robertson, et al., 9–28. London: Routledge.

Turner, Victor. 1964. Betwixt and Between: The Liminal Period in *Rites de passage*. In *Proceedings of the American Ethnological Society Symposium on New Approaches to the Study of Religion*, 4–24. Washington, D.C.: American Ethnological Society.

———. 1982. *From Ritual to Theatre: The Human Seriousness of Play*. New York: Performing Arts Journal Publications.

———. 1967 *The Forest of Symbols: Aspects of Ndembu Ritual*. Ithaca, N.Y.: Cornell University Press.

U.S. Bureau of the Census. 1996. *Statistical Abstract of the United States: 1996*. 116th ed. Washington, D.C.

———. 1977. *Statistical Abstract of the United States: 1977*. 98th ed. Washington, D.C..

Walker, Alice. 1993a. *Warrior Marks: Female Genital Mutilation and the Sexual Blinding of Women*. New York: Harcourt Brace.

———. 1993b. *Warrior Marks* (Video). New York: Women Make Movies.

Werbner, Pnina. 1990a. Economic Rationality and Hierarchical Gift Economies: Value and Ranking Among British Pakistanis. *Man* 25: 266–85.

———. 1990b. *The Migration Process: Capital, Gifts and Offerings Among British Pakistanis.* Oxford: Berg.

———. 1996a. The Making of Muslim Dissent: Hybridized Discourse, Lay Preachers, and Radical Rhetoric Among British Pakistanis. *American Ethnologist* 23: 102–22.

———. 1996b. Stamping the Earth with the Name of Allah: *Zikr* and the Sacralizing of Space Among British Muslims. *Cultural Anthropology* 11 309–338.

———. 2001. *Imagined Diasporas Among Manchester Muslims: The Public Performance of Pakistani Transnational Identity Politics.* Oxford: James Carrey.

Williams, Brett. 1985. Why Migrant Women Feed Their Husbands Tamales: Foodways as a Basis for a Revisionist View of Tejano Family Life. In *Ethnic and Regional Foodways in the United States: The Performance of Group Identity*, ed. Linda Keller Brown and Kay Mussell, 113–26. Knoxville: University of Tennessee Press.

Wyse, Akintola. 1988 The Krio of Sierra Leone: An Ethnographical Study of a West African People. *International Journal of Sierra Leone Studies* 1: 36–63.

———. 1989. *The Krio of Sierra Leone: An Interpretive History.* London: Hurst.

Yamaguchi, Masao. 1991. The Poetics of Exhibition in Japanese Culture. In *Exhibiting Cultures: The Poetics and Politics of Museum Display*, ed. Ivan Karp and Steven D. Lavine, 57–67. Washington, DC: Smithsonian Institution Press.

Yalçun-Heckman, Lale. 1994. Are Fireworks Islamic? Toward an Understanding of Turkish Migrants and Islam in Germany. In *Syncretism/Anti-Syncretism*, ed. Charles Stewart and Rosalind Shaw, 178–195. London: Routledge.

Ybarra-Frausto, Tomas. 1991. The Chicano Movement/The Movement of Chicano Art. In *Exhibiting Cultures: The Poetics and Politics of Museum Display*, ed. Ivan Karp and Steven D. Lavine, 128–50. Washington, D.C.: Smithsonian Institution Press.

Index

Acknowledgments

The origins of this book are complex and varied. Many people along the way played a significant role in its birth, and I am deeply indebted to them. A Rockefeller Residential Fellowship in the Humanities at the Center for Ethnicities, Communities, and Social Policy, Bryn Mawr College, provided me a year off from teaching, which allowed me to complete the final revisions on this book. I would like to thank Mary Osirim, Rick Davis, Sandy Schram, Phil Kilbride, and Azade Seyhan, as well as the other members of the Center who provided a nurturing and supportive environment.

I have always been fortunate in having the company of critical but sympathetic teachers. I have benefited from my conversations with all of them. I would like to thank Alma Gottlieb for the years of advice, friendship, and support. She has guided my interests for nearly two decades, and her voice can surely be heard in these pages. Alma expects a lot of her students, I hope I have lived up to her expectations. I would also like to thank Edward Bruner and Charles Stewart. Each in his own way has contributed to the making of this text. I am grateful to Ed for encouraging me in the classroom and through his writings to think critically about the world in which we live. He has been a guiding influence in shaping the way I have "experienced" anthropology. I would also like to thank Charles for his continual support over the years and for nurturing my interest in Islam. The roots of many of my interests can be found with Giselle Hendel-Sebastian, who introduced me to anthropology all those years ago in an undergraduate class at the State University of New York at New Paltz. I am grateful for her continual support through the many years since we first met. But I am most grateful to her for teaching me what it means to be an excellent and committed teacher.

During the long evolution of this project I have stumbled many times. At these points there have been people who appeared to offer hope and encouragement. In particular, Paul Stoller has been there to offer support and the benefit of his long experience as author, editor, and anthropologist. Paul's advice and friendship saw me through those times when it seemed that I would never finish this book. I can find few words to express the depth of my gratitude. I would also like to thank my editor Peter Agree. He has always taken my anxious calls, provided a sympathetic ear in discussions, and most of all supported this project when others would not. For this I am deeply grateful. Laura Helper introduced me to Peter, and for this I am indebted to her. Laura and I share some life experiences that have profoundly influenced the way in which we do anthropology. Because we see the world through the same anthropological lens, she has helped me through times when I seemed to be losing heart and direction. I want to thank her for always being there.

No project could proceed without the support of friends. I would like to thank my friend Susan Jelly for the continual support and the many engaging conversations that we have had through the years of our friendship. I will always be grateful for her confidence in me. I would also like to thank, Marcia-Anne Dobres, Carole Counihan, Jim Taggart, Ashton Welch, Jim Wunch, Diane Baird N'Diaye, and Debbie Harold, for their advice, friendship, and encouragement. Rosa De Jorio, Ted Swedenburg, and Lynda Coon read critical portions of this work at various stages. I want to thank them for the time and energy they put into those readings. I would also like to thank Rosalind Shaw for reading the entire manuscript. Her comments were most welcome and appreciated.

Simeon Sisay, Fatu Songawa, Sorrie Songawa, Musa Sisay, Fanta Kakay, Isatu Sisay, Princess Mustapha, and her daughter Soa shared their lives with me daily, and for this I am deeply indebted. To all I offer my deepest thanks and respect. I am also indebted to the Sierra Leonean community in the Washington, D.C. metropolitan area. At times I may have seemed like an annoyance, but they put up with my endless questions and welcomed me into their community. I would also like to thank Dr. Abdullah Khouj, the director of the Islamic Center of Washington, D.C., for allowing me to roam freely through the Center talking with whomever I liked (and whoever would speak to me). This was, I am sure, profoundly trying for him at times, but he always respected my need to be able to transcend the gendered boundaries that are so deeply etched into that institution. I am grateful and indebted for his support.

And last, but not least, I would like to thank Joel Gordon and my son Alexander D'Alisera-Gordon. Each in his own way has inspired me to complete this book. I am deeply grateful to Joel for his insightful comments during my fieldwork, and in the writing of this book. Neither could have been possible without his collaboration. I am thankful for my son Alexander who patiently puts up with an anthropologist-mother who disappears into fieldwork and writing for long periods of time. This book is dedicated to his future.

Earlier versions of parts of this book appeared in *Anthropology Today*

14, 1 (1998): 16–19 (© 1998 Blackwell); *Anthropology and Humanism* 24, 1 (1999): 5–19 (© 1999 American Anthropological Association); *Journal of Material Culture* 6, 1 (2001): 89–108 (© 2001 Sage Publications); *PoLAR* 25, 2 (2002): 73–88 (© 2002 American Anthropological Association). They are reprinted here with permission.